# NO WELL-WORN PATHS

By the same author:

*A People Prepared*
*Enjoying God's Grace*
*Explaining Reigning in Life*
*From Refreshing to Revival*
*God Knows You're Human*
*Men of Destiny*
*Praying the Lord's Prayer*
*Receiving the Holy Spirit and His Gifts*
*Restoration in the Church*
*Start*
*Weak People, Mighty God*

# No Well-Worn Paths

TERRY VIRGO

KINGSWAY PUBLICATIONS
EASTBOURNE

First published 2001
Reprinted 2001

Unless otherwise indicated, biblical quotations are from
the New American Standard Bible © The Lockman Foundation
1960, 1962, 1963, 1968, 1971, 1972, 1973, 1975, 1977.

Verses marked NIV are taken from the
New International Version © 1973, 1978, 1984
by the International Bible Society.

ISBN 0 85476 990 0

Published by
KINGSWAY PUBLICATIONS
Lottbridge Drove, Eastbourne, BN23 6NT, England.
Email: books@kingsway.co.uk

Book design and production for the publishers by
Bookprint Creative Services, P.O. Box 827, BN21 3YJ, England.
Printed in Great Britain.

*For Wendy*

Thank you for
your laughter, your energy and your zeal for God.
Thank you for believing in me and sharing the journey –
and the prophets keep telling me that the best
is yet to come!

# Contents

# Acknowledgements

I am indebted to more people than I could possibly mention who have shaped my thinking and practice. Some of the most significant are referred to in the story that follows but countless others have played a huge part. I thank God for every one of them, known and unknown, who have helped me on my way.

I want also to thank the members of the Church of Christ the King in Brighton for their constant love and encouragement and also all my dear brothers and sisters in the wider New Frontiers International family scattered around the world.

Finally, I want to express my heartfelt gratitude to Janis Peters, my secretary, for her patient and enthusiastic typing and re-typing of the manuscript for this book. Her diligence and constant encouragement have made the whole venture possible.

# Preface

A friend of mine tells the story of a man who discovered his small son enthusiastically drawing a picture. He asked what he was drawing. The boy's reply was unexpected. 'God,' he said. 'But no one knows what God looks like,' his father pointed out. 'They will when I've finished!' he boasted.

Some would argue that no one knows what the ideal church looks like. The Bible isn't explicit. How did the thousands of believers in Jerusalem, Ephesus or Rome relate together? What were their church meetings like? How were they structured?

I can't say that I faced my task with the same confidence that this small boy claimed, but I have tried to tell an honest story of how I have been led over the last few decades.

Saved in the 1950s during the days of Billy Graham's greatest impact on Britain, I tried as an outsider to find my way into the Evangelical church. Having no religious background I came into a foreign culture and worked hard at trying to learn the rules. The breakout of the charismatic movement of the 1960s came to my rescue, introducing me to a new dimension of spiritual experience.

But I needed more than a personal experience. I needed to become deeply involved in a community of faith and friendship where God could be known and enjoyed without unnecessary religious trappings. I also needed a vision that would captivate me and consume my desires and energies. I believe I have found it and I believe it is a lot like the early church that Jesus started. Jesus called himself the Way and his early disciples were called followers of the Way. They were on a journey; a pilgrimage of discovery and delight.

There were no well-worn paths ahead of them, but the Holy Spirit was their guide and the ancient scriptures were now illuminated by the leadership and writings of the New Testament apostles and prophets who began to establish the new community – the church.

Jesus loved the church and gave himself up for her. I have come to love the church and I pray that, as I tell my story of following the Lord over nearly half a century through many pains and pleasures, you will find encouragement, provocation and inspiration to help you forward in your personal calling to follow and glorify Jesus as part of his glorious church.

*Terry Virgo*

# 1
# What a Mess!

I wish I could be a fly on the wall and watch that evening again. If only I had a video recording. I came home from an evening out in Brighton. I was 16 and my sister, visiting home for the weekend, was waiting for me. She asked if she could speak to me for a while. I had nothing else to do, so told her to fire away! She told me that since she had been living in London she had become a Christian.

'We are all Christians, aren't we?' I argued.

No, she was talking about something else. Something that brought her certainty and urgency in speaking to me. She knew that she would go to heaven when she died. She knew her sins were forgiven. I thought it was impossible; how can anybody know that sort of thing?

The conversation continued for a long time until there came an extraordinary moment.

'Do you believe that Jesus rose from the dead?' she asked.

'He's supposed to have been raised after three days, isn't he?' I responded.

'If he rose from the dead,' she said, 'he's alive now.'

Suddenly I felt I knew: Jesus is alive! Amazingly, I was

convinced it was true. I had never heard such things before, and had never been aware that there was a gospel. Why hadn't somebody told me this?

That night, I knelt by the fireplace in my living-room, face buried in the armchair, and asked Christ to save me and come into my life – and he did! I felt it happen! I was suddenly ashamed of my failures and dirty lifestyle. To my great surprise, I found myself crying, but I knew that I was born again. I went to bed unaware that an extraordinary adventure was about to begin.

A few weeks later, my sister invited me to visit her in London and attend a guest service at All Souls, Langham Place, where a man called John Stott would be speaking. I sat transfixed by his wonderful presentation of the gospel. At the end, when he invited people who wanted to respond to come forward, I stood with great joy and a sense of wonder. I walked to the front. There was nowhere else I would rather be. It was a privilege to shake the hand of the man who, through subsequent years and many books, would become such a blessing to me and to the evangelical world. I still have the gracious letter he wrote to me the following week, in which he congratulated me on my decision to follow Christ and encouraged me to find a church and commit myself to it.

I started to attend the Anglican church that John Stott recommended. Owning no means of transport, I needed to catch the bus across town to Bishop Hannington Memorial Church. One Sunday, on my way to the bus-stop, the heavens opened with such a heavy downpour that I rushed into a Baptist church that I passed each week on my journey. I knew this building quite well from the outside and, in my total ignorance, had dismissed it as a strange place because it always had large posters outside, advertising its programme. I regarded this as rather commercial for a church. More like a cinema, I used to think. I ducked in, out of the rain. To my surprise and delight, I was immediately aware of a warm welcome and quickly realised that these were born again Christians too! I could feel it. It was wonderful.

Though they never attended church, my parents had always sent me as a small child to the local Sunday school. The church was one of the 'bells and smells' variety, but happened to be nearby. After the preliminaries, the Sunday school teacher used to talk to our little group about football, or anything else that we fancied. Later, as I grew up, I began to enjoy table tennis and played to an acceptable standard, joining a church club that required me to attend the local Congregational church on Sunday mornings. I never met God or anything spiritual in either of these churches, but when I came to this Baptist church I immediately realised that these people were born again, and that I was entering a genuinely spiritual community. The preacher was wonderful. I never again made the long journey across town, but Holland Road Baptist Church in Hove was to become my spiritual home for the next twelve years, and its pastor, E. G. Rudman, became my spiritual father, friend and mentor, though it would be several years before I began to truly know and value him fully.

Sadly, though I was undoubtedly born again, those around me probably saw no change whatsoever, apart from the fact that I began to attend church every Sunday morning.

Many years later, I would preach at the Stoneleigh Bible Week, on the image of Christians being like an arrow for God. An arrow does not start life as an arrow; it had a prior existence, a former identity, namely as a branch in a tree. In order to become an arrow, it has to be cut from the tree and take on a totally new identity. It must be cut from its roots and have its leaves removed and be reshaped. It has to be introduced to such totally new and foreign concepts as flight, speed, target hitting – unimaginable experiences for a branch in a tree. One can imagine a branch asking, 'What is flight? What is speed? How can you hit a target?' While remaining a branch in the tree, it is impossible to also be an arrow. The branch has to be cut away. For myself, I was like a branch still very much attached to my tree, drawing sap as before from my former lifestyle and alongside other branches in the same situation. I had simply asked Jesus into my life. I had never really heard Jesus' invitation to come and follow him. I had not realised that to be his disciple I had to turn my back on my former lifestyle and commit myself to him absolutely. A call, like that of Abraham to leave Ur of the Chaldeans and go out to another place, had not been impressed on me.

So I lived a very unsatisfactory double life. Church on Sunday, but the jazz club on Friday night, and out drinking and partying on Saturday night. Late night card schools, the bright lights of Brighton and the buzz of its young people totally gripped me. My father was a school caretaker and our house stood within the school grounds. On Saturday nights I often hosted parties in an underground hall in the school, which my friends and I decorated with coloured lights. We would bring in barrels of beer and set up a bar. Everybody brought bottles. Modern jazz was the chosen music and scores of young people used to come, dance and drink. I remember one night, when my parents were away, being taken home eventually by my friends, since I could no longer walk alone. They carried me to my bedroom and put me to bed. By the side of my bed was my Bible, so I asked them to read a Bible passage to me, which they thought was a huge joke.

I scraped through my O and A levels at Brighton, Hove and Sussex Grammar School, but not without serious warnings from teachers and even the headmaster. In those days my friends and I perversely used to prize any hostile and frustrated comment by a teacher written in our annual reports. I actually treasured a geography teacher's comment that I received just before taking my final A level examinations: 'After two years of idleness and evasion, I hesitate to forecast even an O level pass.' As it happens, I passed my geography A level, which simply confirmed me in my foolishness.

I was an extraordinary mixture: regenerate, but constantly backsliding. Sometimes I would experience terrible conviction of sin through the pastor's preaching and my troubled conscience, but repentance was always short-lived and I had no idea how to sustain a godly lifestyle. In my eighteenth year, just prior to leaving school, I attended the church's annual missionary week. Throughout the week, missionaries would give their reports, show their slides, bring their baubles and beads from far-off countries. Intense and earnest young men and women would give their accounts. I could never identify with them. I was very girl-conscious at the time, but these women were not the sort that interested me. They were so old-fashioned. They didn't know how to dress, do their hair or look remotely feminine. The young men were from another planet! They didn't speak my language. I couldn't imagine being in their company for any length of time.

At this particular conference, the closing speaker was apparently a famous preacher from the USA. His name was Stephen Olford, and I was urged to attend the Friday night bonanza. Reluctantly, I agreed. To my amazement, he was electric. I was totally captivated. Having built to a passionate climax, he invited young people to surrender their lives and face the challenge of the mission field. Young women poured forward, but hardly any young men. 'Where are the young men?' Stephen Olford thundered! I stood in my place, scared stiff. Gradually, my defences crumbled. 'The mission field needs young men,' he insisted. I was a young man. Perhaps I was what God needed. Certainly, I was healthy. I was also modern and relevant to my generation. Perhaps this was the point: God needed someone young and modern – not quaint and out of date, like so much that I saw around me. Perhaps I could help God sort it all out.

In my naïvety and arrogance, I responded to the appeal and joined the crowd at the front. I can only imagine that the pastor was shocked to see this backslidden teenager volunteering to give his life in missionary service. The song rang out: 'Just as I am, young strong and free, to be the best that I can be.' Only God could unravel the mixture of motives and emotions I felt as I stood singing my response to the invitation. In fact, by the time I had taken the step I was actually on quite a high, emotionally intoxicated and stirred.

We finished our closing hymn, a prayer was prayed, names were taken and we were all dismissed. It was Friday evening and, of course, being a Christian meeting it ended while the night was still young! What should I do now? Well, it was Friday night. Jazz club, of course! Feeling really high, I went to my usual Friday night haunt, excitedly got into the atmosphere, enjoyed the music and the dancing, picked up a blonde girl I had noticed there for the last few weeks and walked her home, kissed her for a while and thought, 'What a great evening!'

What a mess!

# 2

# I Need Power

Two years later, after repeated ups and downs in my Christian life, a day came that turned my life upside down.

By this time I had left school and was working in London for the civil service. The daily 7.37 a.m. train took me to Victoria and the 6.00 p.m. brought me home. Morning and evening found me in the front carriage, which was totally unlike the rest of the train. It was like a club. Everybody knew one another. Seats were jealously reserved for the regulars. Strangers and newcomers were viewed with hostility. At Christmas, the windows would be covered with cotton wool decorations. You could find me playing card games morning and evening: a quiet game of solo in the morning and a noisy three card brag in the evening, where my winnings regularly paid for my railway season ticket. I still have my old diaries recording each week's winnings!

At work, no one knew I was a believer. My lifestyle continued as a shambles, often drunk at the weekend and totally without purpose. Nevertheless, nearly every Sunday morning I would attend my old Baptist church, and I would secretly pray and occasionally read my Bible.

One Sunday, the pastor's assistant was preaching. His text was taken from Galatians: 'You were running well, who hindered you from obeying the truth?' I was totally convicted of sin. I had never before encountered God in such a way. It was as though I was the only person in the building and his words ripped into my soul. For the first time I genuinely tasted the fear of the Lord. Somehow I knew that it was now or never! I shook hands with the preacher at the door, left the building and knew I had to change my lifestyle totally.

I went out for one last weekend with my friends and announced that this was the end. I could no longer be with them. I told them about my Christian experience and never spent my weekends with them again, in spite of their assurances that I would be back with them next week and that this stuff would never last. I broke off a relationship with a girl I had been going steadily with and went through a kind of death. The next weekend came around, and on the Saturday night I found myself driving down to the centre of Brighton as usual. The lights, the crowds and the electric atmosphere still had magnetic power. Nevertheless, after a while, I drove away from the bright lights of Brighton, through the darker streets of Hove until I arrived at home. My parents were watching television and I sat in another room, alone – indoors on a Saturday night! It was agony, and I could hardly believe what I was doing. Truly like dying!

I knelt down and cried out to God to help me. I knew that I was in terrible danger of going back. Sitting at home alone on a Saturday night, it was hard to believe that I had found abundant life, or, as was a popular expression in those days, 'life with a capital L'. Brighton on Saturday night was more like life to me. This seemed more like hell with a capital H! Eventually, I reached for my Bible. I sat and read right through the book of Acts in one sitting, something I had never done before. As I did so, I felt a strange sensation of excitement. What I read was certainly not boring. The early church looked anything but dull and predictable. I found myself inwardly stirred, and finally went to bed strangely comforted.

I stopped travelling in the front carriage of the Brighton train and started a regular habit of reading for two hours a day on my daily journey to and from London. A lady from the church observed my spiritual change and asked if I had ever read *Jungle Pilot*, the story of Nate Saint, who had recently been martyred in the Ecuadorian jungle. As a young pilot, he had trained to serve the Missionary Aviation Fellowship in order to help unreached people in the jungles of South America. I was powerfully influenced by the testimony of this vibrant young man. When I returned the book to her, I was subsequently loaned the story of Jim Elliot in *Through Gates of Splendour* and *Shadow of the Almighty*. Each book was followed by another. I met with great heroes like C. T. Studd, George Müller, George Whitefield, C. H. Spurgeon, Murray McCheyne, J. O. Fraser and, perhaps the one that most touched my heart, the godly pioneer J. Hudson Taylor. His life was so impacted one day when God spoke to him on Brighton beach that he began his great life's work, the China Inland Mission. I read both of Mrs Howard Taylor's classic volumes *The Growth of a Soul* and *The Growth of a Work of God*. My daily two-hour reading habit had a profound effect on my life. My old diaries suddenly changed from recording my winnings at gambling to listing the books that I devoured. And yes, I still have the list of 53 books read in 1961 alone.

My foul language disappeared almost overnight, but the

battle to break my smoking habit took a little longer. I found I liked a cigarette with my morning coffee and couldn't imagine coffee without a cigarette, so I cut out the coffee. I pushed my first cigarette to later and later in the day, until I was down to about five a day. Then I ruthlessly cut it out altogether (though I still had dreams even years later that I was still smoking!).

Alan Pringle, the young assistant pastor whose preaching so impacted me, invited me to visit his home whenever I wanted to. His friendship was a lifeline to me. He subsequently told me that he had prayed fervently all week before preaching that memorable Sunday sermon on Galatians. He had cried to God to break through among the young people who he felt were lukewarm. I asked him if he had prayed for me, but he replied that he hadn't, since he regarded me as a hopeless case!

Now I threw myself into church life. I needed to be busy. I needed to break the habits that had dominated my life for some years. I needed to get out of one culture into another. Every night of the week found me at some Christian meeting – Monday: evening prayer meeting; Tuesday: young people's fellowship; Wednesday: Bible school; Friday: helping at the Boys' Brigade; Saturday night: prayer meeting. Thursday evening was still free, so I had to fill it. I found that the church had a male voice choir, so I joined it! That year, my usual style summer holidays were replaced by attending the Keswick Convention and Filey Week. I had backslidden so many times before that I wanted to leave no opportunity to mess up again, and in the past holidays had been outrageous times. At Filey, I responded to the powerful preaching of Dr Edwin Orr, who was an authority on revival and was encouraging Christians to make sure they were Spirit-filled. I wasn't sure what that meant, but walked forward and was lovingly counselled by Arthur Coffey, who kept in touch with me for years. More recently, it has been my joy and privilege to meet and enjoy the friendship of his two outstanding sons, David and Ian.

Within the year, on the 18th September 1961, the pastor's assistant moved on, but he had the great foresight to see my need of someone to replace him in my life. He deliberately introduced me to a young evangelist who had recently moved to Hove. Affiliated to a Worthing-based organisation called Turn To Christ, he was serving Hove's Clarendon mission. He and his wife, together with their baby daughter, were living by faith and trusting God for all their support. I had never met anyone like him. By now, I had read many missionary biographies and was familiar with the principles of pioneer workers and their lifestyle of faith. Suddenly, I was being introduced to a real-life one in my own hometown! His name was Philip Vogel. He was to have a great impact on my life.

He invited me to call in at any time, but also particularly mentioned that he intended to start a Monday night fellowship in his home. It was not a typical Bible study, but became a very formative discipling context. A handful of us gathered, mostly friends of our own age group. Phil suggested that we should study the book of Acts with the intention of believing every promise and obeying every command! Hardly knowing what we were agreeing to, we gave hearty approval. The evenings consisted of prayer, praise and study. Inevitably, as we started on the book of Acts we encountered the powerful activity of the Holy Spirit in the early church. First-century believers were evidently charged with an energy that we knew nothing about.

Phil encouraged us to become active in evangelism. He spent hours in personal door-to-door work and urged us to join him. The thought of it totally terrified me. Until now, I was beginning to be genuinely excited by my newfound lifestyle and the heroes with whom I regularly rubbed shoulders in the many books I was reading. But I was still shamefully shy about sharing my faith with others. It became painfully obvious to me that I was like Simon Peter before Pentecost, virtually denying my Lord when opportunities arose to own and name him.

One memorable Sunday afternoon, I had actually led a Bible study for the young people at the Baptist church. I was rather thrilled at having that privilege and thought that it had gone rather well. Before the evening service, I thought I would take a stroll along the seafront. I arrived at Brighton's fish market, where a crowd had gathered. Looking down from the upper promenade, I saw what was attracting the crowd. On the lower promenade a group of elderly ladies were holding up gospel banners and singing ancient songs in trembling voices, celebrating their Saviour. The crowds were laughing. Behind my sunglasses, I stood there thinking, 'This is terrible.' In my heart I immediately questioned why this was so awful. Immediately came the reply that Jesus had called young men to serve him in this way, not elderly ladies – and with that came the haunting question, 'Would you do it?' Not on your life, I thought! I would rather die than stand up like that and preach about Jesus in public.

At that moment, some people in front of me turned to one another and said, 'Look at those old fools. Why don't they keep their religion to themselves?' At once came the inner urge, 'At least tell these people that you also believe in Jesus.' But I couldn't! I found I couldn't open my mouth. As ever, I was full of fear. I felt totally humbled, turned away and rushed home. I knelt by my bed and cried to God: 'Surely there is more than this. You changed Simon

Peter; can't you change me? Can I receive power?'

Within a short space of time, I was introduced to a young man in London who seemed to be everything I longed to be. He was the friend of a mutual friend, and we often lunched together. At every opportunity he always shared his faith with any casual acquaintance. We would often be in a café and he would give tracts to those nearby. I hated the embarrassment, but so admired his courage and freedom.

'Why are you so different to me?' I asked one day.

'I've been baptised with the Holy Spirit,' he replied.

'What's that?'

'Come to my church next weekend and I will get my pastor to pray for you.'

To be honest, I had read a few books on the subject by now, but was totally confused. If John Stott disagreed with Dr Martyn Lloyd-Jones, who was I to work out the real truth of how and when the individual believer received the Holy Spirit into his life? Some seemed to say that you have everything at conversion. Others said you must wait until you are more mature before you can receive power from on high. Then there were the Pentecostals, who seemed to insist that you wait until you speak with tongues, but my previous experience of Christianity seemed to say that this was all finished in the early centuries of the church.

By now, however, I was desperate. If there was more, I wanted it. If I could be set free to own Jesus and be a witness to my work colleagues and others, I longed for it. The following weekend I attended my friend's church in London. It was 1962 and the charismatic renewal had barely started. It was about to break out, and I was to have the privilege of being part of it.

# 3

# Being Apprenticed

The following Sunday found me at Peniel Chapel, a Pentecostal church near Notting Hill Gate. On the Saturday evening I met some of the young people from the chapel who were going on a coach trip into the country to take a meeting in another church. Never had I seen such a zealous, vital group. One after another they stood up and gave their testimony in the meeting without any prior warning or preparation. They were magnificent. The young people I was used to would need a few weeks' notice for this sort of thing and even then they would have to read from notes. For the first time in my life I heard someone speak in tongues during the course of the meeting and then, to my astonishment, one of the young Londoners who had been laughing and joking on the coach earlier gave an interpretation. It sounded as if someone like Isaiah had come into the room. It was all in a different league from anything I had ever encountered, but I knew that this was what I wanted.

During the day my friend Derek and I, together with a handful of others, had been fasting and praying about my need to be filled with the Spirit and he had spoken a prophecy. I had never heard this gift being used before, but I received it as if God himself was speaking to me. 'My little sheep,' he said, 'keep very close to me and I will lead you to the living waters and give you your heart's desire.' Having heard that promise, I had no doubt that God was going to fill me with his Spirit.

The following day I was at the chapel. In a small room I gathered with a group of others, eagerly waiting to receive the baptism of the Holy Spirit. After a while, the pastor entered and, following a few words of explanation, began to move around the circle, praying for one after another.

Eventually he arrived in front of me as I sat before him. I don't know what I expected, but I certainly didn't expect what at first I seemed to get, namely a couple of hands on my head, and a prayer. After his brief prayer, he moved on to the next person. I felt nothing! I had come all this way, fasted through the previous day, and received nothing! To my consternation, my friends now not only told me to thank and praise God for my new gift, but also to speak in tongues. I was appalled! Nothing had happened, and they wanted me to thank God for it and, to add to my embarrassment, throw in some tongues-speaking!

I argued with them at length, but their love and patience were exemplary. They brought me back to the promises of the Bible and reminded me of my heavenly Father's faithfulness and encouraged me to draw near to God once again. By now the pastor had gone. I prayed and once again they encouraged me to speak in tongues. Fearfully I started but quickly stopped, claiming that I did not want to make up some silly, meaningless language. Again they patiently prevailed upon me to stick at it and again begin to pray. I did so and carried on this new language for a little while but it was as though hundreds of voices in my head were accusing,

'You are making this up. This is not supernatural. This is mere nonsense!' Quietly, my friend commented, 'You are very clever making all this up.' We laughed, I relaxed and carried on. Suddenly a rush of power went right through my being from head to toe. I found myself not only speaking freely in tongues but also calling out to God in the most loving and intimate terms that I could imagine. God was right here in my heart. His love was overflowing me. I truly loved him like never before. *Abba* Father suddenly took on new meaning.

A few minutes earlier I had been arguing against my tongues-speaking endeavours; now I never wanted to stop! I went to the public evening service that followed, but sat in the back row, hand over my mouth so that I would not disturb anyone, and prayed in tongues throughout the whole service. It was wonderful. I felt that I could never doubt God's love or presence again. He was right inside me. He was actually speaking through me. I was totally overjoyed and flooded with excitement.

I was soon to find that my experience was not going to go uncontested. When I arrived back in Hove that night my sister was waiting for me, wanting to find out what had happened. When I told her that I had been baptised in the Spirit, her response was immediate: 'Please pray for me.'

With little understanding of how to help someone, but only knowing what had just happened to me in London, I prayed for her. Because of my ignorance of how to prepare her to believe God, she was disappointed. She cried and cried that God would fill her, but nothing happened. I was not ready for this sort of thing and found myself assailed by doubts again. Where was the power that I expected to flow? The devil rushed in to suggest that what had happened to me was OK in London but I was back in Hove now and I was no different. It was just a passing experience that had come and gone.

For a week I felt cut off from God. I was in turmoil. Had that experience in London been real or not? There was nobody I could turn to, because at that time I knew nobody in the Brighton area who had had this experience of the Spirit. Finally, the next Sunday afternoon, I got down on my knees in my bedroom and cried to God for an answer. As I prayed, my joy came flooding back and I began to praise God in new tongues again. He had come to abide with me for ever. I was out of the wilderness and never doubted the experience again. Within a few weeks, everyone in Phil's little Monday night fellowship was baptised in the Holy Spirit. The meetings became electric. God's presence was wonderful. Suddenly, my Christianity was taking on totally new dimensions.

A few weeks later, the young people of the Baptist church which I attended were gathered for their annual retreat weekend. I had prayed fervently that the opportunity might arise for me to share my new experience without causing offence. The programme was already arranged but on the Saturday afternoon, when we were supposed to go for a walk, it poured with rain. Mr Rudman approached me and said that he was going to arrange an extra session. It would be an open discussion and he wanted to call it 'Inreach and Outreach', discussing the fact that before we could ever be effective in evangelism God had to work in our hearts by way of preparation. During the discussion he amazed me by saying, 'Something seems to have happened to you lately, Terry. Have you a testimony to share?' I was suddenly on the spot! I had told no one of my recent experience and wasn't sure how well a secret visit to a Pentecostal church, resulting in my speaking in tongues, would be received by my pastor. I began to tell the story of what had happened just a few weeks earlier. The room was totally hushed. When I finished, you could have heard a pin drop. Mr Rudman broke the silence by saying, 'Terry, you must lay hands on all of these young people and I will come at the end of the queue.' I have many great memories of that remarkable man of God, but I shall never forget his extraordinary humility and grace on that afternoon.

Over the next few weeks I had the joy of laying hands on many of the young people and watching them receive the Holy Spirit and speak in tongues. To my great delight, that following summer I led several of them out to Brighton seafront, where we sang and I stood on a box and preached the gospel in the open air. It became our regular programme on Sunday afternoons through that summer and was absolutely thrilling. With growing faith and understanding I prayed again for my sister and her friend, and saw them both filled with the Holy Spirit.

On one occasion, the very remarkable Edgar Trout was guest speaker at Phil's Monday night group. He was actually a Justice of the Peace, a respected and older gentleman who lived in Devon. But he was no ordinary JP; he had experience of casting out demons like nothing I'd ever heard before. He had extraordinary encounters with witches' covens in Devon and was a remarkable man of war! He spoke to us from the book of Judges, liberally scattered with illustrations from his hair-raising experiences of spiritual warfare in Devon. On that evening, Graham, a young man from Holland Road, was there for the first time. He was so amazed at the testimony to the reality of the powers of darkness that he realised he needed power from God. On his way home he drove his car into a quiet area in a car park and cried to God. The power of God flooded and shook the car. He was powerfully baptised in the Holy Spirit and was a changed man.

Meanwhile, Phil began to involve us in door-to-door evangelism and the distribution of *Challenge* newspaper. When October came, we planned to await the conclusion of the Labour Party conference in Brighton and give every delegate a copy. To our dismay, when we arrived on the last day we found that the conference had finished earlier than we had anticipated. What should we now do with our hundreds of *Challenge* newspapers?

The truth was that in addition to becoming increasingly involved in evangelism, we had developed a growing urgency in prayer. In fact Phil's meetings now took place not only on Monday evenings but also on Saturday mornings, so that we could give more time to interceding for revival in Brighton. We had particularly been praying for the housing estates to the north of the town. Phil therefore suggested that we followed our prayers by distributing the papers throughout these estates, which we proceeded to do at every opportunity.

Gradually my life was becoming increasingly crowded with prayer and evangelism and occasional opportunities to speak at small mission halls and churches around the town and county. Life was hectic. Monday to Friday I left home at 7.00 a.m., arriving home in the evening after 7.00 p.m. and rushing off to some aspect of my crowded programme. So I began to wonder: why did I have to spend twelve hours a day simply earning my keep? One day a Jehovah's Witness knocked at my door. I asked him how he managed financially. He told me that he knocked on doors for part of the day and cleaned windows as a way of covering his costs during the rest of the day. I was deeply challenged by his reply and began wondering if God would have me leave my job. The burden gradually grew more intense. I had a good job and came from a very humble family background. My parents were so pleased that I had a safe and secure job with promotion prospects and a safe pension. They were not yet Christian and were very perplexed at my changed lifestyle. They regretted the loss of my old friends and on one evening, when I was praying fervently in my bedroom, my father knocked, opened the door and urged me not to take all this religious stuff so seriously.

As the days went by, I increasingly felt that God wanted me to be more available to him. He wanted me as a man of prayer. Revival was coming. He was looking for my availability. Two challenges faced me. How could I give more time to prayer with such a demanding job in London, but if I left work, how would I make ends meet? Where would my money come from?

One Sunday morning I slipped away to the local Elim Pentecostal church which at that time met in the Lanes in Brighton. During the meeting there were two prophetic utterances. One said that God was looking for those who would spend time waiting on him and giving themselves to prayer. I knew God was speaking to me. The second said that God would always provide for and look after the one who obeyed him and put first the kingdom of God.

The next day I gave in my notice. On the 28th June 1963 I spent my last day in secular work. I was 23 years old.

# 4

# On the Potter's Wheel

Amazingly, the following week was the annual Holland Road missionary event. Five years on from my abortive attempt to respond to Stephen Olford's appeal I was now available to serve God full-time. Life took on a new shape. A number of key building blocks were established in my life. The first was prayer. Phil and I began to meet regularly for prayer, joined by another member of the Monday night group, Keith Frampton, who gave his notice at work the same day as I, though neither knew the other was doing so. Keith stayed with us for four months before he went to All Nations Missionary Training College and on to Bolivia, where he has done a great work for God.

The three of us spent regular extended times interceding for revival in Brighton. We had a great longing and a growing faith that God would come in power to his church. Almost daily we would pray by name for every church across the town and at times would feel an extraordinary intensity of God's presence and great stirrings of faith that he would come powerfully to the town. I remember on one occasion being literally afraid to open my eyes at the end of our prayer session for fear of what I would see – God's presence was so powerfully manifest.

Meanwhile, we also began to systematically visit Coldean, a housing estate to the north-east of town where there was a rather redundant Anglican church, but no evangelical testimony at all. Not surprisingly, we weren't greeted by the residents with great enthusiasm. Jehovah's Witnesses were fairly active in the area and the Mormons had already built a meeting place there and were regularly involved in outreach. In spite of a mixture of indifference and resentment from the locals, we gradually gathered a list of people willing to receive the monthly *Challenge* newspaper that we delivered.

When the schools broke for the summer we hit on a new strategy and invited children to meet with us on one of the open greens in the centre of the estate. We leafleted the area and on the first day (26th August 1963) 118 turned up, sat on the ground, listened to stories, sang songs, did quizzes, played games and seemed to generally enjoy themselves. Happily the weather stayed fine all week. Numbers held and parents watched from the sidelines. To my delight, this changed the attitude of many who opened the doors as we went from house to house. We were now recognised as the young men who arranged the holiday club for the kids. Suddenly smiles and friendliness replaced frowns and suspicion. (Now, nearly 40 years later, I see Kids' Clubs springing up everywhere.)

We decided to start a regular Sunday school to follow up this success. The local school was well placed in the centre of the estate, so each week we hired rooms and gathered our enthusiastic crowd of youngsters, drawing on some young people from the Baptist church to help us staff it. Once a month we had a family service and parents of the children were urged to attend. Slowly, the number of parents began to grow.

Since I had never received any formal theological training, I set myself to work through Louis Berkhof's *Systematic Theology*, gradually filling exercise books with my notes. My pastor urged me to leave the estate work, adopt a more well-worn path and train for Christian ministry by attending Spurgeon's Bible College. But Coldean's immediate needs gripped me and I could see no point in doing so. I was not persuaded that there was any biblical precedent for Bible college. My pastor argued that Paul initially went to Arabia for some years, but I couldn't quite see the connection! Nevertheless, I knew my need to study and, though I had read many books by now, I had never consistently worked through a theological tome. In spite of the small print and the rather colourless style of Berkhof, I enjoyed the discipline.

By this time my sister was actually attending Bible college, prior to doing missionary work in Spain. I asked her to give me a recommended reading list for my studies. When I had left my civil service job in London, my work colleagues wanted to make a gift and collected a substantial amount of money. Most of them thought that I was absolutely mad in leaving my job to do what I was going to do, but they all signed an autograph book and presented me with a handsome cheque. They wanted to buy a particular gift for me but I said I would prefer the money to buy books. In this way, I started my personal library with some commentaries and reference books recommended by my sister's tutors.

On Sunday evenings I continued to attend Holland Road Baptist Church and by this time was part of the small committee that led the young people's fellowship. Opportunities to lead meetings and speak began to grow. Phil would often take me with him when he was preaching and get me to give my testimony. Then the time came when I had the fearful responsibility of actually being the Sunday speaker in a few small churches, chapels and mission halls in the Brighton area and around Sussex. One of the first I ever spoke in was the old Clarendon mission building in Hove, totally unaware of how this building would later feature in my life.

On one occasion, Phil was invited to be padre for a Boys' Brigade camp in Devon. He wrote back to say that he could not come but strongly recommended they ask me. It meant that for a week I had to speak to the boys every morning and evening. I was also required to camp in a tent, the thought of which totally appalled me. It was my most taxing preaching responsibility to date, and involved preparing and preaching about twelve messages.

Each day found me on my knees pleading for the messages. To my great delight, several boys responded to my gospel invitation, coming forward at the end of the penultimate evening and then individually praying with me through the final day. What a thrill. It went well enough for them to ask me back the following year. I did four such camps in all, always seeing a great response. One year I took a short series on Joshua and when I spoke about Achan stealing things from a tent and hiding them in his, one boy responded and confessed that on the previous day he had done precisely the same thing! He returned the stolen property, but thankfully stoning is definitely excluded from Boys' Brigade procedure!

I certainly had no idea as I spoke at these camps that one day I would be speaking at the 25,000-strong Stoneleigh International Bible weeks. But it was a particular thrill to discover much later that an elder of one of the NFI churches, who always attended Stoneleigh, was one of those teenage boys whom I led to Christ in my tent many years ago.

My original expectation, to follow the example of the young Jehovah's Witness who worked part-time in order to support his door-to-door outreach, never materialised. At first I simply lived on my savings from five years of working in the civil service. My father had always impressed upon me to save systematically, so I had enough to see me through for several months. Gradually, I felt that God was speaking to me about faith principles and trusting him for my supply. I dropped the idea of any other work and felt that God also wanted me to give away what remained of my savings and trust him for my needs. After some months it occurred to me that I should actually leave home and move to live on the housing estate and be among the people I was trying to reach.

One of the homes that I regularly visited was advertising a room to let, so I made arrangements and moved in. Though friendly people, they were not Christians and would have been amazed if they had known my financial situation. I was never late in paying my rent but sometimes it would come at the very last minute. I never made my financial needs known to anybody and issued no prayer letter. I had no guaranteed support, but week by week gifts would arrive to cover my costs. Sometimes the lady of the house would put the day's post in my hand, little realising that within a few minutes I would be giving her back the contents of the envelope in the form of this week's rent!

My costs were minimal really. I only needed my rent and money to cover petrol for my motor scooter, buying *Challenge* newspapers, hiring the schoolroom and daily necessities. Luxuries, of course, were unnecessary. I had long since stopped smoking, drinking and buying the latest jazz albums, so costs were low. I also felt that the money I did receive represented other people's income given to me as part of their worship and commitment to God, and therefore not to be squandered by me – though, to be honest, the amounts given did not leave much for squandering!

I well remember approaching my first Christmas, living on the estate and anticipating returning to my parents' home to celebrate with my family. Funds were extremely low. Could I really afford to buy Christmas presents for my parents, brother, sister and sister-in-law? Was it right to use people's gifts to me to buy presents anyway? I struggled with the whole dilemma.

As funds got even lower I took time out to cry to God. He spoke to me very clearly. It was a strange word but very clear. The Holy Spirit told me to ask for an amount equal to as many verses as there were in a certain psalm. I grabbed my Bible eager to find how many verses there were in the particular psalm impressed upon me. Though I remember the experience vividly I cannot remember the psalm number or the number of verses, but I do recall finding it and immediately praying urgently that God would meet my need. Within three days I received the exact amount in pounds sterling corresponding to the number of verses in the psalm, which gave me enough to pay my bills, buy the Christmas presents and give some to Phil, who I knew was in some need.

Life was exciting, if a little scary at times. On one occasion, when funds were extremely low, I cried to God to speak to me from my morning Bible reading. I desperately needed encouragement and the bolstering of my faith. Having prayed, I turned to my regular Bible reading and realised that I had arrived at Paul's letter to Titus. My heart sank as I remembered that the book was largely about administration of the churches and the appointment of elders and deacons. Despondently, I began to read, but within two verses I encountered Paul's wonderful description of the Lord as the 'God who cannot lie' (Titus 1:2). That was all I needed! I shouted for joy, sang and praised the Lord. Faith was rekindled, expectation arose and, praise God, once again funds flowed in. I was getting to know God.

After a while, Phil felt that he should respond to an invitation to become the director of British Youth for Christ. I was now alone in the work.

My time spent working at Coldean, which was two years in total, was a time of intense training. I found door-to-door evangelism exceedingly difficult. I remember one afternoon calling at a council house. A woman who was clearly drunk answered the door and invited me to the party! Walking in, I found half a dozen drunken housewives laughing, singing and generally fooling around. After a brief time, I reckoned that this was not a clever place for me to be. Someone shouted that it was my host's birthday and that they were celebrating (at 3.00 in the afternoon?!). As I left the house, she accompanied me to the door. I wished her a happy birthday. She said, 'It's not my birthday. We do this every Friday afternoon.' Then she told me she had a son. Tears began to flow. Telling me her heartbreaking story about her son, she began to cry even more. 'What can you do?' she asked, rhetorically. 'You have to drink, don't you?' Quickly, she controlled her emotions and forced a laugh. By now the others were calling to her from inside and I left.

Gradually I gained people's trust. They would tell me their stories of heartbreak: broken relationships, rebel kids, marital disloyalty and even experiences with demons. I would spend most mornings in intercessory prayer and working through my Berkhof and other books, and my afternoons going from door to door. It was tough, gruelling work and I was extremely lonely. J. O. Fraser became one of my great heroes. I read and reread his *Behind the Ranges* (later republished as *Mountain Rain* by Eileen Crossman, OMF Books, 1982). He had a highly developed understanding of the power of prayer and approached the whole matter very pragmatically when he said:

> We often speak of intercessory work as being of vital importance. I want to prove that I believe this in actual fact by giving my first and best energies to it as God may lead. I feel like a businessman who perceives that a certain line of goods pays better than any other in his store and who purposes making it his chief investment. (Eileen Crossman, *Mountain Rain*, OMF Books, 1982, pp. 127–28)

Occasionally there were wonderful streams in the desert. I remember once feeling particularly dejected as I went from house to house, and I decided I had had enough for one day. Weary and low I visited Mrs Payne, a lady who had recently accepted Christ. I wasn't sure if she needed a pastoral visit but I certainly knew I did! She greeted me really warmly. Recently she had told me that she could only speak about her Christian faith to me and to her husband and that she felt shy and scared to ever mention Christ beyond that tiny circle to any of her friends, family or neighbours. I had told her that she needed to be baptised in the Holy Spirit and had given her a booklet to read. To my dismay, she saw this afternoon as a golden opportunity to be prayed for to receive the Spirit. Depressed and miserable, I hardly felt like God's man of faith and power, ready to lay hands on someone so that out of my abundant experience she might also receive. But she was insistent. I certainly didn't want to fail her. I briefly went through a few Bible verses with her, explained that I would pray and did so. The room went very silent. I then thought that perhaps I should pray out loud in tongues so that at least she knew what it sounded like. She had only been saved a short while and had never attended a meeting. I waited for a moment, but suddenly the silence was broken as she began to pour out her new language of praise to the Lord. I was amazed and thrilled. God's strength had been available in my great weakness. He was not dependent on my feeling strong. He simply answered the cry of a thirsty child. I went on my way rejoicing, riding my motor scooter and shouting at the top of my voice as I roared down the road.

Not long after this experience I remember speaking at a Bath University Christian Union retreat and in one session I taught on receiving the Spirit. A long queue of students came to my room to be prayed for. In those days I would always pray for people individually after spending some time explaining from the Scriptures what they should expect to experience. The queue continued long into the night. I always recall the last young man. I had thought we had finished, but then one more came. I was so tired but he simply knelt down in my room and said with great yearning, 'I am *so thirsty*.' My faith soared as I knew that he would meet powerfully with God. I laid hands on him and prayed. He was silent for what seemed like an age. When I eventually asked how he was getting on, he told me that he had seen an amazing white light and was totally overwhelmed by it. In hushed tones he talked for a while, then we briefly prayed again. He spoke in tongues, celebrated his new-found experience of God and went on his way rejoicing.

I enjoyed my occasional preaching opportunities and was always refreshed on Sunday evenings by being at the Holland Road Baptist Church. Mr Rudman was a wonder-

ful preacher and a great man of God. But I found Monday
to Friday usually tough and demanding. I remember working my way through A.W. Pink's magnificent book on Elijah
during this season. I so identified with Elijah's lonely experience. I also meditated right through Jeremiah over many
weeks. He was sent to an unbelieving and resistant generation, but God had called him and put his word in his mouth,
commanding him to speak. Sometimes I wanted to leave, to
run away from the estate, but I still have an old Bible with
verses strongly underlined and notes in the margins of
Jeremiah. He had to work in harsh circumstances, but had
promises of a bright future. I knew that I was on the Master
Potter's wheel and that he was dealing with me deeply. As I
look back on my two years of door-to-door evangelism and
trusting God for all my resources, I feel I was probably there
more for my own formation and reshaping than for the sake
of the people of the estate.

Hardly anyone got saved. A church was not planted.
There is nothing at Coldean to show for my labours there.
Sometimes I would sob in prayer for the thousands of lost
people. There is an old folks' home in the centre of the
estate, which is surrounded by hills. It is in fact shaped
rather like a bowl with gently sloping sides. As I prayed it
was as though I could see all the inhabitants walking slowly
down its streets, finishing up in the old folks' home and then
slipping out into hell. As I pleaded with God I felt he gave
me promises not only for Coldean but also for Brighton as a
whole. He then spoke very strongly to me from Genesis
28:15 – 'Behold, I am with you, and will keep you wherever
you go, and will bring you back to this land; for I will not
leave you until I have done what I have promised you.' I
really made it my own in prayer and have underlined it in
every Bible that I have subsequently owned. I have always

believed that I have God's guarantee that he will fulfil the promise of blessing, particularly in the Brighton area for which I was daily crying. One part of the verse I could not understand. It said, 'I will bring you back to this land.' I wasn't going anywhere, so why did he say he would bring me back?

# 5

# The Broader Picture

Although my priorities were concentrated in the local Brighton area, I gradually became conscious of developments elsewhere. Arthur Wallis's book *In the Day of Thy Power*, a classic on revival, first published in 1956, had stirred many to seek God with new zeal. News began to circulate that prayer groups were multiplying. I travelled to London to attend one of George Ingram's half nights of prayer for revival and also began to receive his regular revival newssheet, which channelled information from around the world regarding awakenings that were beginning to take place. One sensed that a new day was dawning. I had always been taught at my Baptist church that we were in the last days and that things would get worse. Our only hope was the return of Christ. There was no hope of anything in this age for the church. We were supposedly in the 'Laodicean age', where lukewarmness would abound, but anyone who heard Jesus knocking at the door could open their heart to him.

Then some tapes came our way, giving testimony to a fresh move of the Holy Spirit among some Episcopalians on the West Coast of the USA. God had suddenly broken out in Dennis Bennett's church in Van Nuys. What became known as the Charismatic Movement was starting. We heard rumours that Anglican curates at All Souls, Langham Place, were now speaking in tongues and on the 29th September 1964 Michael Harper formed the influential Fountain Trust, having left All Souls that July. In 1965 he started publishing the bi-monthly *Renewal* magazine.

Before these developments, however, I was to enjoy the huge privilege of meeting Denis and Beth Clark, a South African couple living in Worthing, Sussex, just half an hour away on the south coast. Denis had formerly worked with Youth for Christ in South Africa but had now come to England carrying responsibility for European Youth for Christ.

In the January of 1964 Denis invited a few friends to be with him for a week of prayer and Bible ministry. He hosted this in his home and because of my friendship with Philip Vogel I was invited along. I had never met a man like him. He preached with amazing passion and authority and no little humour. The prayer times were magnificent. He prayed on a grand scale with great faith and had an enormous impact on me.

It was a totally memorable week and a great way to start the New Year. Indeed, my next few years began and ended at Denis's prayer and Bible weeks. By December 1964 Arthur Wallis and Campbell McAlpine had returned from living in New Zealand. They joined us, and Denis, Campbell and Arthur were a formidable preaching trio augmented by Stanley Jebb and joined for one session by Michael Harper. Again, prayer times were electric. Numbers grew and we had to move out of Denis's home to the nearby Greenhills Christian Conference Centre.

Each year numbers multiplied, and we moved first to Capel (later to affect the highly influential Capel Bible Week) and subsequently to Ashburnham Place. During these conferences I was exposed to powerful prayer and magnificent preaching and the comradeship of three spiritual giants, all of whom became dear and respected friends of mine. The combination of diligent preaching of the word and sustained Spirit-inspired intercession influenced me greatly for the future. The weeks also provided opportunity to meet such men as Barney Coombs from Basingstoke and Peter Lyne from Bristol, both of whom were working out the implications of the fresh move of the Holy Spirit in their home settings.

On one memorable occasion, Campbell McAlpine took Phil and me to a conference entitled The Apostolic Commission, held at Herne Bay Court. Speakers included Roger Forster, Graham Perrins, Arthur Wallis and the remarkable Willy Burton, a Pentecostal missionary home from Africa, who spoke at the breaking of bread with tears pouring down his face. When one of the earlier speakers had finished his talk I felt with longing, 'I wish I knew the Bible like he does.' When Willy Burton concluded I thought, 'If only I knew *the Lord* like he does!' It was a unique privilege to be present and I will never forget Willy Burton's pure devotion to Christ. He had planted hundreds of churches in Africa and seen amazing signs and wonders through his ministry, but what impacted me was his simplicity and deep personal passion for Jesus.

While there, I was also exposed for the first time to the extraordinary word of knowledge gift, especially through the very gracious ministry of a man I later learned was known as Pastor North, who had influence in a group of churches affectionately known by some as the North

Circular. I also met David Lillie, another pioneer in the fresh move of the Holy Spirit, who had longings for God to restore the New Testament pattern of church life.

Gradually I was becoming aware of the fact that what had happened to me in quite a private and singular way was part of a widespread move of the Holy Spirit. Waves of the Spirit were coming up on my beach, but if I looked along the coastline over the breakwaters I would notice that on every beach the tide was moving up. I heard of more and more people getting baptised in the Holy Spirit. Books began to be published. Conferences began to take place. Magazines and ministries began to multiply. *Renewal* magazine kept us informed of developments, particularly among Anglicans, and *A Voice of Faith,* edited by Cecil Cousen, started publishing more radical articles. I waited eagerly for each issue.

In 1964 John and Elizabeth Sherrill wrote the book *They Speak with Other Tongues*, and this was followed by other helpful testimony books written by such men as Michael Harper, Don Basham and Dennis Bennett. There was, of course, considerable disquiet and even opposition from some bastions of conservative evangelicalism who thought that such things as tongues-speaking were long since obsolete and that any modern manifestation must therefore be satanically inspired. David Lillie wrote his helpful apologetic for tongues-speaking, entitled *Tongues Under Fire*, published by the growingly influential Fountain Trust.

In this twenty-first-century climate it is hard to remember how hostile many were at the growing influence of this new development. Tongues-speaking became a very controversial subject in many circles. Books were written against it and many people were deeply alarmed. A very influential and helpful book appeared at this time entitled *The Cross and the Switchblade*. At first, it was hard to obtain. Some books were definitely of the 'brown paper bag under the counter' variety! It was not publicly displayed in some Christian bookshops, but if you asked for it you could get it. Originally *The Cross and the Switchblade* was only imported from the USA in what was a rather unusual format for most English readers, but its effect was explosive.

It was the breathtaking story of a young Pentecostal minister, David Wilkerson, who had dared to invade the drug-infested gangland of downtown New York and had seen amazing conversions and transformed lives among the gangs that fought there. The book, brilliantly written by John and Elizabeth Sherrill, had all the pace of a modern thriller, written in the style of a novel, but reporting extraordinary current events. It was a success story. Christians had not been used to reading success stories. There wasn't much success around, but here was a brilliantly written contemporary account of God acting among young gang members and drug addicts in New York today. I had read many books but this was unique. Finally the dam broke, the supplies poured in and everybody read it. (Later it would be distributed as a film, starring Pat Boone playing the part of David Wilkerson.)

What also made it rather explosive was that at the end of the totally gripping story some teaching was added on the vital importance of individuals being baptised with the Holy Spirit. It became a hugely influential book and added fuel to the growing charismatic fire that was gradually sweeping the country.

Amazingly, and for me very confusingly, one began to hear of Roman Catholics being baptised in the Holy Spirit. I went to hear a South African Assemblies of God minister called David Du Plessis (who had somehow earned the extraordinary title 'Mr Pentecost') speaking in Worthing. He said that God had told him to go to the Roman Catholics and that thousands were receiving the Holy Spirit. This certainly added grave misgivings to many conservative evangelicals and for some was final proof, if more proof were needed, that the whole thing was clearly satanic. In some areas disquiet turned to opposition and even fierce hostility. You could read articles claiming that tongues-speaking was actually people swearing and cursing in foreign languages.

It would take a brave man to challenge the biblical authenticity of speaking in tongues today, but at that time it was a revolutionary and controversial subject. Lines were drawn and many battles were fought, not only in Christian magazines and paperbacks but also in local churches, where growing numbers of traditional evangelicals were beginning to find this strange development affecting their own congregation. Tensions developed and people took sides. Many churches began to experience considerable strain in coping with the growing problem. At home my pastor, Mr Rudman, continued to be very warm towards me, even visiting Denis Clark's prayer and Bible week on one occasion, and continuing to encourage me to lay hands on the young people in the church. But he became quite nervous when some Pentecostals joined the church and tried to push things along in a more aggressive manner. He had enjoyed a successful ministry building a Baptist church with 600 members and very wide influence, and confided in me that he certainly did not want a split church. But he could see danger looming.

Also, he continued to press me to reconsider Bible college and a more conventional way forward. Once again I resisted his appeal. Enigmatically, having urged me to rethink my faith stance, he would then shake my hand (the charismatic hug was yet to be invented) and as I withdrew my hand I would often find he had pressed some folded money into it to help me on my way. To my great surprise, however, I found that a few other voices were expressing similar things to me. I was staggered to realise that within the space of a few weeks no fewer than seven people had urged me to reconsider going to Bible college. Though still very unconvinced, I felt I would be arrogant and stupid to ignore so many loving friends. My life was about to take a fresh turn. Maybe I would step into some well-worn paths after all, though I rather doubted it.

I was pleasantly surprised to discover that Dr Ernest Kevan, Principal of London Bible College, was to be the guest speaker at Peacehaven Evangelical Free Church on the 25th July, which was within a few days. It was extremely late to apply to go to college for the beginning of the new academic year starting in ten weeks' time, but I strongly felt that if I was going to go to college I must go in that immediate year, otherwise I would be faced with a year's wait followed by three years of college. The very thought of 'losing' four years appalled me, so I set this as a kind of Gideon's fleece that if I could get into college this autumn I would take it that God wanted me to go. I secretly felt that I was pretty safe and it would be impossible to be accepted at such a late date, but at least I was showing some willingness!

Dr Kevan spoke to me very graciously, telling me that there might be a place for me providing that I could pass an LBC interview and obtain a local government grant to cover my fees for the college. Once again, I was ridiculously late in applying for such a grant, since applications should have been sent many months before. I attended my college interview as late as the 23rd August and was accepted on the 27th. In obedience to Dr Kevan, I made my approach to the

East Sussex County Council. To my total amazement, I was the first ever theological student awarded a full local government grant – despite having applied at the end of August, and without even having an interview!

To my surprise, it seemed that God did want me to go to Bible college. On the 4th October 1965 a new chapter began in my life as I moved to London to attend LBC, which at that time was still based in Marylebone Road in the West End of London.

# 6

# A Student Again

On the 4th October 1965 I left for London and lived for my first year in digs near Lord's Cricket Ground, fifteen minutes' walk from London Bible College. Though I would often reach the college warm and carrying my jacket, the first thing one had to do on arrival was not only put on one's jacket and tie but also add an academic gown! Life was formal at LBC in those days. Imagine my amazement years later when I was invited to address the student body and found most dressed in jeans and open-necked shirts, worship led by guitars and students addressing the Principal by his Christian name! The transformation was extraordinary. In my day, hymn books and worship accompanied by the organ were the norm. The faculty processed into chapel each morning and the students stood to acknowledge their presence.

Sadly, the esteemed and beloved Dr Kevan had suddenly died just prior to the autumn term. When I began at college Dr H. D. McDonald was acting Principal, a man with a very lively mind and fascinating lecturing skill. He headed a very qualified team of lecturers with such stars as Donald

Guthrie, Harold Rowden, Arthur Cundall, Clement Connell, Leslie Allen, O. J. Thomas, David Jackson, Margaret Manton, Tim Buckley and for me the most inspiring Geoffrey Grogan, who was later to become Principal of the Bible Training Institute in Glasgow. His lectures on dogmatic theology made my heart leap and I never wanted to simply rush off to another lecture when he finished. When he taught, for instance, on the person of Christ and the mysteries of the Trinity, his own personal devotion shone through and his total fascination for his subject was contagious. I wanted to break out in praise and worship. We were also privileged to have lectures on missionary strategy by the great missionary statesman John Savage. I found him profoundly inspirational.

I have to say that some lectures were less than thrilling. They had become dull routine and some lecturers seemed to be simply going through the motions for the latest intake of students. The annual student Christmas concert, to which the faculty was invited, was always the golden opportunity for revenge and outrageous comment on college life. I remember one particular lecturer, who will remain nameless, being parodied in a particular skit. The student (mercilessly impersonating his lecturer) paused, looked at his notes and confessed that he could no longer read them since they had become so faded.

Notable contemporaries among the student body included Peter Lewis, pastor, theologian and writer, who would later have the honour of being the main speaker in a packed Westminster Chapel at Dr Martyn Lloyd-Jones' memorial service; Patrick Sookhdeo, who has become a leading authority on Islamic issues; Biang Kato, who later emerged as a key leader in West Africa before his tragic death in an accident at sea; and Ailish Eves, who was later to become a lecturer at the college. Also Os Guinness, who went through a time of questioning his faith while at LBC but is now recognised as a leading Christian apologist and prolific and provocative writer based in the USA.

I had gone to London with some trepidation. At school I had been a reluctant student and now after a five-year break from study I had to get back to lectures, homework and exams. Most of all, I dreaded having to learn Greek, so I worked very hard at it, realising that if I didn't keep on top I would get totally lost.

Although I arrived knowing nobody, I found that people were generally friendly. I met a young man who I understood to be the first Pentecostal that LBC had ever accepted. He was warm and lively but had been told very clearly at his interview how he was to conduct himself while attending college. No Pentecostal practice was to be promoted. In Dr Kevan's eyes, of course, I was a Baptist, so never received such a warning. I agreed to no such restrictions. The matter was never raised in my interviews and charismatic issues were not considered. Indeed, had there been any such imposed restraint I would have taken that as guidance that I was not to attend the college. It was not my intention to rock the boat or be on a crusade but, of course, I had no intention of being silent if opportunity to testify to the Holy Spirit's activity arose.

On Sunday 10th October I spent my first Sunday in a pattern which was to continue for nearly all my three years in London. In the morning I attended a new church that had recently started meeting in offices in Buckingham Street near Charing Cross, belonging to a firm headed by Mr David Foot. My dear friends who had so helped me in receiving the baptism of the Holy Spirit at Peniel Chapel had recently discovered this church and insisted that this was the place for me to be on Sunday mornings. It was an unusual place. Chairs were packed into a comparatively small room and several people had to sit on the floor. Hymn books were distributed as in the Baptist church I was used to, but there any similarities ceased. The hymn book was not our rather boring and ancient *Baptist Hymnal*, but *Redemption Hymnal* and was full of not only the usual classic hymns of such greats as Wesley and Watts but also other hymns of great joy and celebration and personal devotion. The atmosphere of praise was totally exuberant and unlike any I had previously encountered. The meeting was also completely unstructured. Starting at about 9.30 in the morning it usually ran on to about 1.00, with many bringing sandwiches and sharing their lunch afterwards.

At one point in the meeting, everybody started to sing in tongues together. Although I often sang in tongues alone in my own devotions, I had never heard anybody else do it and I certainly had never encountered everybody singing in tongues together. I immediately buried my head in my hands and asked God if this was all right. He seemed to give me great peace about it so I simply joined in.

The age group was diverse and many of the prayers of some of the older godly people present were quite magnificent. We had no musical instruments, not even a guitar, but the praise and worship were wonderful and the flow of the gifts of the Spirit surpassed anything I had previously encountered. Another new phenomenon to me was solo sung prophecies, sometimes with complicated rhythms. I remember on one occasion when Stuart Stranack, the pastor, began to sing a prophecy calypso style with rhythm and tone of voice in that form. It was extraordinary!

The leading figure in the group was an ex-Anglican called Richard Bolt, whose powerful healing ministry caused us to gasp. At one time he had been on a skiing holiday with David Foot and his family, when he fell and broke his leg. Having passed out, he was taken to hospital and came round with his leg in plaster. His confidence in Christ's power to heal was such that he actually cut the plaster off his leg and walked out of the hospital. On the following Sunday, he arrived at church holding up the redundant plaster and jumping on his formerly broken leg. I was sitting next to a nurse at the time and she gasped, 'That is impossible!' But he was doing it and we were rejoicing.

On another occasion, a boy in the congregation had had a serious face injury. He had been told that he would either remain disfigured or his face would be permanently scarred as a result of any surgery. Richard Bolt prayed, and the boy was perfectly healed. From then on he was known by us as the boy with the round face. Every time I saw him I would sit and stare at the result of his phenomenal healing. One week while we were worshipping, Richard suddenly produced an Autoharp, ran his fingers over the strings and began to sing an amazing worship song totally spontaneously. It was like being in David's tabernacle.

One other experience I must record. It was my birthday and, to my great delight, God particularly blessed me. I had received a birthday card in which a friend had written a particular verse that had, unbeknown to him, always been very special to me. It was a great reminder of God's hand upon me. Later I tore off the date from the page-a-day calendar and found another verse that God had often underlined to me with my birthday date on it. Later, at the Sunday morning meeting, I was helping to distribute the bread and wine and had actually begun to step over one man who was sitting on the floor. As I took my first step he began to prophesy. His eyes were closed. He had no idea that I was standing over him. In the prophecy he quoted both of the above verses. It was quite overwhelming for me as I stood in the presence of God, deeply moved at his ability to speak to me so directly.

As you can imagine, I could not wait to get to church every Sunday morning. I never knew what might happen. I had always enjoyed being at Holland Road in Hove. The preaching was always good and the singing was usually enthusiastic, especially if we sang 'And can it be' or 'Oh for a thousand tongues', but I had never encountered anything like this. God was manifestly there. It was genuinely exciting and unpredictable to be in the meetings. I began to bring sung prophecies myself and get caught up in the Holy Spirit's powerful activity. I was being exposed to a new way of being church, where God's presence was phenomenally real and unrushed worship and praise were the order of the day. Stuart was also a fine Bible expositor, so we were well fed with truth. And on the Sundays Richard Bolt was there, you never knew what might happen! Sunday morning always found me rushing off to Buckingham Street. At first I went alone but by the end of my three years a whole group of students from LBC would join me. But I must not rush ahead.

There was no Sunday evening service, so I had the great privilege for my three years in London to sit at the feet of the great Dr Martyn Lloyd-Jones at Westminster Chapel. One could hardly imagine a greater contrast in church life, but the magnificent preaching of the doctor made up for the formality and impersonal nature of the meetings.

College life was quite a mixture. In those days, most students shared accommodation in the college hostels. Some students shared their rooms with two or three others and several testified that retaining a personal walk with God in prayer was extremely difficult. They were substituting lectures for their own personal devotional reading. By the end of the first term many testified that they were spiritually backslidden and depressed. I was actually glad that I was living outside the college, where it was easier to sustain spiritual disciplines and maintain a walk with God.

On Tuesday nights, I would slip down to the Buckingham Street Church prayer meeting, which was held in another church building in Orange Street, near Leicester Square, and on Saturday evenings I would go to the same address, where the church hall was transformed into an outreach coffee bar and was absolutely packed with people off the streets. I regularly preached the gospel to the rowdy crowd that filled the place. If you could silence them and hold their attention by your preaching it was a real delight. I loved the experience and really felt God's help and anointing in preaching the gospel in that context.

In my second term, I was particularly surprised when one of the senior students, a member of the house committee, asked if I would be willing to stand as Student Evangelistic Chairman in the forthcoming student elections. Knowing that another student had already been nominated, I declined. He was one that I deeply admired and regarded as one of the genuine bright lights of the college. I was shocked when he replied, 'But he's an Arminian and you're a Calvinist.' Suddenly I was being introduced to a college undercurrent of which I had been formerly ignorant.

'How do you know that I am a Calvinist?' I asked.

'I can tell from the way you pray in the college prayer meeting,' he replied.

I was staggered. It was true that some years earlier I had been particularly impacted by A. W. Pink's book *The Sovereignty of God*, published by Banner of Truth. I could not withstand its strong biblical argument. My pastor had never taught reformed doctrine. Although he certainly had a very healthy assurance of God's sovereignty, he was more of a devotional teacher in the Keswick mould. It was through reading and study that I had come to adopt an essentially reformed stance. Subsequently, the writings of such men as Dr Martyn Lloyd-Jones, John Stott, J. I. Packer, C. H. Spurgeon and countless others had helped to establish me in these truths.

When I held my ground and refused to stand as Evangelistic Chairman, he asked if I would be willing to be Student Prayer Secretary. This would mean leading the student prayer meeting every week. I immediately felt that God would have me accept the invitation. Within a few weeks I was elected so that from the third term of my first year and throughout my second year I had the privilege of leading the student prayer meeting every week, always preceding the time with a brief devotional talk. What the senior student had not realised was that, although I was Calvinistic, I was also a charismatic. He could not conceive of a charismatic Calvinist. In the next year, when charismatic issues began to surface, I can imagine he was horrified that I now had such a key role in college life, since he himself was distinctly nervous of the whole development.

For myself, I have always been extremely comfortable with the combination of reformed doctrine and charismatic experience, feeling deeply convinced that they are both rooted in biblical revelation. Years later, we interviewed Joel Edwards, the current leader of the British Evangelical Alliance, in the Millennium edition of our *NFI Magazine* and he said of NFI, 'I think you have an unusual combination of reformed theology and charismatic experience. You're the only reformed charismatic group I know –

and that holds a lot of challenges.'

For me, some of those challenges were going to emerge in the pressures that developed in my later years at London Bible College.

# 7

# Pleasures and Pains

That summer I was asked to take responsibility for arranging what was called a 'Student Trek'. This meant that I had to lead a group of students on a three-week evangelistic mission and had freedom in choosing the locations. We went to Sussex and I led the team first to Seaford, where I had some contacts through Philip Vogel, then to Burgess Hill, where I knew the pastor of the Baptist church, and to Littlehampton, where Mr Rudman's former assistant, Alan Pringle, had now become the Baptist minister. The team, which was chosen for me, included about a dozen students, one of whom had recently caught my eye. Her name was Wendy Morgan. My first encounter had been totally negative, as one day she burst into the student lounge, windswept and carrying a hockey stick, wearing a ballooning skirt, ankle socks and plimsolls. Not exactly my type, but then sadly none of the female students at LBC were. Later, however, I met her again and we were frequently thrown together in what was called 'The Witness Team'. She and Bob Biggs would play guitars and sing and I would preach or give my testimony at various churches in the

London area, one of which I remember was Duke Street, Richmond. The more I got to know her the more I liked her. She was clearly genuinely sold out to God and had not only a beautiful personality but also, when not in 'jolly hockey stick' mode, could look absolutely stunning. I was definitely interested.

On one occasion I had made an evangelistic contact with a young woman at the Saturday evening outreach at Orange Street. I invited her to come to Buckingham Street on the following morning and realised that it would be unwise for me to meet her alone, so asked Wendy if she would come along to make the appropriate female link with the enquirer. Sadly, the girl did not show up, but Wendy came and as a result had her first experience of the Buckingham Street Church. A few weeks earlier I had the joy of laying hands on my first LBC student to receive the baptism of the Holy Spirit, namely Arnold Bell who was to become my room-mate for the remainder of my time at college, as I moved into the college hostel. Other students followed and a grow-ing number began to receive the Spirit. I prayed for one stu-dent just prior to the Student Trek; her name was Catherine and she was also part of the Trek Team. At the beginning of our time in Littlehampton, Wendy asked me about the bap-tism of the Holy Spirit. I spent some time explaining to her, but we were interrupted before there was opportunity to pray. Later that night she was staying in digs with Catherine and urged her to lay hands on her. She did, and Wendy was flooded with the Holy Spirit. At that point Wendy had to leave the Trek and join her parents on a previously arranged family holiday in Scotland.

She wrote to me, but the letter was a mixed blessing. In spite of the misgivings of her Plymouth Brethren parents, she was absolutely thrilled with her new experience of the

Spirit – but she added a tender but cautionary note. Rather apologetically, she said that she had wondered if I was looking for more than a simple friendship and was perhaps hoping for romantic involvement. If this was so, she was very sorry but she was not interested. She was determined to find the will of God for her life and wanted no distractions. To be honest, if I wasn't interested before, I certainly was now! I was absolutely hooked. I had never met a girl so focused. She now seemed to be everything that I was looking for.

After the summer break we returned to college but I kept my distance, though we were often together in a group context. She became a regular worshipper at Buckingham Street, as did a growing number of students. Arnold and I had started to use Sunday afternoons to pray together and the praying group kept on growing. Sundays for me became like heaven on earth. Buckingham Street in the morning, praying through the afternoon and Westminster Chapel in the evening. Sometimes Wendy and I simply found ourselves together in the crowd but she issued me one more cautionary warning of her determination to stay man-free. It was rather perplexing, since we seemed to fit so well together and she seemed genuinely fond of me. I was certainly growing increasingly fond of her.

Early in 1967 I set myself a three-day fast. I had a list of roughly six things about which I urgently required answers to prayer, and Wendy was one of them. On the following day, a Saturday morning, Wendy approached me after morning chapel. 'Can I speak to you please?' she asked. 'Oh no,' I thought, 'here comes the final go and get lost rebuff.' We went to the library annexe and I steeled myself for the inevitable. To my great surprise, she began to be rather embarrassed but proceeded to tell me that she thought she had fallen in love with me and feared that after her previous refusals I might never approach her again. I was absolutely amazed and delighted. We went quietly down to the college chapel, knelt and prayed, committing our lives to God and asking that if this was really his will he would confirm it for us as the days went by. There was no Hollywood style clinch; in fact I pride myself that I did not kiss Wendy until after several weeks of our friendship. I had made so many mistakes in the past and really wanted to get it right this time. We did, however, begin to hold hands and on that afternoon walked to Regents Park together. Since many students often strolled there, we were observed together and in the claustrophobic atmosphere of London 'Bridal' College it was evident Terry and Wendy were now 'an item'.

Meeting her parents, who were alarmed that their oldest daughter was going out with a charismatic, presented quite a challenge. Her rather formidable mother greeted me with, 'So *you* are the paragon of virtue.' Her father was more affable and easy-going. Later, I asked him if I might marry his daughter. On 26th April 1967 I asked Wendy to marry me. It was her 21st birthday and she accepted my proposal.

As the years passed, Wendy's parents came to value all that we were involved with and enthusiastically attended Bible weeks. After retiring, they lived in Lincolnshire and began to attend Stuart Bell's New Life Church in Lincoln. After her husband's death, Wendy's mother joined us in Brighton, having become an enthusiastic charismatic! In her late 70s and early 80s she fulfilled a lifetime's ambition to visit China, smuggling in cases full of Bibles. She was quite a lady! And so is her daughter!

LBC itself was beginning a new phase. A new principal, Gilbert Kirby, had joined the faculty. An extremely warm and friendly man, he had formerly led the Evangelical Alliance and seemed to know everybody in the Christian world. Each week's guest speaker at the college chapel was introduced to the students as his personal friend. Inevitably, when the next Christmas concert came around, Mr Kirby was mercilessly mocked by the students. He was mimicked as introducing everybody (from the Pope to Billy Graham) as his own dear friend. He obviously got the point, and at the next chapel he introduced our guest speaker with no personal reference at all. The man stood and said what a privilege it was to speak to the students at London Bible College and what a special joy it was for him to be with his dear friend Gilbert Kirby. The student congregation erupted in laughter and our guest was totally confused, unaware that his few gracious words had proved to be such good pantomime!

Occasionally, the Students' Committee would also invite guest speakers for Saturday night meetings, which the lecturers rarely attended. As Prayer Secretary, I was now free to arrange such a meeting and invited Denis Clark to speak on evangelism. Not a man to beat about the bush, Denis took Mark 16 as his text and worked through the passage in a very straightforward way. Though his exegesis was perfectly accurate, his theme included reference to signs, wonders and speaking in tongues and proved to be very controversial. At one point, a student actually rose to his feet to withstand him publicly. On the following Monday, Gilbert Kirby asked me to his study and urged me not to invite college speakers who represented extreme views.

The following year, when Arnold Bell had replaced me as Prayer Secretary and I had now been elected as Evangelistic Chairman, we invited Arthur Wallis to speak on the subject of revival. Sadly, this again proved controversial, since Arthur referred to the revival in Indonesia, where extraordinary signs and wonders were taking place. On that particular occasion, some members of the faculty had also attended the meeting and were clearly upset that such things were mentioned. I found it extraordinarily narrow-minded and frustrating.

The following evening found me attending Westminster Chapel, where I heard Dr Martyn Lloyd-Jones, who was currently preaching through the book of Acts. On that evening, he had arrived at chapter 8, Philip's evangelistic breakthrough in Samaria. He was at his majestic and awesome best and to me he seemed to be saying exactly the same sort of things that Arthur had said at college the previous evening. He made clear reference to Philip's preaching being accompanied by visible signs and wonders. He argued for the essential place of the Holy Spirit's powerful activity in biblical evangelism. I was held spellbound. When he finished, I determined to go and speak to him if at all possible. I knew that LBC students occasionally did, but had never done so myself. I also understood that there was often a long queue of people waiting to see him and decided that I would stay only if the queue was short. When I arrived, only one person was ahead of me, so I waited.

He greeted me very warmly and I told him of my dilemma. I told him I had been baptised with the Holy Spirit and spoke with tongues. He smiled, clearly unfazed by that piece of information. I then told him about Arthur Wallis's visit to LBC the previous evening and how he had been received with such caution. I finally told him that he (the greatly respected and revered Doctor) had just preached a very similar sermon. To my amazement, he responded by asking me how many points he had announced that he was going to make in his sermon that night. It was actually quite unusual for Dr Lloyd-Jones to say in advance how many points he was going to make but I clearly remembered his mentioning that he was going to make three.

'Correct,' he said, 'and how many did I actually make?'

I stopped and tried to remember. 'Actually you never did make a second point, did you?'

'Correct,' he replied. 'The first point kept opening up to me. The Holy Spirit gave me the whole thing as I spoke.'

He pointed to a small pile of notes on the table, smiled and said, 'Those notes will do for next week now.' He then continued to encourage me. He said that the great sin of the evangelical world was to put God in a box and tell him what he could and could not do. I said that although I wanted to be open to all that both Arthur Wallis and he had preached, the fact was we were not actually experiencing anything like it. He responded by reminding me that Jesus said, 'Ask, seek and knock,' and every verb was expressed in the present continuous tense. He went on to urge me to keep on asking, keep on seeking and keep on knocking. He was so positive and encouraging. I went from his study thrilled that I had had the privilege of talking to him and even more thrilled with his breadth and depth of vision. He was no narrow-minded, safe, evangelical but a man with a big God who was to be sought for all his many blessings. So it was that the greatly respected and honoured Dr Martyn Lloyd-Jones gave me the same counsel as the (at that time) somewhat marginalised Arthur Wallis.

Gradually more and more students were being baptised in the Holy Spirit but my second year was one of considerable tension regarding the subject. One lecturer, speaking in chapel, dismissed charismatics as being like little children at Christmas, more interested in the glittering wrapping-paper than in the substance of the gift inside. Even some non-charismatics were offended on our behalf with the dismissive style adopted on that occasion. At LBC in those days 'caution' was the key theme. 'Balance' (what J. I. Packer calls 'that dreadful self-conscious word') was to be our God.

Arnold Bell wrote a brilliant exposé of the college's stance in the student magazine *Areopagus*, concluding his piece with the memorable appeal, 'So with both feet firmly on the ground, let us go forward!'

It amazed me that evangelical scholars normally famous for their careful exegesis of the text of Scripture abandoned that approach and argued from experience. For them, tongues had ceased. The supernatural manifestations of the Spirit were finished. Those wanting such things were dismissed as emotionalists and sensationalists. They totally ignored the fact that if their position were to be biblically based, the onus of proof lay with them to demonstrate that normal biblical Christianity was later to be replaced by something else. Of course, no such scripture exists. Specious and flimsy arguments were used, the strongest of which was that now the perfect has come (1 Corinthians 13), therefore tongues had passed away. To them, it seemed that since we now had the full canon of Scripture, the perfect had come. Happily, today such weak exegesis would be rejected out of hand by the vast majority but at that time it still carried weight for some. Copies of Anthony Hoekema's very sad book *What About Tongues-Speaking?* were left around the college for students to read.

Actually, after a very contentious second year, my third and final year at LBC was far more peaceful. A particularly anti-charismatic group of students had now left the college and more and more students were becoming filled with the Spirit. The Sunday afternoon prayer meeting was exciting and other prayer groups grew, which included Brash Bonsall's daughter, Ruth, the lively June Coxhead, later to have her own radio programme in New Zealand, and the future Mrs Rosemary Sookhdeo.

As time went by, I realised that Wendy and I were now

facing the very great question of where we were to go after leaving college. Several alternatives were set before us and I received very clear guidance from God, namely that we were not to take any of them! I was glad that it was clear, but alarmed that I was now approaching Easter and had no idea where I would go when summer arrived and college days were over. I knew that I could not become the pastor of a conventional Baptist church, as Mr Rudman and my friends at Holland Road had hoped. Buckingham Street had ruined me for that. If I were to be a pastor it would need to be in a totally new kind of church.

By this time, the influence of the Fountain Trust was growing. Paperbacks and booklets were multiplying, reflecting the fact that people from all sorts of denominational backgrounds were becoming charismatics, but most seemed content to see this development take place exclusively at specially arranged conferences or, at most, within the limits of their denominational framework. So, for many, their Sunday services were unchanged, but charismatic activity could be found at the margins of church life if you knew where to look for it. The result of this was that the out-working of the baptism of the Spirit and the use of spiritual gifts for many remained a personal rather than a church-changing event. After my three years at Buckingham Street I could never settle for that. I had to be in a church where the power of the Holy Spirit and his gifts played a central part, as Scripture clearly indicated they should. I was not content with personal renewal. I wanted to see the church restored to New Testament norms. Surely we needed a new wineskin or the old skin would crack and the wine would be lost.

Wendy and I set aside some time for special prayer and, to my surprise, I had a prophecy – something which I never expected when only two of us were praying together. The gist of the prophecy was that we were not to worry about the way ahead. Jesus was the way and if we clung closely to him and followed him he would open up things for us. His presence and his word brought us total peace – no specific answers but peace. Within a few weeks, I was approached by the leaders of the new Evangelical Free Church in Seaford on the south coast, 16 miles from Brighton. This was the group that had hosted the first week of our London Bible College Trek two summers earlier. They now knew Wendy and me and liked us. They had bought a plot of land, were going to build a church and invited me to become their first full-time pastor. I liked the people very much and admired their pioneering spirit. But they were not charismatic.

I was very open with them and told them that I was not only baptised in the Spirit but that if Wendy and I were to come I would want to build a New Testament type of church, totally open to the Holy Spirit's activity and reflecting the sort of thing I had experienced at Buckingham Street. They had never seen Buckingham Street but assured me that they had heard me preach and liked my biblical stance. They promised that if my teaching were clearly Bible-based they would follow as the Holy Spirit led into all that he had for us. It was settled that I would join them that summer.

I left college and on the 10th July 1968 Holland Road Baptist Church in Hove was packed for what was for me a very memorable ordination service. Gilbert Kirby preached a fine sermon on Ephesians 3:8: 'To me, the very least of all saints, this grace was given, to preach to the Gentiles the unfathomable riches of Christ', a verse I have always treasured. Mr Rudman spoke to me like a true father and prayed for me very lovingly, acknowledging that the printed programme stated that this ordination was into the 'Christian ministry' and not into the 'Baptist ministry' as he had hoped. He went on to predict that I would 'not walk along any securely tried pathways', but would 'walk a pathway different from the usual', and added, 'I cannot imagine what this ministry is going to lead to in the days to come.'

I then moved to live temporarily with a young couple in Seaford. After a few weeks, I laid hands on them both and they were baptised in the Holy Spirit.

On 31st August 1968 Wendy and I were married by Alan Pringle at Goodwood Hall Brethren Assembly in Leicester. The church bought a house and we set up our home in Seaford, where we were to live for the next eleven years and where we began to work out the principles of local church life. Gradually, individuals were filled with the Holy Spirit, but it was not going to be plain sailing by any means.

# 8

# Building a Church

Since the church at Seaford had only recently started, it had no long-standing traditions, which of course was a great advantage. No one could argue, 'We have always done it this way.' On the other hand, I was soon to discover that every member had their own personal background and expectations. The original group had met one another at a local missionary prayer meeting but travelled out of town on Sundays to various nearby evangelical churches. Now, through various stages of development and being influenced by a few different people, including my friend Philip Vogel, who had helped them for a while, they had begun meeting on Sundays in a hired hall with mid-week meetings in homes. They were a small group of fewer than 40 adults but other young couples began to arrive soon after Wendy and I moved in.

At first, all was calm. I preached on most Sundays but the other two elders were both experienced lay preachers and would occasionally speak. The meetings were formal, with the old classic style of a hymn, a prayer, a hymn, a reading, notices, offering, hymn, preach, hymn and finish. Very different from the last three years at Buckingham Street! It was very hard for Wendy and me to say goodbye to those magnificent Sundays in London.

Gradually, a few more came to me for prayer to be baptised in the Holy Spirit. Wendy and I would watch to see who might be next. We would often select a target couple, secretly fast and pray for them through our lunchtimes, invite them to a meal, lend them a book or a tape, and if they were interested they would soon ask to be prayed for. Slowly the numbers grew.

There were two church prayer meetings. One, which already existed before I arrived, was held on Tuesday evenings and was led rather formally by one of the elders. I then added a second, which took place on Friday evenings and which, though open to all, began to be attended by those who were filled with the Spirit. Gradually, it became a rather exciting place to be and the manifestation of the Spirit's presence grew increasingly strong there. I remember one Pentecostal lady attending the Friday meeting for the first time. She was amazed at the intensity of God's presence and eventually left at the end almost overwhelmed and asked, 'Is it always like this on Fridays?' Praise God, it increasingly was.

After a few months, we celebrated the opening of our new building. The Mayor of Seaford attended, Mr Rudman came with a large coachload from Hove, and other friends from Eastbourne and around attended. Our building was totally packed. Hilary Vogel cut the tape and we were officially open. Campbell McAlpine followed up with a week of special meetings and we were off to a good start.

We continued having our mid-week prayer meetings in homes. Now it was time to try introducing some more freedom into the Sunday meetings. I asked for ten minutes of 'open worship' in the midst of the normal prayer sandwich. People were initially unsure of what I was after, though one of the elders was from a Brethren background and was familiar with the concept. I explained to the people that they would be free to lead out in public prayer, or read a scripture, select a hymn, or start singing a song of worship.

At first, it was totally painful. One elderly gentleman asked if we could sing his favourite hymn 'For those in peril on the sea'. This was not exactly what I had in mind, and did not really reflect the Buckingham Street style meeting that I was longing to see reproduced. Another lady felt that she suddenly understood what it was all about. She remembered a chorus from her childhood and asked if we could sing 'A little talk with Jesus makes it right, all right'. My heart sank! One of my co-elders held his head in his hands. He was far from impressed with my bright ideas of 'open worship'.

Gradually, more people were getting Spirit-filled but why did the irresponsible types have to lead the way? Why couldn't a bank manager or other respected citizen become a tongues-speaker? One of the earliest to receive was a very extrovert and unpredictable lady. She knocked on my door one day and announced, 'I want the tongues.' Could I refuse to pray for her? I had very mixed feelings as I laid hands on her but sure enough she got 'the tongues' and after a while she started attending the Friday evening prayer meeting. Gradually, the Sunday morning ten minutes of open worship began to come alive and grew to 20 minutes. The Friday evening group began to realise what was possible. Could Sunday morning really become like the Friday evening prayer meetings? I was determined that it would. Eventually, Eleanor, our unpredictable lady, crossed the line for us. One Sunday morning, during the open worship, she spoke out excitedly in tongues. An interpretation followed. The atmosphere was tense but we survived. More people began to take part as weeks went by but it was noticeably the ladies who took the lead. The men were slower and more reluctant.

One elderly and very godly former Exclusive Brethren couple felt that they had to leave us at that point. It was terribly sad but they felt that if women were going to pray publicly in the meeting they could no longer be part of the church. It was a truly painful moment. They were a beautiful and beloved couple but their conscience would not allow them to break with their understanding of the Scripture's requirements regarding women participating publicly in the meetings. We remained very good friends and I continued visiting them regularly but there was consternation in the church that such a godly couple had left us.

Another older gentleman, who was far from happy with the way things were going, decided to stay and fight. He wasn't going to withdraw but if the worship choruses were becoming too bright he would interject very serious and sombre readings. So a couple of lively songs would be followed by his strong voice urging us now to turn, for instance, to Isaiah 53 which he would read slowly and deliberately with all the defiance of an implied 'follow that if you can'. He also used the horizontal prayer method of teaching us a few things while apparently addressing the Lord. Everybody knew what was happening and the meetings lurched on week by week. My co-elder from a Brethren background strongly endorsed his stance and began to be increasingly unhappy with developments. Sunday mornings were a mixture of pain and pleasure for me. I was always wondering what might happen next.

Because the open worship was so female-dominated I decided to arrange an occasional men's meeting in order to bring the men through to more spiritual liberty. Again, it was a publicly announced meeting but not all bothered to come, including the other two elders. It was an unstructured evening, always held in someone's home rather than the church building and it gradually became a centre of magnificent fellowship, praise, worship and unpredictability. The men at the heart of the church increasingly became friends who really enjoyed being together in the presence of God. Sunday mornings began to feel the impact of these liberated men and the open worship grew in length and intensity of God's presence, but we were still very vulnerable to being torpedoed at any time by those hostile to our progress.

I decided it was time to change the atmosphere of the church building. We got rid of our old, very upright wooden chairs and replaced them with something more comfortable. We also carpeted the whole room and rearranged the chairs from simply sitting in rows facing the front to sitting in ever-increasing circles facing inward. I taught from the Scriptures on the church coming together as family for worship in the presence of God. Gradually the whole service became open-style and the hymn sandwich became obsolete.

I selected approximately a dozen men, who by now had some experience in open worship, and arranged for them each to 'partner' another inexperienced man, who was given responsibility to open the worship. So the inexperienced one would bring a Bible reading, make a few comments, select an opening hymn and get our worship started. If he floundered, his more experienced partner would step in and take responsibility. I was determined to overcome their passivity and bring more men through and felt that God had spoken to me from the illustration of eagles pushing their young out of the nest in order to teach them to fly. Increasing numbers of people were taking part and the meeting sometimes began to touch something wonderful, though I would have to say the worship was often sweet rather than exuberant. We would sing gentle worship choruses and, to be honest, as time went by I began to forget how exuberant and totally uninhibited the worship had been at Buckingham Street. Nevertheless, progress was being made, albeit in an atmosphere of occasional tension and with strong misgivings being expressed by my two co-elders.

At this point, another unexpected development took place. Some friends of mine, Philip and Agnes Ball, formerly of Holland Road, who had been among the first to be baptised in the Holy Spirit there, had now moved to a village called Scaynes Hill near Haywards Heath. They had met another very godly couple in the village called Nigel and Janita Ring. Together, they had begun to make friends with a few Christians in the area and invited me to speak to a houseful of believers who were increasingly interested in the activity of the Holy Spirit in the church today. I agreed to go and took a car full of men from Seaford with me. The room was full. We had a great evening and people were eager to meet regularly and asked if I would come every week. I declined, but offered to come on alternate weeks. Gradually the group grew until people were sitting on the floor, in the hall and even up the stairs. Eventually Nigel arranged to have his wall knocked down and extended the size of the room for the meetings. People were getting filled with the Spirit and worship gradually developed, beautifully peppered with gifts of the Spirit. I always took three or four men with me and it proved a great discipling context for their development. I would always teach from the word and people seemed to be genuinely appreciative.

After a while, Phil and Agnes moved house to a small village near Horsham. Once again, they gathered some local

Christians and invited me there. Soon I was spending alternate weeks at the two growing house fellowships. Gradually I was drawn into other towns like Hastings, Crawley, East Grinstead and Burgess Hill. Unexpectedly, a sphere of influence was developing in the county. It was an exciting development that provided a welcome context of ministry away from the growing tensions at Seaford.

One day, I received a call from Ian McCullough, a former friend of mine who had attended Denis Clark's prayer and Bible weeks and was now living in Eastbourne. He knew of a conference that was going to take place at Halford House, Richmond, hosted by Arthur Wallis. It was going to feature teaching on Ephesians 4 and the ministry gifts listed in that chapter. I had enormous respect for Arthur so eagerly agreed to go. The place was packed and I knew a few faces there but not many. I was looking forward to hearing Arthur.

To my surprise, Peter Lyne took the first session. Chairs were arranged facing the front from three different angles and I noticed a particularly strange young man in the front row on the right-hand side. He was not sitting in what I regarded as a normal conventional way but seemed rather spread over two or three chairs, lounging very casually and looking around carelessly. He seemed to be frequently saying Amen loudly and, I thought, inappropriately. I wondered why he was in this meeting and how on earth he got to be in the front row near the revered Arthur Wallis.

When the next session started, Arthur announced that it was to be focused on the role of the prophet and once again, to my dismay, he was not going to speak but was delighted that David was there and would address this session. I looked around to see who David might be and, to my amazement, the man in the front row stood up and began to speak. I was shocked, but my sense of outrage was quickly replaced when David Mansell began to warm to his subject. It was a sermon that opened my eyes to God's glorious purpose in the church. David was almost hysterically funny in his delivery but his content held me spellbound. God wants a glorious church, a city set on a hill that cannot be hid. That day, as David spoke, I was captivated with a prophetic vision of God's purpose for the church that has never left me. My heart was pumping with excitement. I loved this man's message and I increasingly loved the man. How could I have been so stupid as to judge him before he even opened his mouth? Later, I learned that David had actually written the majestic song 'Jesus is Lord, creation's voice proclaims it', which was rapidly becoming almost the anthem of the charismatic movement. It was being sung everywhere and was the first classic hymn to come out of the recent move of the Holy Spirit.

Directly the session concluded, I pushed through the crowd, grabbed him and asked if he would speak at our church. We were rapidly approaching the third anniversary of our building's opening and I booked him to come for a week's meetings. David arrived at Seaford in April 1972 and we enjoyed an extraordinary week of phenomenal blessing. His preaching on the love of God was life-changing. His teaching about the church as a committed community of love was totally eye-opening. Added to great teaching there was a breakout of powerful physical healing. I was personally healed from a long-standing back pain that had made it impossible for me to stand for any length of time without serious pain and discomfort. David prayed for me. My leg grew about half an inch and my pain completely disappeared.

In addition to this, David was totally free from any religious jargon or attitude to church life. By this time I was already beginning to get glimpses into the truth of God's grace as a result of my own reading, study and prayer. But I was not free from legalism in my own soul and often battled with a sense of condemnation that had dogged me for years. I always felt that I wasn't good enough for God and worked hard at my sanctification. I also had a dutiful attitude to work and a fairly uptight view of money. Wendy and I never spent any on ourselves and regarded the holes in our carpet at home as proof of our commitment to higher things and indifference to the things of this world.

David was totally different from anyone I had ever met. He was a free spirit. He clearly loved God fervently and was full of faith but he was not remotely religious. He was full of humour and came among us like a breath of fresh air. On the final evening of our week of meetings, we were enjoying a meal together and one of our friends went ahead to the church building to unlock the doors. We joked that he had a church unlocking ministry. I then realised that David had exactly the same! He had somehow unlocked the church through his visit and lifted us into a new place in God.

Tony Gunstone, my antagonistic elder, was very angry and defiant. He also had serious back trouble. When David, whom he intensely disliked, invited people forward for prayer, Tony stepped forward, sat in the 'prayer chair' and announced, 'Third vertebra damaged.' He had had a serious back problem for years. He was going to show up David for the charlatan he obviously was. David laid hands on him and prayed. His prayer was as powerful as it was peculiar. 'Come in, number three,' he said simply. Tony was immediately healed. Not surprisingly, he was absolutely amazed and for a season became a transformed man, enthusiastically endorsing David's visit and even laying hands on people himself, expecting them to be healed. His wife had recently had an operation, as a result of which she was no longer able to place the sole of her foot flat on the ground. Tony sat her down and prayed for her; there was a crack, her foot went down flat and she was healed. These were happy days. We had definitely moved forward.

I also began to be invited to other meetings being held in London, with which David was identified. The first was held at hired rooms in the Leprosy Mission's headquarters in London. I arrived late and rather embarrassingly my entrance was at the focal point of the room. A man called Maurice Smith was leading the meeting and greeted me very warmly. The seating fanned out from the centre and I made my way towards the few remaining spaces at the back. The first thing I noticed was the exuberance of the worship. I hadn't met such enthusiasm in worship since Buckingham Street. It made me realise how much ground I had lost through the slow slog of Seaford in gradually changing it from its rather formal background. Here there was a shout in the camp and a manly vitality about the atmosphere. Also, tambourines were much in evidence, which rather surprised me. It was a remarkable meeting, yet the most memorable thing came right at the end.

I had been perplexed by a very youthful looking guy at the centre of the gathering. He wore a leather jacket, had noticeably long hair, was thin and had the look of an adolescent. Why was he there at the centre with the leaders, I wondered? Maurice Smith concluded the meeting and then announced that the Festival of Light, a great event on the streets of central London, would be taking place very soon and he would like Gerald to say a few words about it. I wondered who Gerald might be. To my amazement the long-haired youth stood up. His passion for Christ, his spiritual authority, his skill of communication took my breath away. Tears began to flow. The meeting came alive with the urgent passion for the nation that he was communicating, and he was supposed to be simply announcing the forthcoming Festival of Light! For the first time I was encountering Gerald Coates.

When he finished, the atmosphere was electric. Maurice Smith joked that the glory always fell after he had pronounced the benediction. I realised I was beginning to touch a powerful stream of spiritual life totally free from the normal trappings of denominational traditions, similar yet different from Buckingham Street. These were the leaders of the emerging house church movement and they were exciting people to be around. They later became affectionately known in some circles as the 'London Brothers' and included other stars such as John Noble, George Tarleton and some great song writers like Ian Traynar and Dave Bilbrough. Soon the magnificent 'Valley of Achor' worship cassette was produced by some of the London group. A new style of beautiful worship was emerging in the body of Christ, no longer rooted simply in old choruses but genuinely expressing the breath of fresh air that was coming in the house churches. Great songs had already been coming around the world from New Zealand. Dave and Dale Garrett had been pace setters, but now the English were beginning to make a contribution. Great songs began to come from a vibrant, fast-growing church in Southampton led by Tony Morton and later Graham Kendrick's songs would begin to emerge.

Within weeks, thousands of us would assemble at Trafalgar Square for the Festival of Light. I found myself standing next to Barney Coombs. The wholehearted singing reflected the new life emerging in the body of Christ. The platform, which was very broad, included Peter Hill who was leading the festival, Gerald Coates, Lord Longford and Malcolm Muggeridge, strange bedfellows but undoubtedly illustrating that things were gaining momentum. We sang enthusiastically, 'Great is the Lord and greatly to be praised, in the city of our God, the mountain of his holiness.' The city of God was beginning to look good for the first time in my Christian experience. A huge column of rejoicing humanity made its way to Hyde Park, where Arthur Blessitt addressed us all and invited the assembled crowd to kneel and pray. It was an awesome sight. Surely God was doing something new in the land.

# 9

# A Growing Sphere of Influence

Now life began to advance on three fronts: the local church in Seaford, the growing sphere of responsibility through Sussex, and increasing fellowship with leaders from London and other contacts. At home the tensions grew ever greater at leadership level, while Sunday meetings gradually grew stronger. Tony reverted to his earlier unhappy position, in spite of the genuine blessing of the David Mansell week. The other elder and I went together to a conference held at Torbay Court, hosted by George Tarleton and Barney Coombs, entitled 'Our Generation'. It was an extraordinary conference addressed by Arthur Wallis, Cecil Cousen and others, and gathering many of the people I had begun to meet in recent months. It was also a meeting place of two streams. Some of the house church leaders from London were there (with their tambourines!), and others who reflected a more conservative denominational renewal preference were in evidence.

By this time I noticed that the house church leaders had started greeting one another with Russian-style hugs, while others used the more conventional handshake. I recall watching Barney greeting a line of men, hugging some and shaking the hands of others, depending on their background and expectation.

Friction was quite evident in the conference. Clearly those being more influenced by the essentially quiet, gentlemanly, Anglican-style that the Fountain Trust reflected anticipated a different approach to worship and relationships from the noisy, exuberant house church men. Tambourines were definitely not their scene! The house church men, with their very relaxed, open, friendly approach, found the formality of the denominational men strange. I observed it all with interest, feeling that I did not particularly belong to either camp. I was not in a denomination, nor was I in the house church stream.

Everybody was asked to give a brief word of testimony. I happened to be the last to speak and mentioned that although we all came from different backgrounds I was perhaps somewhat typical of the group that had gathered. Saved in the 1950s indirectly through Billy Graham's visit to London (I was a Billy Graham 'great-grandchild', my sister having been led to Christ by a Billy Graham convert), baptised in the Spirit in the 1960s and now in the 1970s trying to work out the full implications of the new wineskin which the charismatic movement surely demanded.

To be honest, the conference was rather a disappointing affair. The preaching was rarely of great significance and a lot of the time was spent in dissecting prophecies that came early in the programme. On one occasion I was in my room between sessions calling out to God because I longed for more of him and had come to Torquay with high expectations. He drew very near indeed and spoke to me in an amazing way, taking me to David's words to Solomon as recorded in 1 Chronicles 28:10: 'Consider now, for the Lord

has chosen you to build a house for the sanctuary; be courageous and act.' The whole passage was strongly impressed
upon me, particularly the closing exhortation in chapter
28:20, 'Be strong and courageous and act. Do not fear or be
dismayed, for the Lord God, my God, is with you. He will
not fail you nor forsake you until all the work for the service of the house of the Lord is finished.' It was reinforced
by the sense of God's presence in the room. I was also
reminded of the earlier promise that God had given me from
Genesis 28 concerning Jacob, that God would bring him
back to the land and would not leave him until he had done
all that he had promised him. Both promises seemed to have
a similar guarantee of fulfilment, and this new word came to
me with the same kind of authority as Genesis 28 had come
those years before. The conference itself had been a disappointment but what God said was indelibly stamped upon
my consciousness. He had chosen me to build a house. I
wasn't fully sure what that meant but I was unmistakably
sure that I had had an encounter with God and had received
a fresh commission from him.

The other positive outcome of the trip to the West
Country was that I had enjoyed some of the best fellowship
I had ever had with my friend from Seaford and we returned
much happier with one another. I believe that he saw the
breadth of what was happening in the country and that I
was not simply trying to wreck his church in Seaford with
my own crazy ideas. We were part of a phenomenon taking
place across the UK and many men were obviously grap-
pling with the implications and tensions in their home base.
I was truly grateful for the change of heart that he was
expressing.

Sadly, as with Tony, the change was not long-lived.
Relational pressures continued to grow. We had actually

drawn in a fourth elder, an extremely warm and friendly man, clearly filled with the Holy Spirit. His home usually hosted the Friday night prayer meeting. I had hoped that his presence would help pacify the rather painful elders' meetings. But he himself went through a very difficult time. Greatly influenced by the Fountain Trust meetings recently held at Ashburnham Place, he and his wife were particularly stirred by Graham Pulkingham, an American Episcopalian charismatic who was highlighting the value of communal living. Deeply moved with the vision, they sold their home, moved into a larger house and with great kindness opened it up to take in a number of people to live with them. After a while, friction began to emerge in the home and the future looked bleak. Instead of eldership tensions growing less, they actually increased.

Although Sunday meetings were undoubtedly gaining momentum and the church seemed to be making real progress, I knew that God could not ultimately bless a church whose leadership was so divided. In some areas the elders enjoyed real harmony and friendship, but in others we experienced serious strife. I longed for deeper unity and spiritual progress. Little arguments about little things seemed to dominate our discussions. One day I sat and wrote a letter of resignation. I explained my dilemma and said that I had to withdraw. Having completed it I felt that I heard God's word in my heart very clearly. He seemed to say, 'Very good, but did I tell you to write that?' I knew that he hadn't. I had no permission from God to withdraw. I had to see it through. I supposed he knew how he was going to resolve my huge dilemmas.

Soon after this, our church in Seaford experienced one of the most remarkable Sunday services that we had ever known. Ian McCullough from Eastbourne had arranged a

Saturday night celebration and his speaker would be free on Sunday morning; would we be interested? We agreed to have Alex Buchanan to speak. We had never met, though I had heard him preach before. During the worship Alex stood and began to prophesy. At first it was warm and affirming but suddenly it took on a serious tone and became a prophecy the like of which I had never heard before. 'You my sons who oppose the work of my Spirit in this place, unless you repent, I will remove you from this place and remove your ministry from you. Young men prepare yourselves for ministry, for my hand is increasingly upon my shepherd in this place. I will increasingly take him out from this place. Here he will grow less and less and you will grow more and more. Young men prepare yourselves for ministry.' Some were trembling. We had never heard such prophesying. As we walked home for lunch after the meeting I asked Alex who had told him about our church. He replied that he knew nothing about our church but that during the worship he had seen a vision of a huge wave coming up on a beach and some men standing trying to stop it. In a very relaxed way he said to me, 'It's impossible. They can't stop what God is doing among you.' I was staggered.

Within a few weeks our 'horizontal pray-er' died. He was working in his garden and dropped dead. He was indeed an elderly gentleman but it was a shock to us all. But a greater shock came on a Sunday afternoon when I returned from a family holiday and preached in the evening service about Simon Peter. I had been taking a series on Peter and had arrived at the verse which says, 'Simon, Simon. . . Satan has demanded permission to sift you like wheat; but I have prayed for you, that your faith may not fail; and you, when once you have turned again, strengthen your brothers.' When the service was over I was taken aside by two of the elders. They were obviously deadly serious and had some terrible news to share with me. While we were on holiday the elder who had accompanied me to Torquay had allowed a secret relationship with another woman to totally ship-wreck his life. He had left his wife and children and gone off with the woman. I could hardly believe what I was hearing. He was a businessman with an exemplary family life, greatly respected among Christians in the Eastbourne area. I went home broken. Wendy and I talked and then went to bed. I wept for ages and felt I would never be able to get to sleep. I was broken-hearted. My friend was spoiled. My friend was ruined. What about his family? I sobbed and sobbed. All our previous differences regarding the church seemed as nothing.

The following week I went to find him at his workplace and pleaded with him to repent and return. It was like talk-ing to a brick wall. His mind was totally closed. He did not want to see me or speak to me. He was completely infatu-ated and willing to lose everything. We gathered the church and amid tears and pain we shared the terrible news. Everybody was broken-hearted. His wife was magnificent and truly walked with God through the whole terrible experience.

A few weeks later the community house established by the fourth elder came into such friction that he felt that he must give priority to the safety of his family and unravel the household. People would have to go. He was in an agony of conscience, determined to care primarily for his own family but aware of the repercussions for some who had to leave. He felt he must resign his eldership.

Soon Tony decided he had had enough. He resigned his eldership, left the church and went through a season of sad backsliding. Some years later I was preaching at the Downs

Bible Week and made an invitation for backsliders to return to God. To my amazement the first person to come forward from the gathered thousands was Tony. I didn't even know that he was there. He was wonderfully restored to God and lived the remainder of his life fully committed to one of our NFI churches. Indeed each of these three men have experienced God's favour in their lives, the first having had an extraordinary restoration to God after being in a spiritual wilderness for 18 years. His wife had always believed that there would be a recovery, even from the night when I preached on Simon Peter's ultimate restoration, though I knew nothing of her husband's situation.

And so suddenly I was the only elder at the Seaford church. The men I had trained came into their own, as Alex's prophecy had said. It was a strange feeling that I was now free to lead without any restraint. The church surged forward. The young men were also far from happy with what they discovered about Wendy's and my home situation, namely that we were living in what was called the church manse on a very small income. No one else in the church had previously known how little we were receiving but the new regime determined to change it. They reckoned that Wendy and I should own our own home like everybody else in the church and they opened an account for people to make contributions to help us make a deposit and get started on a mortgage. The people gave very generously. The manse was sold, releasing some cash for improvements on the church building, and Wendy and I bought our first home with a salary that could sustain a mortgage. We felt like real people; no longer simply church employees in a supplied house!

On the wider front, I began occasionally to attend some public celebrations in London, hosted by David Mansell and the other brothers, in the Bonnington Hotel and other locations. Realising that I had a growing sphere across Sussex they encouraged me to follow their pattern and host some meetings in Brighton, the key town in the county. The first was held in Hove's Dudley Hotel and charismatics from all around the Sussex area pressed in to a lively gathering. A series of meetings followed, which subsequently took us to locations such as Brighton's Art College, the Royal Pavilion and ultimately the 1,300-seater Hove Town Hall. Guest speakers included David Mansell, Gerald Coates, George Tarleton, Barney Coombs, John Noble, David Pawson and others who were evidently emerging in the nation. As the meetings grew in significance so also my influence grew across the county and I added to the list of churches that I was serving in such towns as Heathfield, Lewes, Uckfield and Horsham.

The celebrations in Brighton were clearly becoming a growing feature and people travelled from around the county to appreciate the opportunity for charismatic fellowship. As time went by I began to take some speaking responsibilities myself and also invited Charlie Pocock, a local charismatic Baptist in Hove, to co-host the events so that we shared speaking responsibilities.

Another fresh development came when a group of ministers from south London, who together led the Lewisham Evangelical Fellowship, invited me to take a weekend of ministry. I had a good time with them, which resulted in Richard Haydon-Knowell, the pastor of Allerford Chapel, Catford, inviting me to come to his church for a nine-day visit, including two weekends and a full week. His was not a new charismatic church but an established evangelical free church of many years' standing. Within his congregation there were clearly three groups of people. A number had been freshly filled with the Spirit, others were very uneasy about this development and a middle group was unclear about the situation and uncommitted either way. Richard and his wife Sue were Spirit-filled and wanted to lead the church forward. I spoke each day of the week, rather like David Mansell had for us in Seaford. Several were baptised in the Holy Spirit, others were healed and God gave us a great time. Richard asked if I would be willing to come regularly and it was agreed that I would come for two days on a bi-monthly basis, spending the first evening with the leaders, the next day with Richard and the second evening with the church. A relationship between us formed and gradually the church began to change. I also spoke on some Sundays and after a while the Sunday services were transformed beyond recognition. The church gradually began to grow numerically and later completely outgrew its premises.

Soon, other nearby pastors asked if I would do a similar work in their churches and I took on responsibility to help a growing number of churches in south London. Among them were South Lee, Downham Way, Thornton Heath, and Bermondsey. My contacts also reached out into Kent, where I had the joy of being drawn into the vibrant church at Biggin Hill, being led by the dynamic and inimitable Ray Lowe, a friend for life.

At about this time, I was invited into a small, recently formed house church in Sidcup. A young man who was just about to conclude his three years of training at London Bible College was expected soon to take over as its pastor. I loved the group and was extremely impressed by the young man. I felt I should take the initiative to make further contact with him, with a view to spending more time with him. I wrote, and amazingly on the next day received a letter from him that had crossed with mine in the post. He had written to ask if it was possible for him, when he finished his studies at LBC, to come and be with me for some months before he took up his responsibilities for the Sidcup church. Hence, within a few months, David Holden came to live with Wendy and me in Seaford and a friendship began to form with great relevance for the future. He also fell in love with and married Liz Etherton, one of the girls in our church.

It seemed that my sphere of responsibility was now stretching away from the south coast and encompassing not only some of Kent but also parts of London. By this time I was working with about 20 churches. I was less and less at Seaford, as Alex had prophesied, but God had spoken to me about building a house for him. What kind of a house was he talking about, and what sort of a builder was I meant to be?

# 10
# All Change

At this time another major development took place. The Abinger Convention became transformed into the Capel Bible Week. Fred Price, who was host of the convention, had been baptised in the Holy Spirit, which radically changed his outlook. Denis Clark's midwinter prayer and Bible weeks were at that time using the Capel Elim Bible College facilities each year, and now the grounds proved ideal for a summer tent convention. Obviously, with hundreds camping and meeting in a big tent, the week could not easily follow the pattern of the prayer and Bible weeks. The prayer aspect stopped and it was simply known as the Capel Bible Week.

Denis Clark, Campbell McAlpine and Arthur Wallis were the main speakers, joined by Jean Darnall, an American evangelist currently based at Post Green in Dorset. I had recently met her in connection with the magnificent 'Come Together' worship concert that had been written by Jimmy and Carol Owens and performed in a number of major cities in the UK. The concert was a ground-breaking experience requiring a large choir. Magnificent Scripture passages were read and sung, and the music was contemporary, strongly affected by the Jesus Movement that was now taking place in the USA. When I first saw a film of it, which Jean Darnall showed to a number of ministers gathered at Pilgrim Hall in Sussex, the impact was phenomenal. 'Come Together' had provided another context for raising the profile of charismatic worship and an opportunity for gathering many charismatics in a context of joy and celebration.

Pat Boone had come over from the USA to be the main singer and compère of the evening in major cities such as Edinburgh, Birmingham, Liverpool, Belfast, Bristol and London's Westminster Central Hall. Thousands of people were trained to sing in choirs across the country and the 'Come Together' album was a huge success. The concert also introduced greater emphasis on audience participation in worship and really helped us to teach the things that God was impressing upon us. Though Pat Boone was the master of ceremonies of the first major presentations of 'Come Together', later the musical was produced by others and we enjoyed a magnificent evening at Brighton's 2,000-seater Dome, when Barney Coombs, who had a rich and full voice, did a brilliant job as the MC. I was almost overcome with emotion when the great choir burst out in song, 'You are the people of God and he loves you and has chosen you for his own.' I was beginning to love the church and long for her success. Somehow, 'Come Together' said so many of the things I was feeling deep inside.

The Capel Bible Week was a small camp by modern standards and had only 750 people camping in any one year. But in the evenings people would travel in and be added to the growing crowds, so that by its final year approximately 2,000 people were in attendance to hear the extraordinary Ern Baxter from the USA. Another regular Capel speaker was a Welshman based in Bradford called Bryn Jones, one of the most powerful preachers I had ever heard. Worship was often led by Barney Coombs or Gerald Coates and the chairman of the event for nearly all of its seven years was Harold Owen, who was leading an increasingly charismatic church in Woking. When he resigned, he was replaced by Mike Pusey from Farnborough, a man I had originally met at the Apostolic Commission conference at Herne Bay Court a few years earlier.

For Capel's last few years, I was invited to become a member of the steering committee responsible for the programme. We were called 'advisers' and came from a wide range of churchmanship. What we had in common was that we were all charismatics. As the years went by, the preaching became more radical and differences of opinion became more marked among the advisers. Some were clearly looking for what came to be known as renewal in the existing churches, with its outworking essentially for the individual believer, whereas others were looking for a more thorough-going restoration of New Testament church life. The differences between the 'Renewal' people and the 'Restoration' people were becoming more marked as time was going by.

But where were the roots of these Restoration ideas? On his first visit to Seaford, David Mansell had told us that he had recently started to meet with a small group of men gathered by Arthur Wallis. It had been Arthur's purpose in gathering them to share views of the prophetic scriptures. He realised that his own eschatology was under review and felt that there would be value in gathering some key prophetic teachers together to share their views in private. To their surprise, they experienced an overflow of prophetic utterances. This led them to believe that they were becoming a workshop for the development of truths that would be restored to the church, and they laid the foundations for a new style of church life that would be recovered in the nation. The six who gathered were: Arthur Wallis, Bryn Jones, David Mansell, Peter Lyne, Graham Perrins and Hugh Thompson. They were later joined by John Noble, which led them to be mischievously known in some circles as 'The Magnificent Seven'.

Certainly, the truths they were discussing about restoration in the church in terms of body ministry, a committed community, grace, spiritual authority and a prophetic hope were exciting themes. They confirmed to me my own conviction that God wanted a new wineskin and that old structures would not cope with the new life being outpoured on believers across the nations.

During this time, there were also a number of random leadership meetings taking place to which I was sometimes invited. I was amazed one day when I heard some men discussing the role of apostles in the church and even wondering if they were themselves apostles. I must confess that I was somewhat scandalised that they should even consider such things possible. Nevertheless, as time went by the influence of these men was growing. *Fullness* magazine was published by the London group of men, with fascinating and radical articles. First it was published in a small format, but later, designed by the extremely skilful Nick Butterworth, it became an impressive production. John Noble also wrote the provocatively titled *Forgive us Our Denominations* and also *First Apostles, Last Apostles*. The influence of this group was clearly rising. Meetings grew larger, until they even booked and filled London's Royal Albert Hall. But not having a great preacher of the Bryn Jones style among them, they hardly seemed to know what to do with it. Messages of little content and interviews with such men as Malcolm

Muggeridge took place – things that hardly required a Royal Albert Hall event. Although they could gather a crowd of over 5,000 people and it was great fun to be there, it seemed that the house church men were not yet ready for such a big platform. David Mansell began the evening by announcing that they had invited everybody to the Royal Albert Hall because they could not fit them all into their front room!

'The Magnificent Seven' was soon doubled to the similarly mocked 'Fabulous Fourteen', adding Gerald Coates, George Tarleton, Barney Coombs, Maurice Smith, Ian McCullough, John MacLoughlan and Campbell McAlpine. I thought very highly of the whole group and respected them enormously. I was grateful that such a radical team was emerging in the nation. One of the things that David Mansell had told me was that they were deeply committed to unity and speaking with one voice. A little later they decided that the fourteen should grow to twenty, and I was among the six who were added to make up the number.

To my surprise and dismay, I realised at the very first meeting that this was not a united group at all. There were deep differences of opinion among them. At first I was shocked at the forthrightness of their conversation when confronting one another, though to be honest I also admired their edge as a genuine strength. My background prepared me for a rather more religious and unreal attitude to relationships and the handling of differences. I had never seen encounters that were quite so raw and lacking in the normal niceties of Christian debate which so often seemed to fudge issues.

The fact was that this group, in spite of its supposed claimed unity, was in trouble. For instance, attitudes to the application of our being 'not under law' were varied. Some felt that others were holding views almost bordering on antinomianism. They would make very dismissive comments about the Bible and prayer meetings. It was said that early Christians did not carry a big black Bible around with them and some clearly saw prayer meetings as little more than the outworking of legalism. Others who were more cautious, not only for themselves but also for how others would interpret their remarks, were appealing for a less provocative line. On top of that there were personality clashes and strong differences of opinion about the need for discipline for one member of the group. I attended only two or three gatherings and pressures were evidently growing. Ern Baxter then visited the country to speak at a conference and added fuel to the fire by making comments and criticisms of the style and emphases of the so-called 'London Brothers' and their associates.

Eventually, hoping to bring resolution, Arthur Wallis wrote a letter, which later he deeply regretted writing. He listed the differences of opinion and brought things to a head. Instead of those receiving it simply replying to Arthur, the letter was duplicated and passed around. More people became involved and tensions multiplied. Things came to a tragic and ugly climax. Differences of opinion were even more magnified and an inevitable split took place. It seemed that people were almost forced to take sides, either essentially with Arthur Wallis, Bryn Jones, David Mansell, David Tomlinson, Peter Parris and those who were associated with them (later to be immortalised by Andrew Walker as 'R1' in his book *Restoring the Kingdom*), or with the London Brothers associated with John Noble, Gerald Coates, George Tarleton and Maurice Smith (Andrew Walker's 'R2').

Arthur came to see me and shared his reasons, and though I found the whole experience deeply painful and felt like the hurting child in the middle of a tragic divorce, I genuinely felt that I had more in common with Arthur's stance and from that time on found myself in the world of the R1 group, which actually reflected my values more. (Years later, in his final update of *Restoring the Kingdom*, Andrew Walker included his view of my personal involvement and the development and emergence of NFI.)

I continued to bump into Gerald regularly at Capel as we both attended the advisers' meetings, but rarely saw the others in R2 for several years. Instead, I found myself drawn into occasional small groups attended by Arthur Wallis, Bryn Jones, Keri Jones, David Tomlinson, Hugh Thompson, Tony Morton, David Mansell and others. On one occasion I was introduced by Arthur to a group of men with the words, 'This is Terry Virgo. He is doing an apostolic work in the south of England.' This shocked me considerably. I would never have introduced myself like that. What did he mean by saying I was doing an apostolic work?

Eventually, it was felt that the Capel Bible Week had fulfilled its purpose. It was undoubtedly an extraordinarily significant annual conference. It provided a platform not only for the excellent preaching of Bryn Jones, but also opened a door into the country for a group of men with growing significance in the USA, including not only Ern Baxter but also John Poole and Dick Williams, who brought superb teaching on such themes as the church, family life and the kingdom of God. Indeed, there was a resurgence of teaching on family life, highlighted by the book *The Christian Family*, a bestseller written by the charismatic Lutheran, Larry Christensen. If anything, Dick Williams' teaching was even more penetrating. He also began to testify to the kind of church life he was experiencing in Chicago, where commitment was at a high level and a very healthy church was being developed.

I had already been exposed to some excellent teaching from Keith Bentson and Orville Swindoll from Buenos Aires, regarding the increasingly strong churches developing there. Soon the powerful impact of Juan Carlos Ortiz's book on *Discipleship* would sweep the country; he, too, came from the same Buenos Aires stable. Discipleship was soon going to become a subject of considerable discussion and heated debate.

Ern Baxter was a powerful prophetic preacher, able to paint a huge picture of the magnificent end-time church. He was deeply rooted theologically, very widely read but also profoundly steeped in a powerful Pentecostal background. He was also in strong relationship with four other men in the USA who were beginning to have great influence; namely Bob Mumford, Derek Prince, Charles Simpson and Don Basham.

Capel had strengths and weaknesses. Its strengths were its platform for great prophetic preaching and a context for many charismatics to be together in exciting worship and fellowship. Its weaknesses were that behind the scenes its team of advisers was often in serious disarray. Bryn Jones was occasionally called upon to try to bring peace to the troubled waters.

When Capel closed, Bryn opened the hugely significant Dales Bible Week, which had all the strengths of Capel but none of its weaknesses. Bryn ran it with his own united team. He used Capel speakers such as Ern Baxter and himself and later Bob Mumford. He also ran it during school holidays (Capel had always been held in June). He used the Harrogate Agricultural Showground, a far larger setting in a more strategically based centre at the heart of the nation. People began to gather in their thousands, pulling their caravans and trailers from all over the country. It grew phenomenally, backed by the radical *Restoration* magazine, which was published monthly from Bryn's Bradford base under the Harvestime label.

One particular year, 1977, when Ern Baxter was the main speaker, we had the most extraordinary and unprecedented experiences. Angelic singing was heard by many. Even local residents from the surrounding area complained about the sound of singing in the night coming from the main shed, where, upon inspection, nobody was physically present. Many heard the singing and testified to its beauty and for them there was no question that they had been privileged to have a phenomenal encounter with angelic choirs. Children testified to seeing angels and one young child, lost in the huge camp, was supernaturally led back to her parents by a white, dancing angel. The atmosphere of the week was electric. The following year the numbers soared even higher. People were keen to have encounters with angels! One day, Bryn scared the life out of me by asking me if I would please lead the worship in one of the great evening celebrations. I had sometimes led worship at the Hove Town Hall meetings, but I'd never led several thousands. This was a new experience and pretty scary. I did it and survived and became a frequent worship leader at Dales Bible Week in the next few years.

The influence of Ern Baxter and his friends was growing even greater in the USA, and their monthly magazine, *New Wine*, became their radical trumpet voice now being read all around the world. At the huge charismatic conference in Kansas City, in 1976, they had obviously arrived in a place of extraordinary influence in the charismatic world. Their sphere of influence became known as the Shepherding Movement and their impact was growing fast. Conferences where they were the speakers were multiplying throughout the USA.

At that time, three things happened to me that were strongly intertwined in my experience. First, I had invited David Pawson to speak at one of our Hove Town Hall meetings and he, in turn, had invited me to speak at his charismatic Baptist church in Guildford, which met at the Millmead Centre. Soon, he invited me to speak on a monthly basis in his church, in order to help them make further transition. It was even suggested to me that I might be invited to become the team leader at Guildford, releasing David to a wider teaching ministry both inside and outside of Guildford, while I would become anchor man and also be free to travel. It was a strange but flattering thought. I said to Wendy that I thought it was unlikely to happen. Millmead was perceived to be a very significant charismatic centre at the time, but I always knew that somehow I would eventually return to Brighton. Hadn't God said to me those many years ago that he would bring me back to this place? I knew I had promises from God for Brighton that he had assured me he would fulfil. Even if we were to go to Guildford for a while, I knew I would ultimately return to Brighton. I continued with the monthly preaching responsibility at Millmead for several months, but the idea of moving there was dropped. Nevertheless, my roots in Seaford had unexpectedly felt a sense of being loosened. Was I meant to be considering relocation?

A second development that took place was totally surprising and unforeseen. People who were nervous of the growth of house churches and the burgeoning Bible week phenomenon, accompanied by the radical and influential magazines that were circulating, began to raise very negative questions. Suddenly, I was accused of trying to take over churches.

Nothing could be further from my thinking. I was rushed off my feet simply trying to keep up with the invitations I was receiving from pastors. It never occurred to me to try and take over anything. How would you do that, anyway?

Even in the Brighton area, a rumour circulated that Terry Virgo was encouraging charismatics to leave their churches and join him. This was scandalous and totally untrue. It never occurred to me that anyone in Brighton would leave their church and come to Seaford, where I was based. The rumours were, however, both powerful and painful. I experienced old friends avoiding me and some who used to attend the Brighton celebrations stopped coming. It was a tough experience and I had to overcome the sense of injustice. And, to make matters worse, no one ever spoke to me direct or asked me questions that would have provided opportunity to answer and show how wrong the stories were.

In reality, invitations were leading me further away from the south coast. I began to be involved in Woking with the church being led by Harold Owen, and then in north London, first of all helping briefly in the North London Community Church and then later in the Watford area where Alan Vincent had recently returned from India and was leading a small but vibrant group of churches. We became good friends and he asked if I would one day accompany him to India, where he hosted annual conferences in Bombay and had links elsewhere across India and Nepal. He and his wife Eileen had pioneered and worked in a sacrificial way there for many years but also longed to see New Testament churches formed.

Thirdly, to my great surprise, Bryn Jones asked me if I would like to accompany him on a trip that he was soon to be taking to the USA. It was an exciting thought. I had never been there before and gladly responded positively to the invitation. Just before we left, I had a phone call from a man in Hove saying that he and a small group had left a charismatic-style Baptist church there and were starting a new church. I was really distressed. There was hardly any genuinely charismatic life in the Brighton and Hove area at the time and this church probably represented the most hopeful context for a charismatic breakthrough in the town. It seemed tragic that it would split and therefore give apparent proof that charismatic issues were divisive, as some anti-charismatics argued.

'What are you going to do?' I asked.

'We are starting to meet in a local school and we want to come under your oversight.'

I was appalled. I pressed them about their desire to look to me for counsel but, when they assured me that they definitely wanted to do this, I said, 'If you want to ask for my oversight, here is my first instruction. Abandon the idea of leaving and try to work out your differences and stay together. I refuse to help you if take the course you are suggesting.' They reluctantly agreed to return and for some weeks I tried to help heal the evident wounds in their local church, which I had known quite well for years, though to be honest the pressures were extremely great. Relationships were desperately strained and things certainly were not going well. In all honesty, it did not look as though it was going to work, but I insisted that they try.

A few weeks later, Bryn and I left for Los Angeles, where Bryn was to speak at a conference alongside Ern Baxter and Charles Simpson. It was a fascinating conference, and I saw things that both impressed and alarmed me. The preaching was excellent and the hospitality afforded to Bryn and me was remarkable. What surprised me was the level of respect and honour afforded the two American speakers by their followers. In the UK leaders were very accessible to the churches they served. The British house church style was extremely informal and we built on friendship and comradeship. My wonderful old pastor, Mr Rudman, was always troubled that I never wore a dog collar and that people didn't call me 'pastor', but even the newest teenage convert would greet me simply as 'Terry'. He used to tell me that I was far too informal and would never gain respect from the congregation. But I wanted to build the church on a far warmer relationship and be real friends with the people in the churches that I served. Here in the US it seemed that these men were being given a deference by their followers that slightly disturbed me. But then again, who was I? The USA was another culture. I was a new boy looking and learning, hardly qualified to assess what I was witnessing.

To our great surprise, while we were in California, Bryn received an emergency phone call from a dear friend of his based in St Louis, Missouri. After lengthy phone conversations, Bryn told me that he must go to help this man who was in the midst of a huge crisis. I would have to cover the rest of the itinerary alone. For me it was an extraordinary experience: for the next three weeks I would be speaking dozens of times and travelling from town to town for approximately three-day visits, speaking to leaders' seminars and public celebrations in Spokane and Yakima, Washington; Portland, Oregon; Fresno and Sacramento, California; Rapid City, South Dakota, and Chicago, Illinois. To my delight, I also experienced a brief visit to Disneyland (how I longed to have Wendy and the children with me!). I also stood viewing Mount Rushmore, with its towering presidential heads carved out of the mountain looking down on me. I even sped to the top of Sears Tower, Chicago, at that time the tallest building in the world. It was quite a trip.

But while I was in the Sacramento area a life-changing event took place. I was provided with hospitality in a very small town called Auburn, about an hour out of Sacramento. The key man in the area, who was overseeing the main meetings in Sacramento, seemed to me to be very unstrategically placed. 'Since this guy is heading up the developments in Sacramento and the whole region, why is he based in the small town of Auburn?' I thought. 'Surely it's obvious he should move to Sacramento!'

No sooner had the thought entered my head than God said to me as clearly as anything, 'That's what you should do.' God had arrested my attention and now strongly impressed on me that it was time to leave Seaford and move to Brighton. I should not simply help to oversee the Hove-based group but should join them and indeed lead them. They should become my new home church. I was profoundly shocked. 'But Lord, they are not a church, they have no premises and there are only about 30 of them! Not only that, this is exactly what people have been saying in the town, that Terry Virgo is calling charismatics in the Brighton area to follow him. If I do this I will walk right into the fire. I don't really need this!'

But I could not resist the strong sense of guidance that I was feeling. When I returned from the States, the Hove-based group were quickly on to me, complaining that it was totally impossible to work things out in their church. They had tried but it was useless. They wanted to leave and start a new church. To their great surprise, I replied that I would not only oversee them, I would also aim to join them in the following year. It was now September 1978 and within six months I would move to Hove. The Brighton and Hove

Christian Fellowship was launched, with Henry Tyler as pastor and under my oversight and direction.

# 11

# A New Home Base

A huge upheaval took place in my life. Eleven historic and life-changing years at Seaford were to reach a conclusion. In my last year there, because of my travelling responsibilities, I preached on only five Sundays, but it was very much my home base and an extremely loving community where my family was cared for. When Wendy was pregnant with our third child, Joel, her waters broke in the twentieth week. When the crisis took place, we were warned that Wendy would probably lose the baby. I was away at a conference but because church members immediately came to care for Ben and Anna and run the home, Wendy was able to rest completely. The rapid and wholehearted response of the church saved the baby's life, and eventually Joel was born on time, a healthy and massive 9lb 9oz!

We have many wonderful memories of Seaford and had come through extraordinary experiences together. It had also provided a model church from which so much had sprung up in the Sussex area and beyond. We had occasionally gathered the pastors of those churches in my home for retreats and prayer times. Seaford had become a much loved centre of activity.

On our last Sunday, Wendy and I were presented with a magnificent painting of the famous local landmark, the Seven Sisters (the spectacular white cliffs overlooking the sea just outside the town) which still holds pride of place in my lounge at home. The church insisted on paying my salary for the first two years following the move to Hove. Many were weeping as we extracted ourselves from the loving community of dear friends. In Seaford, many of us lived in very close proximity to one another. For instance, five church families lived within ten front doors in the street in which we lived. Everybody was nearby. Homes were constantly invaded and small children often overflowed from house to house. In contrast, when we moved to Hove our nearest neighbours from the new church group lived a 15-minute walk away, a distance that would probably have covered nearly half of our Seaford congregation. It was a very strange transition.

On the wider front, Bryn Jones had suggested that I ought to consider forming a team to help me with the growing number of churches that I was serving. Thus far I had simply been busily travelling from church to church, usually alone or, if the church I was visiting was nearby, taking a group from Seaford in my car. Now I realised that I could not really serve many more churches unless I asked others to help me. Richard Haydon-Knowell, for instance, had personal experience of his own church being radically transformed and thus was equipped to represent me and help others in his area if I should ask him to do so. Things were clearly growing larger. We received a prophecy which called us to leave our market gardening approach to ministry and begin to take on more of a combine harvester approach.

If we were to grow I needed help. Not only did I need a

team but I desperately needed an administrator. The final proof of this, if proof were needed, was that Bryn Jones and the men running the increasingly massive Dales Bible Week felt it would be good if an equivalent conference could be launched somewhere in the south. Men in our ranks in the south were beginning to think similarly. Hundreds were making the long journey north every year. It certainly seemed to make sense to start a southern one, but the administrative implications appalled me. How could we run a Bible week?

I approached my friend Nigel Ring from Scaynes Hill, whose house fellowship by now had grown out of his home into a developing church led by David Coak, a dear friend formerly at Holland Road but now at Haywards Heath. When I mentioned the Bible week idea to Nigel, he rubbed his hands together with glee! He was a brilliant administrator and relished the opportunity to serve and make it work. When, a year later, I asked him if he would join me in Brighton and help me with the wider work with which I was increasingly involved, he agreed to leave his job at Chailey Heritage and come. His response was totally positive. He sold his house and he and Janita and their two children, Jez and Nicky, followed us to Hove. It is impossible for me to put a value on or express my appreciation for the friendship, companionship, unswerving loyalty and excellence of serving spirit which Nigel has brought to me in all that we have done together ever since.

Our first Downs Bible Week in 1979 attracted 2,900 people. Because we had already started distributing audiotapes of the Hove Town Hall meetings and already developed some organisational responsibility we felt the need to have some identity and came up with the title 'Coastlands'. A picture of the Seven Sisters was on each cassette label. This coincided with artwork we had used for the Seaford church. Probably because of the artwork, the title was always thought to represent the fact that I was working essentially on the south coast. But actually I had taken the word 'Coastlands' from the New American Standard Bible translation, where it usually represents the far-off nations waiting to hear the gospel (Isaiah 42:4).

The first Downs Bible Week was a replica of the Dales. The team from Harrogate came south to Plumpton Racecourse, where we erected a huge circus tent and Bryn and others spoke, though Bryn insisted that I should also be a main speaker. This represented a major challenge to me. I spoke on Gideon, whose story had always fascinated me. I must confess that I had often found personal encouragement in his story and identified with his reluctance and awareness of personal limitations. I took three sessions and spoke of the Prophet's Explanation (of the situation of decline in Israel), the New Anointed Leader, and finally the Committed Army. I felt truly thrilled that God had given me what I felt was a genuinely prophetic word speaking into the church situation in our day as I understood it. Having said that, I was confident that the Bible week was not really my responsibility. I felt secure because I knew that Bryn would carry the day and that other speakers would do a great job. Worship leaders, speakers, children's workers, the bookshop and everything were brought straight from the Dales to the Downs. It was quite an operation but it was wholly success-ful and we had demonstrated that we could gather a large crowd and administrate a great Bible week.

Meanwhile, in Hove, we started our new church in the Connaught school. Only 38 adult chairs were available, after which we had to use plastic boxes and other makeshift furniture. Some people brought their own deckchairs. As with Seaford, we had to start all over again regarding establishing a New Testament church with the centrality of worship and expecting the manifestation of the presence of the Holy Spirit and the development of spiritual gifts. It was quite tough, as we missed the levels of spontaneity and wholeheartedness we had developed in Seaford. But it was not the first time that we had learned to go back and start all over again, and we were happy to do it here in the Brighton area. The room was far from pleasant, and it was not unknown for the school caretaker to forget to turn on the heating. So we endured some truly dreadful meetings in cramped and cold conditions.

As regards teaching, I was committed to establishing a foundation of grace in the church. By this time I had become convinced of God's grace in a way that had transformed my Christian life. Under Denis Clark and other people's influence I had become a zealot regarding Bible reading, meditation and prayer. I had learned a fairly typical legalistic view of my faith from my Baptist church background and had added to that a zeal and commitment that I applied religiously. Often I was despondent because I felt that I did not pray enough or was in one way or another unworthy of God. Indeed, condemnation used to be the norm in evangelical circles and I always remember the heavy atmosphere of guilt that one encountered in prayer meetings, the opening part of which often consisted of people confessing their failure and need of forgiveness. Today, it is hard to remember the sense of oppression that used to rest on evangelical believers and how prayer meetings were often a place for sharing that sense of failure corporately.

From having been a heavy drinker in my early years, I had now become teetotal. I never attended cinemas and had no time for television. We never spent any money on holidays and, when Wendy and I were engaged, I even questioned whether it was appropriate to spend money on an engagement ring. As with most legalists, I felt inwardly condemned most of the time. I was never able to live to the standard that I felt was required. I probably would have said that the second part of Romans 7 was a description of my life.

Gradually, during the Seaford years, God began to open my eyes to his grace and total acceptance of me. When I first caught a glimpse of the truth of the grace of God it was almost too good to be true. I felt like the early disciples when they heard that Jesus had risen from the dead. 'They still could not believe it for joy' (Luke 24:41). I felt the same. I could hardly comprehend that all my striving to be acceptable was unnecessary and that feelings of condemnation could be a thing of the past.

Moments of extraordinary revelation brought me into increasing freedom. I remember preaching on one Sunday at Seaford on Zechariah 3 where Joshua, the High Priest, stood condemned before God as Satan accused him of his unworthiness, pointing out his filthy garments. God wonderfully intervenes in the story, giving Joshua clean clothes and a mitre on his head, while also rebuking Satan. Before he could offer his excuses, God justified him freely. On the night that I preached this sermon at Seaford, I suddenly saw more strongly my total acceptance in God and the free righteousness that we had been given, together with the magnificent truth of Romans 8 that it is God who justifies. Who can condemn? It was a moment of revelation that deeply stirred both me and the congregation. The worship following the sermon continued late into the evening as people grasped the liberty that grace brings. Many were dancing all around the building. It was a breakthrough night.

Later, David Mansell's teaching strongly underlined God's grace to me. Then, working systematically through Dr Martyn Lloyd-Jones' great series on Romans settled it for me, especially his treatment of Romans 7, which was wonderfully releasing. I had been freed from the law! I understood that Christians are not under law but under grace. I realised that many attitudes in me had to change and the legalistic lifestyle that I had adopted had to yield to the truth of God's word. I felt totally emancipated and almost as though my Christian life had started all over again.

It became very important to me to make sure that the Brighton church was built on these wonderful principles of grace. I had seen the church in Seaford become a grace-filled community. I wanted the same in Brighton and in every church where I had responsibility for laying foundations. With this in view, I started a series on Romans and worked through it on the Sunday mornings for several months. I wanted to see people not simply free from legalistic religion but also able to understand the New Testament doctrines of grace. Free, and knowing why they were free! Further, I wanted them to be free not only from law but also genuinely released from sin's power. So I needed to work right through Romans 6, meticulously teaching the liberty that Christ has brought and proclaiming what Jesus has provided for his people.

The congregation started to grow. Within a few weeks David and Rosie Fellingham and their family joined us from an Anglican church (though actually from Salvation Army roots). A group also chose to come with them. That brought our number up to about 70 and we were beginning to fill the small school room. I began to pray that God would provide a more satisfactory meeting place for us. One day the old Clarendon church mission building in Hove came strongly to mind. It was one of the first places in which I had ever preached back in the days when Philip Vogel was based there in the early 1960s. I had often preached there subsequently, having enjoyed excellent fellowship with two of its former pastors, Mr Hewitt and Mr Money, each of whom had been there for several years. It was a large building, erected in 1883, with a possible seating capacity of 500 if really packed. But it had not had a significant-sized congregation for many years and was now gathering about 25 mostly elderly people and hosting a youth club. I began to ask God in prayer if we could have that building for the church. One day Henry Tyler, Dave Fellingham and I were praying together and made a specific request that we might have it. While we were still praying we experienced the supernatural joy of certainty that God had heard and answered our prayers. I had no idea how it might happen but in my heart I felt it was done. It was just like the kind of assurance I used to receive in those early days at Coldean when praying in the money I needed for my rent.

Soon after this, quite out of the blue, I received a phone call from the residing pastor. Having seen the success of the Hove Town Hall meetings, he wanted to host some charismatic meetings in his building and wondered if I could recommend any speakers. I gave him the names of some of my friends, including Ray Lowe and Arnold Bell, who both spoke for him. Soon he called me again and asked if he could speak to me personally. I prayed, wondering how I might be able to raise the matter of his building. To my surprise and delight he almost immediately raised it himself. He knew of our growing congregation, meeting in the small school room, and he wondered if we would like to come and join the former mission, now known as Clarendon Church. Would we like to make it our home?

I told him we would be extremely interested but that we could only do this if we could actually run the church in the way that we understood church must be run, which would be very different from the way in which the mission had traditionally functioned. We had full discussions and set out on paper how it should happen, agreeing that I would be overall leader and that Henry Tyler would be the pastor. The church would have to undergo a total transition into the sort of new wineskin that we were convinced was essential. Certainly, we needed a new building but we could not accept a building at the expense of giving up the values that God had so strongly impressed upon us. The existing pastor would be drawn into our corporate life since we very much believed in team ministry. However, we made it very clear that it would be quite impossible for us simply to be added to what was already there. In real terms, it was very evident that our numbers would totally overwhelm the handful who were there at the moment and we would obviously become the majority of the congregation. We all agreed that any alternative would be unworkable.

Having arrived at the Clarendon Church building we grew even more quickly. New people came virtually every week. The actual structure was in a terrible state of disrepair. We discovered widespread dry rot. It had not only the 500-seater hall but a number of ancillary rooms and halls. Most of them, however, were full of junk. Generations of people had deposited their unwanted ancient suites of furniture in room after room. A small army of dedicated workers took load after load to the local tip. The finances of the church were discovered to be in a sad state. The phone had been cut off, since the bills had not been paid.

An exciting yet demanding programme of renovation was essential. The old pipe organ took up too much space, and the ugly and old-fashioned dark brown wood panelling needed to be ripped out. Specialists came in to deal with the dry rot. We drew up a plan to fit a dropped ceiling into the main hall, which was exceedingly high. Not only the heat but also our voices were lost into the huge space over our heads. It was hopeless for the kind of congregational participation that we wanted to develop. Little by little we set to work on reclaiming the whole building, moving from room to room with renovations as we could afford the bills. We began to have regular gift days, asking God for what seemed like huge sums, such as £20,000 a time, in special offerings. It was a great opportunity to learn to pray together and devote ourselves to God. Having accrued more, we could press on with the next phase. After a few years, we realised that looking back we had spent about £250,000 in completing the work for the renovation. It was a great thrill to see the old building come to life again and even greater to see it packed on Sunday mornings.

We had installed an extra floor at one end to make adequate space for our growing demands for offices. These were needed to handle the work of both the local church and the extension ministry that was increasingly involving Nigel and me as God seemed to be drawing us further afield in serving the growing number of churches across the southeast of England.

Alan Vincent from Watford asked me again if I would accompany him to India. Whoever would have believed that I would get to visit that magnificent far-off nation with its completely different culture? I was very excited and counted it a huge privilege to be invited to accompany him and his wife Eileen on my first ever visit to Bombay. I will never forget the heat, the crowds, the smells, the slums, the animals on the streets, and the wonderful hospitality of the saints in the church. Alan had gathered a beautiful church and taught them wonderful truths, which they had genuinely built into their lives. They received us with extraordinary warmth and love. We also travelled beyond the city for a leaders' conference. I remember that they had to chase some rats out of the room in which I was going to sleep. As we said our goodnights Eileen remarked, 'They do have their way of getting back in again.' I lay awake all night waiting for their arrival. The mixture of colossal heat, jet lag, noise levels and the fear of rats meant that though God was well able to give his beloved sleep, on that particular night I was in no condition to receive it!

Nevertheless, we had a great conference and I fell in love with the people. I was eager to respond positively the following year, when Alan asked if I would accompany him again. Later, he would ask me if I would be willing to oversee the work in an apostolic way. Indeed, it was when we returned from India and Alan asked me to speak to a leaders' conference in the Watford area on the subject of apostles that I first researched the subject for myself in a more thoroughgoing way. As I prepared my talk and worked at my study I felt that God told me not only to bring an objective Bible-based teaching but also to own up personally to the fact that this was the ministry into which he had called me. Though others had used that term to describe the ministry that I was now fulfilling, I had never felt comfortable with it myself. I was increasingly happy to see that others were called apostles. I could argue from the Scripture that this ministry was clearly available not simply at the birth of the church but throughout the church age. But I had never before felt such a personal word from God telling me that I was to own this as my ministry. Clearly I was no longer pastoring a local church. I was not doing the work of an evan-

gelist. Nor was I essentially a prophet, though I often prophesied. The fact was that I was involved in the planting and
overseeing of scattered local churches, laying foundations of
truth, and providing ongoing love and care. I was increasingly gathering a team of men who also served those
churches. In the New Testament this was what apostles did.
God reminded me of the powerful word that he had given
me those years ago at the Torbay Court Conference, where
he said, 'The Lord has chosen you to build a house for the
sanctuary. Be strong and do it.'

Paul described his ministry as 'a wise master builder' and,
as such, he had laid a foundation at the church in Corinth
(1 Corinthians 3:10). I now found myself increasingly occu-
pied with foundational issues in church after church. It was
impressed upon me that, with the growing numbers of celebrations and charismatic meetings, I could visit many places
simply to bless, but God wanted my life committed not simply to blessing but to building! God wanted me to be
involved in building him a house. Words from Jeremiah 1
that God had spoken to me years earlier on the Coldean
housing estate in Brighton came back with force:

> 'Do not say, "I am a youth," because everywhere I send you,
> you shall go, and all that I command you, you shall speak. Do
> not be afraid of them, for I am with you to deliver you,'
> declares the Lord . . . 'See, I have appointed you this day over
> the nations and over the kingdoms, to pluck up and to break
> down, to destroy and to overthrow, to build and to plant.'

I felt freshly commissioned by God to an increasingly wider
work among churches. God was sending me and he would
supply the grace to do the job.

One of the prophetic men with whom I worked saw a

vision of me first driving along country lanes, then driving along motorways. He then saw the picture change to an airport and the flags of different nations. The vision resonated with me because, in the past, when travelling from Seaford to serve churches in London, I often found myself late at night driving home along narrow country roads. Now that I was living in Brighton I was already beginning to feel the benefits of the motorway system that feeds the town. But soon Gatwick and Heathrow were to become familiar places, as God began to extend my sphere of responsibility.

# 12

# Under Attack

For years my instinct has been to bathe everything in prayer, so as the new church got started in Brighton, Henry, David and I often met to pray. We particularly set aside Thursday mornings to seek God. Soon Philip Poston, who was now full-time in Seaford, asked if he could join us. Then David Coak, the pastor in Haywards Heath, came along, soon followed by other pastors from around the county. At first, the weekly prayer meeting took place in my home. Later, as numbers grew, we started meeting at the Clarendon Church building. Gradually some pastors from London and elsewhere were making the regular Thursday morning trip. We enjoyed excellent prayer fellowship and great freedom in prophecy.

Later, this group was sub-divided into three, one remaining in Hove and the others developing in south London and to the west of London. Today, Thursday morning prayer meetings take place right across the UK and beyond as NFI pastors gather in multiplied regional centres.

Another significant development regarding prayer resulted from my inability to read what Scripture plainly says.

For some unknown reason I misread the instructions that God gave Moses to gather the men three times a year. I read that they should gather 'empty-handed' (though the passage clearly states that they should *not* come empty-handed!). In my stupidity I tried to consider what 'empty-handed' might mean and felt that it should be interpreted that I should gather the pastors with whom I was working three times a year for three days of prayer and fasting with no set agenda, but simply to wait on God. We first gathered about two dozen men at Pilgrim Hall in Sussex. The pattern has continued ever since, though now it is for only two days and takes place three times a year at Stoneleigh, gathering approximately 400 each time. It has proved to be one of the keys to our fellowship, unity and openness to the leading of the Holy Spirit through prophecy.

The church in Hove was also learning to pray together. God gave us wonderful promises in prayer. He told us that he had set before us an open door which no one could shut. Our faith really grew as we set about the costly refurbishing programme and needed to see regular offerings of about £20,000. We would really give ourselves to prayer on Saturday mornings prior to the Sunday gift days. We would pray and pause and ask, 'Do you believe that we have it yet, or shall we pray on?' Usually we were clear in faith before we left the prayer meeting and on the following day would have the thrill of regularly receiving £20,000 offerings, which 20 years ago in a small congregation were really exciting and encouraging. We learned to pray and the building gradually took shape.

However, in spite of the joy of numerical growth and blessing, not everything was peaceful. Both locally and nationally the so-called 'new churches' were not received with unmixed enthusiasm. Many were very disturbed at the new developments. Some were also confused about the kind of church life that was being established. One of the controversial features was spiritual authority. Some of us had come from Baptist backgrounds and had experienced the 'church business meeting'. I must confess that my own first encounter with the church business meeting at Holland Road, which I knew to be a good Baptist church, left me profoundly shocked. As a young man I was certainly no authority on church government, but I was amazed at the atmosphere of open conflict that I discovered there. Ideas were proposed, seconded and voted upon in a very hostile atmosphere and the pastor had no more voting power than anybody else. The church, I discovered, was run as a democracy and I, as a new convert and backslidden at that, had as much authority to vote as the pastor! It was plainly wrong, even to my eyes.

Later, as we began to start new churches, people gathered to loving, relaxed communities where leaders were evidently gifted to lead. In the early, informal days of meeting in homes there was virtually no church life to organise. As churches grew, however, we had to establish principles. Who made the decisions? How was the church to be led? We were persuaded from Scripture that democracy was not the norm. Clearly, God anointed leaders and gave them abilities and responsibilities. The biblical pattern of eldership was studied, considered and put into practice.

Like many Christians in those days I had been blessed by the writings of Watchman Nee. Such books as *The Normal Christian Life* had become extremely successful in the popular market, rapidly followed by other devotional studies, such as *Sit, Walk, Stand* and *What Shall This Man Do?* Nee was obviously a gifted and inspirational writer and had great influence. I was then introduced to some of his lesser-known writings, such as *The Glorious Church, Spiritual Authority* and *The Normal Christian Church Life*. These were more controversial volumes and though I could not embrace all that he said in them I found them instructive, radical and thought-provoking. His approach to church was fundamentally different from my Baptist background and he clearly expected leaders to have freedom to lead within the churches for which they were responsible. He anticipated that God would have a glorious church in the earth. This really excited me. Being Chinese, he wrote without centuries of Western Christian tradition. He had also come freshly to the Scriptures to see the biblical place of apostles in the church, especially in connection with her mission of world evangelisation.

We embraced a number of his principles as being clearly biblical. We also saw the need to explain our vision and values to new people joining our churches so that they could be added to us with clarity. If we were going to build strong churches, people should clearly understand in advance what they were being added to. Many pastors drew up their own individual commitment courses. Richard Haydon-Knowell from Catford prepared a particularly thorough, accessible and helpful one which we felt was so good that we asked if we could make it widely available. We subsequently published it under the title *How to Join the Church*. The first 'how to' book published by Coastlands, its chapter headings were as follows:

PART ONE    BECOMING A CHRISTIAN
Lesson 1    Judgement to Come
Lesson 2    Repentance and Faith in the Lord Jesus
Lesson 3    Baptism in Water
Lesson 4    Baptism in the Holy Spirit

The chapter on learning about the church included teaching on Ephesians 4 ministries, with simple and clear descriptions of the roles of apostle, prophet, evangelist, pastor and teacher. It showed the duties and responsibilities of elders and the biblical teaching on how people were to relate to them. For several years we had seen the value of small house groups to which church members would be added and where they would be able to work out their life together in Christ. We had noted that the New Testament had over 40 'one another' verses, where instructions were given to the believers to, for instance, 'pray for one another' or 'encourage one another', or 'admonish one another', all of which required developed friendships of love and trust. Small groups provided an ideal context in which these things could be worked out.

My former experience had been that the pastor was responsible for all oversight of the church, by which we meant that he handled the meetings. There was hardly any discipling taking place. We began to see that Christ's instructions were not simply to go and have meetings but rather to go and make disciples. There was a sense in which we all had responsibility to build one another up in the Lord. Much of this was beginning to happen fairly spontaneously in the early house churches but as we grew into larger congregations it was vital that we found contexts to maintain intimacy and mutual care. People joining us needed to know from the outset that this was how we were running the church, hence the commitment course. Those joining us seemed to really appreciate our approach and people were being added continually to my home church in Brighton and across the country. We were building on the principles experienced successfully in the Seaford church, where we had already pioneered house groups through the 1970s.

Sadly, many who heard second-hand about these developments began to caricature them and attack them. We were accused of running churches that were like cults. Crazy stories circulated, suggesting that people had to get permission before they could change their wallpaper or arrange their holidays. It was absolutely ludicrous but many even went into print, attacking our kind of churches. More than once I saw references to our being like the famous Jim Jones cult, a tragic group in South America that had recently committed mass suicide. It was absolutely staggering that evangelical brothers in England could write about us in terms that suggested we were similar to this ghastly sect.

At that time in our Brighton congregation we had two solicitors, a barrister, several school teachers, some policemen and, as we grew, hundreds of other happy, fulfilled ordinary Christians who were delighted to find a church that enjoyed the presence of God and took commitment to Christ and his church seriously. From the reports in some of the publications you would have been tempted to think that the stewards on the doors were carrying machine guns! The hostility towards the new churches and what we were thought to represent became very great. People who have been saved more recently and added to us, find it hard to believe that we ever went through such a difficult and painful patch.

At one point I was asked to speak at the Westminster Fellowship held at Westminster Chapel, a fraternal for pastors formerly hosted by Dr Martyn Lloyd-Jones. The initial invitation requested me to address the subject of Restoration churches. I replied that I did not believe in Restoration churches; I believed that God wanted to restore his whole church to New Testament norms. I had no desire to see a small group of churches being pigeonholed as having the title 'Restoration'. They wrote to me again, having adjusted the invitation accordingly.

The room in which the meeting took place was packed. Dr R.T. Kendall, whom I met for the first time on that day, told me that he had never seen so many pastors there, even in the days of 'the Doctor'. Some sliding wall sections that he had never seen opened had to be opened to get everybody in. I spoke for about an hour on principles of restoration, as I understood them, highlighting the fresh move of the Holy Spirit, the resulting renewal of a sense of sonship, grace rather than law, and the priesthood of all believers expressed in open worship. I spoke about the Christian community and the important place of friendship. I finished by referring to the ongoing place of Ephesians 4 ministries and the functions of pastor/teachers, evangelists, prophets and apostles, as I understood them.

My talk was followed by a question time from the gathered pastors. To say that the questioning was hostile would be something of an understatement, but I tried to answer my brothers honestly. I was glad to escape for the lunch break into Dr Kendall's study. We became friends that day and have remained good friends ever since. I had been in that study once before, as an LBC student, when Dr Martyn Lloyd-Jones had urged me to keep asking, seeking and knocking for all the fullness of God's blessing. In contrast, on this visit to the chapel it seemed that the vast majority had totally written me off as an upstart heretic who needed to be put soundly in his place. Question after question communicated strong criticism. Because I had argued for the ongoing role of the apostle in today's church, I was accused of making myself equal to the apostle Paul. In my talk I had mentioned the informality in our church life, so that anyone in the church would call me 'Terry'. One man gained some approval in the room by prefacing his question with, 'I will not call you Terry!' As it happened, I recognised the man, so began my reply using his Christian name. I managed to raise at least a brief chuckle from some.

Peter Lewis, a close friend of the late Dr Lloyd-Jones, was outraged at the treatment I received. He was chairing the meeting and had been somewhat responsible for my being invited to speak. He accused them of 'coming from their backstreet Bethels with their deep-frozen Berkhofs and thinking that they spoke for all of Christendom'. It was a remarkable day! Weeks later, I was told by someone who had been in attendance that the hostility even continued into the next meeting a month later when, of course, I was not present. In my talk I had mentioned the value of the commitment course as a way of adding people carefully to the community and that all of those joining us as members would go through the course and therefore come into a clear understanding of our values. At one point I was asked where the new members of our church in Brighton were coming from and how many of them were new Christians. I honestly replied that I simply did not know but could only make a guess. At the following month's meeting it was said publicly that I was obviously a liar because if new members came through a commitment course I would certainly know where they came from, therefore my answers of the previous week were self-contradictory. The fact was that since I did so much travelling I was never personally involved in running the commitment course and by now we had over 350 members, with people being added continuously whom I did not know personally. Sadly, my brother assumed that I was a liar and was happy to say so publicly.

Within a year I was invited to make a similar presentation at an Evangelical Alliance consultation meeting. I took the same outline and received a similar response when I finished, though the questions were far less hostile and more reasoned. Directly I finished speaking, one of the Church of England ministers present asked a question, though it was not really a question but rather an attack on Bryn Jones, whom he took to be a 'restoration man' and with whom he had a bone to pick. Bryn was not present and I was, so I was the one to be challenged! He made accusations against Bryn regarding 'sheep stealing'. I defended Bryn by saying that he was an honest man and a genuine church builder.

'Well, I wish he wouldn't use my bricks to build his church!' he snorted. Everyone laughed. Then Philip Mohabir's voice came from the back of the room, 'Perhaps you shouldn't leave your bricks lying around, brother.' The second laugh was greater than the first and the atmosphere became far more friendly, though one man stood to accuse me of arrogance. He happened to be the former student from LBC who many years earlier had asked me to stand as Prayer Secretary for the student body because I was a Calvinist and the man already standing was an Arminian. He was now a pastor and evidently far from happy with me. I publicly apologised for any arrogance that I had communicated.

An Anglican minister was outraged that I could even consider starting new churches. He asked the not unreasonable question, 'What gives you the right to start new churches?' But before I could reply, Morgan Denham, the former chairman of the Evangelical Alliance, mischievously called out, 'I would rather belong to a church founded by Terry Virgo than one founded by Henry VIII!' At least the non-conformists present thought it was funny.

These were painful days for many people who had been personally baptised in the Holy Spirit and, therefore, were in difficulties with their existing church. They had to make a choice. They had to either deny or stifle their experience. The alternative, if they valued their new experience and treasured the manifestation of the Spirit, was to become a potential problem in their church or to leave it. Many were choosing to be true to their new experience and therefore left their churches. Some jumped and some were pushed. Some left quietly; others were told to go.

Many found their way through to the new churches, so it was easy to see the new churches as the cause of the problem. If it could be argued that the new churches were also cult-like, it was even easier to be angry with them and leave them outside the established and accepted world of evangelicalism. In some places there may have been excessive application of the principles of authority and submission in the local church but these abuses were exceedingly rare. We were actually preaching and rejoicing in grace. Meanwhile our brothers were accusing us of legalism. It was a strange and painful situation.

At the next Downs Bible Week I felt that God led me to take a four-part series in the main evening celebrations on Joseph as a type of the new charismatic churches. He was a man of dreams and visions, just like charismatics. As a youth he may have been unwise and even arrogant towards his brothers. Maybe we were guilty of the same. As a result, his brothers threw him out. He then went through a season of serious testing regarding attitudes to his brothers, his past and his present situation. He was also tested morally regarding the possibility of sexual sin with Potiphar's wife. We spent a whole evening on that issue, with many responding to the closing appeal. Finally, he stayed true to his gift of dreams and visions. His character had stood the test of severe trials but he never abandoned his vision or his faith in his charismatic gift. He was released and vindicated, tried and tested, and found faithful. His wise oversight made provision possible for a starving world. When his brothers heard there was food in Egypt they came to him. When Joseph proved he could feed the hungry, his brothers believed in him. In conclusion, his attitude to his brothers was exemplary. He continued to love them and embrace them. He had no desire for self-vindication or revenge but looked rather to the sovereign hand of God in working out his purposes. Many responded to the ministry wholeheartedly and felt that God was helping them to understand the pressures through which they were passing.

At a subsequent year I preached a series about David. I saw him as a man of fresh anointing; his defeat of Goliath; the hostility and persecution of Saul and David's excellent attitude to Saul in spite of the way he treated him. I then spoke on the gathering of a new community in Adullam's cave and the ultimate emergence of a united army in covenant relationship. Finally, after a searching evening on David and Bathsheba, when powerful conviction of sin swept through the tent and many responded in tears of repentance, I concluded by looking at the magnificent Temple that Solomon was commissioned to build, as a type of church that God wants.

On a further year, I took studies on Nehemiah, the man who was broken-hearted over Jerusalem's walls being down and who, against the odds, rebuilt the city. He faced mockery, lies and slander, fear and disloyalty but committed himself to building the wall and getting the job done. We saw how he was accused of being in rebellion and having the secret motive of the pursuit of power and wanting to be king. But the Bible shows us clearly that his true motivation was to see Zion restored.

The Bible weeks continued to grow in numbers and provide a helpful context where thousands of believers could be exposed to preaching on themes that helped them to build churches in their locations in the midst of difficulty and misunderstanding. At first I preached at the comparatively small Downs Bible Week but in 1980 I also spoke at the massive Dales Bible Week. It was a fearful responsibility, but I felt that God wonderfully helped me. Years later I was thrilled to hear that it was when I spoke on Nehemiah at the 1983 Dales Bible Week that God called into full-time ministry Ken Gott, who went on to build the successful work in Sunderland. Meanwhile, the Downs continued to grow and in 1984 had to be repeated through a second week, which coincided with the Dales week. My visits to Dales were therefore over. Soon we began to publish our own magazine, so my occasional contributions to Bryn's *Restoration* magazine stopped. Attending the editorial meetings for the *Restoration* magazine and speaking at the Dales were the two main reasons for regular fellowship with Bryn Jones and his team. Since from 1984 onwards they no longer existed, I saw very little of him as our lives became extremely busy in our various spheres of service.

# 13

# New Frontiers

The Downs Bible Week now had its own identity and we provided the programme, the speakers and the children's workers. After the second year of Downs we stood on our own feet and those who ran the Dales no longer needed to travel south to help us. We were on our own. I invited various speakers and was thrilled to have Alan Vincent as a regular contributor. He also continued to invite me to be involved with him in India. I agreed to provide apostolic oversight to the church in Bombay that he had founded, provided that the elders all resigned. They were not in good relationship with one another and the work was beginning to suffer seriously. They each agreed to my rather radical surgery and Henry and Dorothy Tyler went, at my suggestion, to live in Bombay for four months (January–April 1981) to look after the church during a season of transition, allowing new leadership to emerge. Henry and Dorothy were a truly loving couple and cared for the church magnificently. Eventually they returned to Brighton and a temporary leadership appointed by Henry led the Bombay church.

On my next visit with Alan, I had a most extraordinary

experience. We were in Hyderabad and Alan was speaking at a leaders' conference. While he was speaking, I was sitting in the front row and suddenly I felt that God was beginning to speak to me. I felt that he told me to leave the meeting immediately and go outside because he wanted my full attention. I was extremely reluctant to move, since Alan was speaking and it seemed inappropriate for me to leave the front row and walk out. Eventually I could stand the pressure no more, so, rather embarrassed, I stood and slipped out. I took my Bible and walked out of the conference centre grounds to a nearby hill overlooking a stream. For a moment I watched a kingfisher on a branch overshadowing the river. It dropped like a stone into the water, re-emerged, flew up to its perch, waited and did the same thing again.

I sat on a rock and waited. Once again I felt the intensity of God's presence and thought it right simply to open my Bible. It fell open at Isaiah 41. I stared at the opening verse, which immediately arrested my attention. It said, 'COAST-LANDS listen to me in silence.' In the New American Standard Bible, which I usually use, Isaiah 41 verse 1 sets out the word 'COASTLANDS' in capital letters. I was transfixed. God certainly got my attention! I was trying to listen in silence. The whole chapter, with all its promises of God's support, captivated me, particularly verses 9–15. These concluded with a verse that had been special to me for years and was prophesied over me on my birthday at Buckingham Street those many years before, '"Do not fear, you worm Jacob. . . I will help you," declares the Lord. "Behold I have made you a new, sharp threshing sledge with double edges; you will thresh the mountains, and pulverise them."' I sat awestruck in God's presence. I then looked up at the stream before me, which on my left looked like a small meandering stream, but as I looked to my right I realised that I could see for a long distance. The stream became ever larger and clearly took on the proportions of a growing river. I felt that God was speaking to me and telling me that what I had seen so far was nothing in comparison to what would follow and that it would grow and flow ever greater and ever fuller. I sat there for a long time, stirred and thrilled by God's presence and the promise of future blessing.

When I returned home Wendy said that she had something to tell me. One day while I was away she had been cooking and the Lord had said to her very clearly, 'I want to speak to you about your husband.' Her response was to carry on cooking and to plan to pray later. She was suddenly shocked by a sense of urgency, 'Now!' She turned off the gas hob under the pots and pans and went to kneel by the bed to pray. Immediately she saw a vision of me running in what seemed like a marathon, carrying a torch. I was running along back streets, alone. Gradually a few others joined in and ran with me. The numbers grew until a huge company was running behind me. We then approached a large arena and ran towards it. As we did so, people were there at the entrance with sticks trying to trip us and black snakes were wriggling on the ground trying to obstruct our way in. Suddenly, having entered the vast stadium, the scene became massive, but things grew dark and the light of the torches being carried was reflected in the eyes of many. Many pulled hoods down over their eyes to prevent the light getting to them. A great battle then ensued. Wendy found herself interceding with floods of tears, feeling that great conflict was taking place. Eventually, the darkness gave way to light, the battle was over and the runners, now dishevelled, bruised and battered, were triumphantly holding up a trophy of victory.

Though I am a serious Bible student and love to preach

expository sermons, it would be true to say that over the years prophecies and visions have also played a very large part in forming my thinking and expectations. Very soon we were to be confronted by another prophetic vision which greatly affected our way of working and our expectations for the future. I was with a number of pastors in prayer when John Groves, who now leads the burgeoning King's Church in Hastings, began to prophesy. He told us that he saw a herd of elephants running together towards a jungle. The way ahead looked totally impenetrable, but the elephants kept running forward and burst through the undergrowth, making a way where there was no way. Their combined strength broke through and a path was formed that others could subsequently use. The opening words of his prophecy were, 'There are no well-worn paths ahead of you,' and it continued, 'Together you can accomplish more than you could ever accomplish alone.'

When John finished, we sat and discussed the prophetic vision at length. It had considerable impact upon us. The fact was that, until this time, I had resisted the idea of the churches that I served seeing themselves as in any way being joined together. They simply had in common the fact that I had helped them to get started or I had helped them through a time of transition from a traditional style to something more like a new wineskin. Each was connected to me and the team with which I was working. Some would have been happy to say that they were 'covered' by me – a word that I was not very happy with because of its lack of definition or biblical backing.

Each church had its different name and title, such as King's Church, New Life Church, Community Church, and had no common denomination. The title 'Coastlands' simply covered us for conferences and cassettes. The churches were not 'Coastlands' churches. By this time I had met C. J. Mahaney and Larry Tomczak, who had spoken at the Dales Bible Week and led a group of churches in the USA who worked corporately under the title People of Destiny International. (Later they dropped this title, with which they had become increasingly uncomfortable. Retaining the PDI initials, they adopted a fresh identity 'Proclaiming grace; Developing local churches; Influencing our world with the gospel'.) I loved these men, thought they were magnificent, even spoke at their leaders' conference in the USA and their home base Covenant Life Church in Washington DC, but was still uneasy about a group of churches working together under a common title. I was scared of denominationalism.

John's prophecy shook me. God was clearly speaking to us about churches working together. The words had included the statement that we would accomplish more together than we could apart. After some days of reflection, prayer and discussion I felt sure that we were meant to take definite steps. At the next prayer and fasting days at Pilgrim Hall in Sussex, I told all the assembled pastors about the prophecy and said that I believed God was inviting us to form a new kind of relationship together. We were to join together on a mission. I believed that this could be well expressed in embracing a new name. The name would be 'New Frontiers', reflecting the burden of the prophetic vision. Having been as open as I possibly could, I acknowledged to the men that when they had got involved with me there was no such expectation. Things were about to change. The number on the front of the bus had changed, with them already on it. I told them that they were totally free to get off the bus if they could not identify with this new direction. None wanted to leave. All embraced it as an authentic word from God that was to be obeyed.

We thus moved into a new phase. Andrew Walker was later to record in *Restoring the Kingdom* that we dropped our inappropriate 'Coastlands' title, with its parochial 'hi-de-hi' feel, replacing it with the altogether more challenging legend, 'New Frontiers'. Each church continued to retain its individual name, King's Church, New Life Church, Family Church or whatever, but from now on each church unashamedly added that it was in association with New Frontiers ('International' soon to be added). A common identity based on a sense of mission was established.

At one of our Downs Bible Weeks I was approached by a small group of South Africans, led by a delightful gentleman called Derek Crumpton. He had enjoyed the week and wondered if I would be open to the possibility of speaking at a conference at East London, South Africa. Soon Bryn Jones and I received formal written invitations to go. I immediately felt that this was God's will and greatly looked forward to the privilege of going. We were informed that we must obtain written consent from the South African Embassy before we could go ahead with our arrangements. There seemed to be endless delay. Weeks and even months passed and still the paperwork was not forthcoming. Bryn decided he could wait no longer and dropped the idea, responding to another invitation that took him to the US. I remained certain that I should go and pressed the South African Embassy, who began to make promises that the paperwork would come soon. Eventually I bought my tickets but even on the very day of the flight the paperwork had failed to arrive. Finally, my secretary, Pam Haworth, went to the Embassy in London in the morning and met me at Heathrow, put the required forms in my hand and I flew out that evening.

I arrived in Johannesburg and was met by Dudley Daniel, who took me to his home in Bryanston. I spoke to some of his leaders on the Saturday night and was then taken to Pretoria on the Sunday morning, where I spoke to the huge crowd at Hatfield Church, which at that time was meeting in a vast tent while its new premises were being built. Ed Roeburt, the pastor, and his wife were extremely warm and friendly and provided excellent hospitality. In the afternoon I returned to Bryanston and spoke at the evening meeting in Dudley Daniel's New Covenant Church. We then flew to East London and I spoke to the leaders' meeting, which gathered men from virtually every background across the churches of white South Africa. Because Bryn was not there, I had a very demanding schedule but enjoyed an excellent time and was befriended by the leaders of groups and denominations from many different contexts, which resulted in my being invited back to South Africa repeatedly over the next few years to speak at a variety of conferences.

When I had finished at East London I was immediately taken to a smaller, more focused conference for people keenly motivated to pursue the sorts of thing that I was doing in the UK. Finally, I was invited to speak to a church in Cape Town by Graham Ingram, who used to pastor a church in South Lee, London – a church that had become a New Frontiers church while he had been living in South Africa. He had heard good things from his former church and was keen that, since I was in South Africa, I might come and speak at his church there. He had been baptised in the Holy Spirit, had left his former church in Cape Town and a number of his people had followed him, resulting in him starting a new church. It was one year old and they were celebrating their anniversary. He asked me if I could speak at some special meetings. I was staggered at Cape Town's beauty but also thrilled to meet the church. While I was there, several were baptised in the Holy Spirit and we enjoyed excellent fellowship.

The following year, when I was invited by another group to return to South Africa, I again visited Dudley's groups in Johannesburg and Durban but finished my time there in Cape Town. This pattern was repeated a number of times in the years that followed, so my friendship with Dudley and the churches that he served grew. Johannesburg and Durban became regular stopping places for me, resulting in strong friendships with Rob Rufus, Chris Weinand, Mike Hanchett and Malcolm Du Plessis. But I always completed my visits to South Africa by visiting the church in Cape Town, where the link became very strong.

One of my visits followed soon after the establishing of our new identity as New Frontiers International, which resulted in a group of about 50 people from 18 different NFI churches in the UK accompanying me to Cape Town. There, we subdivided into a number of different teams. Some did street evangelism, some helped build houses in the black township of Khayelitsha, some helped educationally, others in a clinic and some even did work as mechanics. I spoke at pastors' events and evening celebrations. It was an excellent time and a real eye-opener regarding the identity of NFI. Some people whom we met assumed that we must all have come from the same church, since we enjoyed such excellent fellowship together as a team and clearly held the same values. We accomplished much more together than we could have done alone. (Amazingly, many of the team that accompanied me on that occasion have since returned to live in South Africa and make it their home, in spite of the tendency of white flight from South Africa during these challenging years in that great nation.)

While I was in Cape Town in March 1984, I was suddenly crippled by an agonising slipped disc. I hobbled through my final days there and prepared for the journey home. Before I left, a pastor of one of the churches approached me and said it would be wonderful if I could meet John Wimber. He commented that I reminded him of John, though he said John was much stronger than I was on teaching on the kingdom and on the power of God in healing. He said that I had more to teach on themes like grace and the church but felt it would be excellent if we were to meet. John Wimber had recently had an extraordinarily successful visit to South Africa, taking a team with him from California. I had heard of John Wimber a few months earlier at the British Charismatic Leaders Conference, when David Watson testified to his having met him and found him to be a wonderfully stimulating man of God. David had waxed very eloquent about John and had evidently been deeply impressed by him.

I agreed with my friend that it would be very nice to meet John Wimber. However, in my mind I thought that it would be very nice to meet a number of other people, like Billy Graham or Yonggi Cho, but I guessed the chances of doing so would be pretty remote! When I arrived in England, the pain from my slipped disc was intense. I had to cancel week after week of meetings and was actually out of action for eight weeks. During that time I listened to hours of John Wimber ministry from cassettes that the South African pastor had pressed on to me. His teaching on healing was unlike any that I had ever heard before. I found his theology rooted in the kingdom of God wholly acceptable. His manner was totally disarming, as he acknowledged many mistakes and was clearly unimpressed by himself. His humour was delightful. Through listening to his tapes I felt that I was getting to know the man and very much liked what I was getting to know. It certainly would be wonderful to meet him, but how was that ever likely to happen?

I recovered from my disc problem in time for the summer Bible weeks and then enjoyed a refreshing family holiday. A short time later I had a very surprising phone call from a friend who said that John Wimber had been in touch with him and wanted to meet me. Was it at all possible for me to meet with him in his hotel in London and spend a morning with him? This was immediately prior to his memorable conference at Westminster Central Hall in October 1984. We met and immediately became excellent friends. I stayed not only for the morning but throughout the day. Although he had an appointment with Dr John White and his wife, he urged me to remain with him and Carol as they joined us. Our resulting friendship was to prove extraordinarily important and had many repercussions for the days ahead.

# 14

# John Wimber

The following February, I was due to speak in Mexico. A member of the NFI church in Hastings had been posted to work in Guadalajara and his Mexican pastor had requested that I visit the church where he was working. Don Smith, the Hastings pastor, had already visited at my request and felt that it would be very worthwhile for me to go. Ray Lowe from Biggin Hill was to accompany me. When John Wimber heard about this, he invited me to go to Mexico via Anaheim, Los Angeles and spend some time with him and Carol and see the church there. We had a wonderful time and further cemented our friendship. He arranged for us to stay at a nearby hotel in order to attend the Anaheim Vineyard, and to accompany him to the Fuller Seminary, where he was currently lecturing on signs and wonders and where I met C. Peter Wagner and Eddie Gibbs.

After an excellent week of fellowship, Ray and I flew on to Guadalajara, where we enjoyed a further week of ministry to the local church and to Mexican leaders. A friendship was formed with El Camino Church in Guadalajara that has continued to this day. Ray particularly developed a close link with John Evans, a young Englishman on the eldership team. He had married Flor, a Mexican girl, and was raising his family there. The church was vibrant and eager to learn. Gradually, other Mexican churches have gathered to us and we have encouraged them to plant new churches so that the sphere across Mexico continues to grow.

When I returned to the UK I was amazed to learn from Nigel Ring that Blaine Cook from the Anaheim Vineyard would be in Brighton on the following day. While with John, I had mentioned that in Brighton there was a superb conference centre that he might like to consider for any of his future visits to the UK. John's visit to London's Westminster Central Hall had phenomenal impact on the British church. He had proved immensely popular. His humour and non-threatening style appealed to British people. It was also evident that God was powerfully with him. The gentle worship style that came from the Vineyard was also immediately popular with many English charismatics, though some found it rather restricting and lacking in the prophetic. The popular 'Hosanna' seemed to be the only up-tempo song in their repertoire!

John's loving and winsome ways led to his having a huge influence in the British charismatic scene. Of course he had his critics, but his popularity was remarkable. Probably no other American Christian, apart from Billy Graham, had such influence in the UK church in the twentieth century. All of his books became bestsellers and the Vineyard worship cassettes were being played everywhere. It is my conviction that charismatic renewal had been fading in the UK outside the new churches but John powerfully renewed the renewal! Thousands of denominational Christians, particularly Anglicans, rallied to him. He revived the hopes of many scattered charismatics and, since at that time he had no intention of planting Vineyard churches in the UK, he was perceived to represent no threat at all.

So why was Blaine Cook arriving in Brighton? After I had left John to fly to Mexico, he had immediately phoned the Brighton Centre from Anaheim and found that they had dates available in the following October. Blaine told Nigel that if Terry were happy John would like to hold a conference there. We were certainly happy! Because of our experience of running large conferences, such as the Downs Bible Week, John asked if we would be willing to handle the administration at Brighton. We felt it a privilege to provide that service and the conference was highly significant. The Brighton Centre was absolutely packed. Indeed, John Wimber was the first person ever to totally fill it and the local council used a photograph that they took of the full hall for their advertising for years to come. A very wide cross-section of charismatics attended and God's presence was wonderfully manifested. John's teaching and his personal presence were a sheer joy. He was relaxed and unpretentious, everyone's favourite uncle. He gave us his testimony and taught us about what he called 'doin' the stuff'. The intensity of God's presence in the large meetings exceeded anything that we had previously experienced.

John publicly expressed his appreciation of our administration of the conference and also mentioned his personal friendship with me. The conference was a mixture of predominantly Church of England and other denominational charismatics, though NFI people were also present in great numbers. We were fans and friends of John Wimber.

When Carl Tuttle and the band started their one up-tempo 'Hosanna' song, they were shocked when lots of our people started to dance enthusiastically. This was normal for

Bible weeks but not for Vineyard conferences. Carl and the band were quite thrown, not expecting the reserved English to be more extrovert than Americans! Carl searched for another up-tempo song for us but could only come up with 'When the saints go marching in'! I was appalled.

We gradually came to appreciate their gentle worship songs and I loved seeing John sitting at his keyboard, surveying the gathered thousands. His style was unique: outwardly casual and relaxed but in reality burning with zeal for God and his glory. I loved him very much and deeply appreciated his friendship. A few months later he arranged for Wendy and me, with all our family, to attend a conference in Anaheim at his expense and to take in Disneyland as well. What an extraordinary man he was.

John returned to Brighton for conferences on four more occasions. I later learned that some people whose attitude had been seriously negative to us were amazed that the wonderful John Wimber would have anything to do with the questionable NFI! Actually, after his first conference I received a very gracious letter from a Church of England vicar who told me that he had been very troubled about the fact that NFI had been invited to administrate the conference. He feared the worst. He wrote a few days after its conclusion to say how much he appreciated our low profile and that we had obviously served very efficiently and had not used the opportunity to promote ourselves at all. He asked for our forgiveness for his previously suspicious and unfair attitude. I was happy to respond to him very warmly.

At John's next conference in Brighton, he invited me to speak at one of the seminars. I later heard from a lady that she had been horrified that John had asked me to do that. She had attended the first conference, determined to avoid the NFI presence. She came to the second, warning her friend to avoid the Terry Virgo seminar. At John's third Brighton conference he invited me to take not only a seminar series but also two main sessions. If you were to attend, therefore, Terry Virgo could no longer be avoided! The place was once again totally packed and I had the joy of fully expounding and teaching on the grace of God, a theme on which I love to speak. When I had finished John publicly said that he had never heard such a clear and releasing teaching on God's grace. He claimed that it had a powerfully releasing impact on his own life. (He later flew me over to Anaheim again to preach the same message to his home Vineyard and told everybody that he played the tapes ceaselessly in his car because it had been so releasing in his personal life.)

The extraordinary spin-off from this whole development was that at last I was being heard by thousands of people, many of them leaders, on the subject of grace, acceptance and no condemnation, when many thought that I had the reputation of a leader in a legalistic group who imposed laws on their members. The lady who wrote to me said that she had been amazed. She had to rethink all her presuppositions and wondered why she had ever believed all the negative stories that she had previously held. She is now a happy member in an NFI-related church!

John subsequently invited me to speak at another Brighton conference on spiritual warfare and at the Worship Conference with Graham Kendrick in another visit to Anaheim. Graham was a great success and the delegates were staggered at his huge repertoire of songs, their magnificent doctrinal content and great diversity of style. At one point in the conference he even invited all the delegates to march right around the large warehouse complex in which the church meets. We walked and sang Graham's 'Make

Way' and other appropriate songs. The Vineyard people enjoyed exposure to the wonderful breath of fresh air that Graham brought. Wendy and I also had the joy of sharing a holiday break with John and Carol in their home. I prized their friendship so much. John even arranged for me to visit Australia and travel across the nation on an itinerary arranged by his friends there.

NFI churches were clearly impacted by John's teaching on signs and wonders. His style of encouraging members of the congregation to be involved in praying for the sick and expecting more manifestations of the Holy Spirit's presence had a profound effect on the churches that we served. Everyone was also deeply impressed with the love and commitment of the American teams that John brought with him. Their willingness to pray over people for a long time was deeply impressive. Their kindness and friendliness were totally winning. There seemed to be no token praying or brief encounters. They served people with their love and power. One was conscious of God's love flowing powerfully through them. Even when there were no obvious healings taking place, one felt that God's love was being imparted. All of these things had a deep impact on us all.

Just as some charismatics were surprised that John Wimber was happy to relate to me, so some of my restoration friends were surprised that I was so enthusiastic about John Wimber. It was pointed out that John Wimber was not 'restoration'. He did not believe that all the Ephesians 4 ministries were still available to the church today. He also had a different view about being baptised in the Holy Spirit. He was working to a different vision. These observations were absolutely true but we knew what our vision and values were and we remained committed to them. John's ministry wonderfully complemented our objectives.

He helped to fill us out where we were weak. Also, we actually shared much in common, particularly regarding his view of the kingdom of God. Many will also remember him at Westminster Central Hall thundering out that God was saying, 'Give me back my church!', a sentiment I wholly embraced. John's approach to ministry in the UK was almost exclusively through conferences and cassettes. Our main emphasis has always been through building local churches, though we also run conferences to support that objective.

John was to meet and be impacted by the remarkably gifted Paul Cain and other prophets who related to Mike Bickle from Kansas City. Mike, who has certainly embraced many restoration values, helped John rethink some of his attitudes to Ephesians 4 ministries; but he stopped short of accepting the possibility of there being apostles in the church today. Eventually he established the Vineyard Fellowships with a denominational structure, feeling that that was the responsible way to proceed in caring for the many churches that came within his sphere.

From my point of view, John's friendship and his whole-hearted acceptance and endorsement of New Frontiers International had a wonderful side effect. People's attitudes seemed to change. I was invited to take the main morning Bible readings at Spring Harvest and have done so on four occasions. I found myself being asked to speak to the students at London Bible College and at Spurgeons. I was also invited to address the Elim Conference at Bognor and to write articles in various denominational magazines. Suddenly, it seemed that we were back in from the cold. Though we had changed nothing in the way we were building church, we were no longer being attacked as being cultish or into 'heavy shepherding' or oppressing our members. Though we continued exactly as we had been before hostility started, it seemed that the hunting season was over. The crazy stories stopped. It had been a sad season of misunderstanding in the body of Christ and I was glad that it was over. I am personally convinced that John Wimber's friendship played a large part in making that healing process possible.

It was during that season that I felt that God told me to write the book *Restoration in the Church*, in which I set out much of our vision and values. I felt that God said to me that it would go to the nations as well as to the UK. How true that proved to be. It went into five British reprints and was published in German, Italian, Dutch, Czechoslovakian, Mandarin, Russian, Armenian, Iranian and Swahili. It was even translated into American and published and distributed there! It was first published in England in 1985, in time for our first double Downs Bible Week. We had outgrown the Plumpton Racecourse and needed two weeks to handle the crowds. It was also the first year in which I invited C. J. Mahaney and Larry Tomczak to join the speaking team. I was deeply impressed with them as men and with the high standards of godliness and church life that they represented in the PDI group of churches. They were an immediate success with our people.

But Downs '85 was memorable for two other reasons. It represented a turning-point in several ways.

# 15

# Restoration, Too Small a Thing!

When we arrived at Plumpton Racecourse for Downs '85, we set up camp in dry conditions for week one, but we were barely settled in when it began to rain. Plumpton Racecourse offered virtually no protection from aggressive weather conditions. It had no hard roads and virtually no solid buildings. All the meetings, seminars and children's events took place in tents. It continued to rain every day and night. We had hardly a break, but managed nevertheless to have a great Bible week. When the first-week campers left, several passed second-week delegates arriving. The first-week people were envious: they had endured a week of terrible conditions; obviously week two would be better. Once again the rain held off as the first week broke camp and the second-week people arrived. But, to everyone's consternation, the second week turned out to be even worse. The unremitting downpours set in again with a vengeance. Larry Tomczak and C.J. Mahaney had brought a dozen American pastors with them. They were all amazed at the English spirit of endurance on display. C.J. told me that if this had happened in the US everybody would have gone straight

159

home! But I still have mental images of people standing in wellington boots and raincoats with frying pans in one hand and umbrellas in the other, cooking in the rain. Some who had not come fully prepared were barefoot in the mud, which grew ever deeper day by day.

Because the whole camp was on a gentle slope, the water gradually flooded away from the Downs, from south to north. People began to dig protective channels around their tents, to avoid being totally waterlogged. Eventually it became almost impossible to continue and for the only time in our Bible week history we had to abandon one main meeting. The stream of water running through the circus tent was so deep in places that wellington boots were inadequate to cope with it. The neighbouring villages around Plumpton opened school halls, church and community halls to take in our people. Many slept on the floor, with blankets and sleeping bags hanging out to dry. Some who were attending the Bible week and who lived locally rushed home to clean up but still came back for more. It was a truly testing and difficult time and I was so proud of the people, many of whom had tiny children and babies with them yet kept smiling and kept praising.

It occurred to me that God never asked Job's permission before he tested him and put him on display before principalities and powers to see if he would curse God in his deeply trying circumstances. As part of one sermon, I made reference to this and said that we would never have chosen such circumstances for our Bible week camp but God was pleased with the evident joy, peace and praise that prevailed on the campsite. When I said this I was interrupted by an extended outburst of praise, applause and worship. These poor, bedraggled people wanted God to know that they trusted him and loved him and that if he wanted them to go through a week of severe endurance (and even pay money for it!) they were going to trust him and praise him. I was deeply impressed with the phenomenal attitudes on display. Some people want to dismiss charismatic Christians as mere 'happy clappies'. These were very happy and clapping, but their joy was real and profound and not dependent on outward circumstances. The following year they were back again in their thousands, many of them sporting T-shirts with the logo 'I survived DROWNS 85!'.

The other significant development of the week was our choice of subject. At a recent prayer and fasting gathering of the pastors, there had been a very important prophecy. God had stirred us to lift our vision to the field of world evangelisation with fresh commitment. He told us that whereas themes relating to church life had hitherto thrilled us, we were about to turn a page and start a new chapter. From now on, 'nations' and 'cities' were going to stir us with equal passion. Thus far the 'city of God' excited us. Now the 'ends of the earth' were going to motivate us in a new way. God strongly impressed on me Isaiah's word that it is too small a thing to restore God's people. He has made us a light to the nations (Isaiah 49:6). This passage had a powerful impact upon me and I made it the theme of that year's Downs.

Having prayed about it, I selected Jonah as my character study and spoke about the parochial and reluctant prophet whose gaze had to be lifted so that he remembered the heathen of Nineveh and became awakened to God's attitude to the lost. God was similarly calling us to a new perspective and to greater commitment to world evangelisation. We had spent a number of years with restoration as our main preoccupation, but God was saying that this was too small a thing. Restoring the church was for a purpose; namely to get the church fighting fit and ready for battle. However, we were not to spend all of our time simply mending our nets, but needed to be reminded that nets were to be mended in order to hurl them once again into the sea where the fish were. Jesus said the fields were white for harvest; our perspective had to change.

It would be true to say that we already had some world vision and were involved in outreaches in India, Africa and Mexico, not to mention some links in Western Europe. But it could hardly be said that we were aggressively committed to mission and world evangelisation. I invited Patrick Johnstone, author of the famous resource book *Operation World,* to address us at the Bible week. We genuinely wanted to make transition. We developed a Frontier year programme and Frontier outreach teams for young people who were willing to take out a full year to be trained in evangelism geared to church planting or get involved in one- to two-week evangelistic programmes.

Later, I was to receive a very unexpected phone call from a friend of Larry Tomczak. He had just read my book *Restoration in the Church* and was phoning to invite me to speak at his upcoming conference in Fort Worth, Texas. His name was Bob Weiner; his organisation was called Maranatha. As it happens, I had already visited this conference as a guest in September 1984 when Larry Tomczak was speaking there and it had had a powerful impact on me. Richard Haydon-Knowell and I were on our way back from a visit to Mexico and I was due to speak in Washington DC at the PDI church on the way back. Larry and C.J. suggested that since my flight took me via Dallas I could use the opportunity to meet them there, since Larry was speaking at the Maranatha conference. Thousands of leaders from the Maranatha group had gathered from all over the world and the speakers whom Bob Weiner had invited were among the most famous of the American charismatic scene, including Kenneth Copeland, Gerry Sevelle and Bob Tilton (whose dubious financial dealings were later to be exposed on America's *20/20* TV documentary programme).

At one point, in this context of fervent missionary passion, accompanied only by a superb solo violinist, Bob Weiner read out the names of all the nations of the world in alphabetical order, over 200 of them. The exercise took several minutes to complete. Many were kneeling to pray. I found the whole experience deeply moving and was on my knees in tears as I heard nation after nation being mentioned and imagined the vast numbers that each briefly uttered word represented. On and on it continued . . . Chad, Chile, China . . . India, Indonesia, Iran, Iraq . . . Paraguay, Peru, Philippines . . . Zaire, Zambia, Zimbabwe. I had never before seen the kind of zealous enthusiasm that the delegates at that conference displayed. Maranatha was an international mission focused particularly on university campuses around the world, so many who gathered were young and totally vibrant. At certain points in the times of praise they would race around the building carrying dozens of different national flags of the world.

On one afternoon the programme simply said 'Concert with Phil Driscoll', who was a trumpet player and singer unknown to me. We were not really interested in a concert, so Richard and I went for a walk around downtown Dallas to take in some of the sights. In the evening meeting Phil Driscoll was invited to do one more number. It was fantastic and I don't think I have ever quite forgiven myself for missing the opportunity to be present at a full Phil Driscoll concert. I now have to content myself with owning one of his wonderful CDs.

Bob Weiner's own zeal was something to behold. I don't think I had ever met a man quite like him for intensity. The whole conference was quite an experience; much of it deeply impressed me while other parts demonstrated American charismatic Christianity at its most outrageous! One speaker, deploring what he regarded as the chaotic political and economic situation in Mexico, suggested that the USA should buy it, like they had bought Alaska, and sort it out. On some occasions it seemed that the gospel of the kingdom of Christ was confused with the 'American Way'. To evangelise the nations or to 'Americanise' them seemed to amount to the same thing! As we left the building C.J. said to me, 'I would love to see you on that platform.' I laughed in incredulity and thought, 'I'd like to see pigs fly and it's about as likely to happen.' I was amazed three years later, therefore, to pick up the phone in my bedroom at home one evening and hear a voice booming through from the USA, 'This is Bob Weiner. I'd like you to speak at this year's Maranatha conference at Fort Worth.' Staggered, I agreed to go and invited David Holden from Sidcup and Ben Davies from Bracknell to accompany me. I wanted these two key men in our movement to be exposed to the extraordinary urgency that I had witnessed at the Maranatha conference on my previous visit.

Just before I left England I attended a conference held at Fairmile Court in Surrey entitled 'Forward Together'. It was a fascinating get-together of leaders of the various new church groupings in the UK with a number of leaders of the historic missionary societies, such as the Worldwide Evangelisation Crusade, Overseas Missionary Fellowship, Bible and Medical Missionary Fellowship (now Interserve), Operation Mobilisation, Wycliffe Bible Translators and others. It was a very open get-together where problems were honestly faced. I was deeply impressed with the humility of the leaders of the established missions. They pointed out that although the new churches were burgeoning they were not, in the main, sending their young people through to the established missionary societies, which were essentially non-charismatic. One of the leaders publicly acknowledged and highlighted the dilemma that the leaders of the new churches obviously faced. We had hammered out a new kind of charismatic church life and were hardly likely to encourage the cream of our young people to apply to non-charismatic missionary societies. I was so pleased to see that we were not encountering hostility but true sympathy, understanding and very mature and genuine fellowship. Having faced up to our dilemma, there was a wholehearted appeal given to the new church leaders not to turn our backs on the challenge of the mission field and to be aware of the thousands of young people in our ranks. Those fine and mature men encouraged us not to reinvent the wheel but to be aware of their huge resources and know-how, particularly in connection with cross-cultural expertise and the vast databases that they had established. I regarded it as a very worthwhile conference.

While I was there I also heard a strange name being mentioned by a few of those present, one of whom was Roger Forster. He and others were speaking with real enthusiasm about a 32-year-old church leader who was emerging in Bangkok, Thailand. His extraordinary name was Dr Kriengsak Chareonwongsak (later to be known in the West as Joseph Wongsak). I interrupted the conversation and asked more about him. I was thrilled with what I heard. What an amazing guy, and what a phenomenal story! What excited me even more was that Roger, who knew that I was going to speak at the Maranatha conference in two weeks' time, told me that Kriengsak was going to be another speaker there. I certainly hoped that I might have a chance to meet him. So Dave, Ben and I flew to Fort Worth to what was yet another extraordinary conference and a life-changing encounter which was going to have a major influence on the development of New Frontiers International.

It was a privilege to speak to the great crowds that assembled at Fort Worth Conference Centre, and Bob Weiner was extremely friendly. Other speakers at the conference included Francis Anfuso, Todd Burke, Mahesh Chavda, John Dawson, Larry Lea, George Otis Jr, Dennis Peacocke, Paul Petrie, Winkie Pratney and Dr Ralph Winter, the founder and president of the US Centre for World Mission in Pasadena, California. The conference took place in a huge arena and once again Bob provided dynamic leadership. I also enjoyed excellent private conversations with him, which I found very stimulating. After I had given my two main sessions he spoke tremendously affirming things, even saying publicly that my sessions were evidently the main reason why they had gathered that year. I was flattered, encouraged, but unconvinced, especially later when Dr Kriengsak spoke. I was wondering if I would get to meet him before he spoke publicly and was trying to keep an eye open for him in the huge crowd when, to my surprise, I was approached from behind by an immaculately dressed, smiling, oriental man. He introduced himself as Dr Kriengsak and said that he had been looking out for me. He had read my book *Restoration in the Church* and would really like to have some fellowship.

I was taken aback by his warmth and his initiating the contact. We arranged a meeting in my hotel room and talked together for ages. After a while, I realised that he was asking all the questions. I was dying to hear his story but he kept on enquiring about how we worked among the churches, our understanding of Ephesians 4 ministries, future plans for growth and so on. I had to interrupt and force him to speak about himself. When he did so he had a remarkable story to tell. He was a brilliant young Buddhist scholar and had been funded by his government to do a PhD in economics in Australia. While there he had been deeply impressed by a very godly Christian and asked him about the secret of his lifestyle. The man told him about his Christian faith and led Dr Kriengsak to Christ.

A short time after this he had returned to his student room one evening and suddenly found it was bathed in supernatural light. He was powerfully baptised in the Holy Spirit and began to speak in tongues. He had no idea what was happening to him but felt that God had come to him in an intensely personal and powerful way. God also commissioned him to plant churches in every region of Thailand, nearly 700 of them. Overjoyed at his new experience, he knocked at the door of the student who had led him to Christ, barely able to stop speaking in tongues. His friend was deeply confused and disturbed and enquired from Kriengsak who had laid hands on him. He then went on to warn him against the experience and on the following day provided him with a pile of books that tried to disprove its validity. Happily, Kriengsak stayed on course and later returned to Bangkok. Very soon he hired a room and dragged a handful of people, mostly relatives, to a small meeting. He preached and one was saved. Since then he had never had a meeting in Bangkok without someone being saved. By now he already had a large congregation. He had also already planted many churches across Thailand. It was a breathtaking story. I could hardly understand why he had bothered to waste time by asking me questions about our little ministry when he had such a magnificent experience to recount.

But if I found his personal fellowship warm and stimulating it could never have prepared me for his public ministry. He spoke on John 4:34, 'My food is to do the will of him who sent me and to accomplish his work.' He was electrifying! His personal warmth still came through, but his passionate commitment to Christ and especially his reckless faith in what God could and would do surpassed anything I had ever heard.

It had the strangest effect upon me. I was supposed to be a leader and had recently been publicly honoured from the platform for my contribution to the conference. But when Kriengsak spoke I was undone. His passion and zeal burned deep into my soul. I felt like a pathetic wretch in comparison. His dynamic faith made me wonder if I had ever trusted God for anything. His pure and passionate devotion to Christ made me feel lukewarm. His energy and expanse of vision made me feel like a total slug. In the UK we had perhaps seen ourselves as radicals but compared with what he had accomplished so quickly against such a tough background, it all seemed so tame and pathetic. What had I been doing with my life? The power of the Holy Spirit upon him was unlike anything I had ever encountered. I had not felt such conviction of sin since my terrible days of teenage backsliding and I have never felt anything like it since. His message was in no way condemning or finger-pointing, but the Holy Spirit was so powerfully upon him that it resulted in my feeling utterly ruined.

When he concluded his message and appealed for young people to give their lives to Christ's service in mission, hundreds ran forward. It was like a stampede. Most of them knelt and many were in tears. I slumped down into my seat, sobbing with conviction of failure and ineffectiveness. In comparison with his burning zeal, I felt that I had wasted my life. What had I ever done for God? It was an awesome, holy and fearful time and it cut deep into my soul. If the essence of sin is 'falling short of the glory of God', I can only say that I had a small revelation of how much my life had fallen short of its full potential, and so badly missed the mark of God's high ideal. I felt that God allowed me to see something of both his high ideals and my total failure to take full advantage of his grace and live my life to the fullness of all that he wanted and was so willing to give. I believe that it was the nearest I have ever been to a genuine revival situation. It seemed as if heaven's power was all over us. When I later returned home, I could not speak about the experience for many days without shedding tears.

As I was slumped in my chair I heard my name being called out over the sound system. It was Bob Weiner, who was now on the platform alongside Kriengsak, trying to oversee the chaos at the front of the meeting. 'Where is Terry Virgo?' he was saying through the speakers. 'Yes, where is Terry Virgo?' I thought. 'He's a hopeless mess in comparison with this man of God.' I turned to Ben and Dave and found that they were in a similar condition to me. Eventually I waved to Bob, indicating where I was. 'Please come up here,' he appealed. I pushed my way through the crowds of young people that had thronged the front of the hall. He invited me to stand next to him and Kriengsak on the platform. Stretching out our hands over the hundreds of young people who were offering their lives to God we were to pray for them as they stood and knelt before us. It was an awesome time and one that I will never forget.

The following year, Kriengsak and I were both invited by Keith Hazel from Canada to speak at a leaders' conference in a town with the unlikely name of 'Medicine Hat'. When Keith told me that the other speaker would be a man from Bangkok with an unpronounceable name, whom they were calling 'Dr Sak' for short, I immediately agreed to go. When I arrived, Kriengsak told me that he had agreed to the invitation with exactly the same motivation, hearing that I was to be the other speaker. We were thrilled to get more fellowship and our friendship grew deeper. His commitment to evangelising his nation and his passion for world mission were phenomenal.

God used these contacts to stimulate my desires that NFI should also see itself as a light to the nations. Restoration, though obviously essential within the church, was evidently too small a thing. I determined to make arrangements to bring Kriengsak to England so that all of our leaders could be exposed to him.

# 16

# Consolidation at Home

The following year we felt that the Downs Bible Week had finished its course and should close. We had tried repeatedly to obtain the nearby Ardingly Agricultural Showground, which seemed ideal as a larger venue but it had been consistently refused to us. We decided that Downs '88 would be our last and we closed with the theme 'World Changers'. David Fellingham, who had repeatedly written magnificent songs to help us in our worship, wrote a song to match our chosen theme and I spoke on Abraham as God's means of blessing the world. God had chosen the unusual method of blessing an individual and making promises to him so that he could become God's channel for world blessing. God had also chosen us to bless the nations. Increasingly, young people in our ranks were approaching me about the possibility of overseas mission and we felt a growing awareness that we should encourage them to go, though we also needed to see more doors opening. We also felt a growing sense that instead of inviting people to come to us in a field in Sussex we should perhaps go to a number of cities in the nation with a series of mini conferences on the theme of grace.

From early days I had recognised the importance of a strong home base. We have never developed a headquarters mentality within NFI because God had impressed upon us the importance of decentralisation. We felt the need to be like an armada of ships. Of course there were inevitable jokes about what happened to Spain's famous armada in Francis Drake's day! England had recently sent a task force to the Falklands, so we thought that perhaps 'task force' might be a better term than 'armada'. Nevertheless, we were impressed that within an armada every ship had its own captain and crew. Each vessel had to know how to advance by catching the wind in its own sails. But in an armada each ship is also caught in a wider purpose. The ships are not joined together by rods of steel but by common purpose and loyalty to the admiral. We considered that in a modern task force different ships had distinctive contributions to make to the whole group. For instance, an aircraft carrier or minesweeper might be included. Each ship had its own internal responsibilities to fulfil but also might have a partic-ular specialist role related to the whole group.

With this in mind, we had no intention for my home base in Brighton to care for all that was happening within NFI. Other churches took responsibility for certain specific areas. For instance, the church at Wimbledon had in its ranks Malcolm Kyte, an excellent children's worker, and so as a church they took responsibility for our growing children's programme. Since Arnold Bell headed up our growing Equipped for Ministry training programme, the Odiham church, where he was based, took responsibility for admin-istrating that training programme. Another ministry among our senior members, entitled 'Crowning Years', developed under the leadership of Alun Davies, so his church at Horsham handled that for us. Other specialist ministries have been distributed similarly and from time to time have changed as the ministry has changed or as people have relocated.

Although we have always maintained this policy there was some inevitability that since Nigel and I were based in Brighton a certain amount of administration would be focused there. As our need particularly for effective communication grew we saw the necessity of a good magazine. We also wanted to start publishing books, teaching cassettes and other materials. Nigel was fully employed in handling those areas that were already developing, and I felt the need of the further support and involvement of a creative thinker and manager for our growing operation. While I was praying about our need and wondering how it would be supplied I was approached by a man in our church who was at something of a crossroads in his own career. As he described his experience and told me of the choices he faced for the future I immediately knew that he was exactly the man I needed. His name was Adrian Willard and I totally surprised him by inviting him to join the team. His expertise proved invaluable. We began to develop our NFI magazine and literature programmes under his excellent oversight and he also brought fresh perspectives first to the later stages of Downs Bible Week and subsequently to many other aspects of our development within the UK and overseas.

Meanwhile, the Clarendon Church was itself growing and had gone through various stages of development. We had filled the Clarendon mission building in Hove and decided to plant out a second congregation into Brighton, which also immediately grew. The spaces in the original building also filled again quite quickly so we sub-divided again from two congregations to five, three school buildings and the central Brighton Art College becoming the venues.

At one time when I was praying about growth and expansion, and particularly the need for more personnel to take responsibility for the ministry, I felt that God brought to my attention the phenomenal success of the current Liverpool Football Club who were so dominant in the 1980s. They seemed to be able to produce an impressive number of brilliant young players from within their youth programme but, when necessary, were unafraid to go outside and buy very skilled and experienced stars. They mixed youth and experience very successfully and maintained a formidable team for several years.

We had some fine young men coming through our ranks and I invited Steve Walford, Chris Wisdom and Alan Preston, all of whom had come to Sussex as students, to come full-time and help oversee three congregations. I also invited two experienced former Baptist pastors to join us. I had first met John Hosier some years previously while he was pastoring in Swalecliffe, Kent, but more recently he had just fulfilled three years of lecturing at Moorlands College. He came to lead the original congregation at the Clarendon building while John Wilthew, who had been pastor at Littlehampton Baptist Church, joined us and led another congregation to the west of town.

After three years, we felt that we should bring all five congregations together again to be one strong, visible church. So we hired Brighton's Odeon cinema, using the large studio for the main meeting and all the smaller studios for our children. It was a great place to meet but became increasingly expensive. We also had to make sure that we vacated the premises promptly because people began appearing, tickets in hand, to see the afternoon movie rather earlier than expected. There was also the weekly hassle of carrying in and out all the amplification, children's equipment and so on. Eventually, we felt sure that we should buy our own large building but in the short term we decided to return to Clarendon Church building and hold repeat Sunday services for two separate congregations. I had a growing conviction that as a church we were beginning to go on a journey of faith and felt that God directed me to preach on the story of Moses. The series lasted many months.

Having a large team of pastors proved a real blessing. On Sundays we could draw on different men to preach, and behind the scenes each man had a sphere of pastoral oversight for a number of house groups in his area. The multi-gifted David Fellingham continued to write magnificent songs that were not only enjoyed by us in Brighton but could be heard all around the world. He also had clear teaching, evangelistic and prophetic skills and actually helped us to plant a new church to the west of Hove, in Lancing. Meanwhile, our relationship with the church in Cape Town continued to grow stronger and we loaned them John and Sue Hosier for an extended period to pastor the church while their pastor visited the UK and had opportunity to get a clearer view of the kind of church life we were developing in the UK.

The conviction that we should buy a large centre that could seat 1,000 people grew, and we, as leaders, were constantly praying about it. At last we learned of a large industrial building being placed on the market which was in the heart of Brighton and was currently owned by Comet, the electrical firm. Although the church knew about our intention and had been praying for God's guidance, it would be true to say that a handful in our ranks were not thrilled with the thought of our spending a lot of money on a building. I was not at all unsympathetic to their perspective, since for years I had said that money should go into ministry not into buildings. But God had clearly led us, so we pressed confidently forward.

We arrived at the time when financial commitment had to be expressed by the people. In our series on Moses the first gift day coincided with our studying Exodus 15, Moses crossing the Red Sea. Strangely, the story seemed wonderfully appropriate. We were going to commit ourselves to a great step of faith that seemed way beyond our ability, yet we felt we had arrived here by simply obeying and following. Just like Moses at the Red Sea, we had to seek God's powerful intervention. In prayer we had asked that on the gift day we might raise £100,000, a figure way above anything that we had raised before. In the prayer meeting on the previous Saturday morning, I had felt a definite surge of faith. I believed that we definitely had £100,000 and began to feel freedom to ask for more, maybe even approaching £200,000. We prayed with fervour and faith. One man, who sadly subsequently left the church, told me that we would never reach the stated £100,000 goal. He reckoned that I was totally out of touch with the feelings of the congregation and he doubted that we would even reach our previous gift day totals of around £20,000. I genuinely believed that we would make it.

We had a great Sunday. It was an extremely exciting day and we were going to cross our Red Sea. As I spent my final moments of preparation in my study at home, I was suddenly reminded of the great speech in Shakespeare's *Henry V*. I quickly grabbed my Shakespeare to make sure I was word perfect and concluded my sermon, with some passion, with the quote, 'And gentlemen in England, now a-bed, shall think themselves accursed they were not here.' It was a dramatic day! We concluded with the offering.

Later that night, Wendy and I were preparing for bed when I heard the letterbox clatter open downstairs and what sounded like an envelope plop onto the mat. I rushed down and recognised the writing on the envelope. It was from the church. It would undoubtedly be the news we were waiting for, telling us the morning's total. I took the envelope back upstairs, opened it carefully, unfolded the note and read the figures of that day's total offering. It was fractionally short of £250,000. My knees buckled and I sat down involuntarily on the bed. We had done it! We had more than done it! I could hardly believe it. We had raised a quarter of a million pounds!

We were on our way. It was incredibly exciting and the sense of God's pleasure and commitment to us was wonderful. In the days ahead we had huge battles to fight with the local authorities who, having initially allowed us to think there would be no problem with planning permission, later unanimously refused our application to change the use of the industrial building to a place of worship. We went through many storms, but eventually all necessary permissions were granted and battles regarding VAT were fought and won. The total price for the finished job continued to escalate over the years but we finally got our great meeting place at the cost of £3.7m. Hundreds of stories could be told regarding the sacrificial giving of church members over a period of nine years. Many gave and repeatedly gave as we developed a rhythm of three gift days a year, usually aiming for £100,000 each time. It is difficult to comprehend where the money kept coming from. We are not a wealthy group of people but God was faithful and all our bills are paid. There is no debt.

Some of our members had feared that if we concentrated our giving on a building we would stop giving to missions

and other needs but because throughout our building project we gave away a tenth of all our building offerings, we
actually gave away far more than we ever used to before. As
a church we always give a tenth of our regular general fund
to NFI anyway, as do most NFI churches.

One story must suffice to show the faithfulness of individuals within the church. In order to make sure the details are
correct I have asked her to tell the story in her own words.

For quite some time I'd wanted to visit my friend, Gail Diani, in
Mexico. In January I found a cheap flight departing at the end
of April but didn't book it immediately. In February we had our
gift day. I prayed about what to give and decided on a figure.
Then God challenged me about it so I 'upped' it a bit. I put the
cheque and paperwork into an envelope, sealed it and drove off
to the Sunday morning meeting.

Terry was preaching, and 'giving' was naturally the theme. I
thought I'd listen quite attentively to the message, agree wholeheartedly with it and then put my gift in the offering. It was a sort
of 'closed envelope, closed mind' mentality. You don't really need
to listen hard to a message on giving if you've already decided
what you're going to give. Anyway, God had other ideas.

As Terry spoke, the Holy Spirit crept up on me and suggested
that maybe I could give more. By the end of the sermon I was
externally my usual calm and collected self, while inwardly
there was war going on. 'What about Mexico?' I protested to
God. 'You know I haven't got any savings. If I give more, there's
no way I can go.'

The band came together for the final song and I glanced at
the offering bowls – large flowerpots stationed at the front.
Everyone stood to sing and go forward with their gifts. I
remained seated, wrestling over what to do, crying out to God
for direction. 'Is this you, me or the enemy?' I asked. 'I don't
want to be forced into something that you're not saying at all.

Maybe I'm just getting too "stressed out" over this. Surely, I prayed about my gift and I'm giving what I believe you told me to. So why the sense of unease? What should I do?'

People all around me were singing and streaming forward. Then God spoke. It had to be his voice because I could never have made up what he said or said it in the way he did. Frankly, I was bracing myself for the words, 'Yes, I want you to give more and this is the figure – plonk!' Instead, he responded with such tenderness. 'Yes,' he said. 'I know that I approved your gift before you got to the meeting,' and then almost with a fatherly smile, he added, 'but wouldn't it be fun to give more?' 'Fun?!' I repeated, pondering the idea for a few seconds and fingering the nicely sealed envelope in my hands. 'Fun? I think it would be quite fun to go to Mexico!' But God's gentle approach and gracious answer had caught me totally off guard.

Finally, I opened the envelope, wrote out a cheque for double my original figure, changed the paperwork and stuffed everything back into the envelope which I sealed as best I could. Then I got up and put my gift in the offering – probably the last person to do so. As I returned to my seat and joined in with the final song I felt happy, but I couldn't deny that there were tears in my eyes, because this sacrifice was costing me something. Needless to say, from that point on I gave up thinking seriously about going to Mexico – until the following Thursday, when I received an unexpected letter from my mother.

'Daddy and I would like to give you some money for a new kitchen extension,' she wrote. 'We'll give you half the money this month and the rest later. What was that final figure? Was it five times what I'd given? Ten times? Twenty times? No, none of these. God multiplied my gift by 22 times! So where's that number in Scripture?! Written into verses like Luke 6:38: 'Give, and it will be given to you; good measure, pressed down, shaken together, running over, they will pour into your lap.' My lap was brimming with provision from God, and my heart with gratitude to him.

But the story didn't end there. For over 20 years as a Christian I've operated a 'receive to give' principle. Whenever I'm given money, I give at least 10 per cent of it away, and sometimes a lot more than that. Now in this case I naturally wanted to honour my parents by using their money for a new kitchen extension – which, by the way, was badly needed. But no sooner was the first instalment in my bank account than I was thinking, 'Now, what do I do about the tithe?' One morning, God gave me the answer. 'Go to Mexico,' he said. 'Give Gail and her pastor's family a holiday by the sea and pay for it all.'

I booked the April flight – which, to my great joy, was even cheaper than before because the departure date was closer. Then I met Flor Evans, her son Johnny, and daughter Florecita in Puerto Vallarta. Her husband, John, couldn't be with us and Gail joined us later in the week. We saw the sights, sat on the beach, swam in the sea, went on boat trips, had meals in restaurants and drank massive pina colladas – all at the heavenly Father's expense. One day, Gail, the two children and I were sitting on an inflatable 'banana' boat, being towed along by a speedboat. Eleven-year-old Florecita squealed with joy as we hit the waves and God spoke to me. 'Wasn't it fun to give more?' he said.

At the end of the first week we went inland to Guadalajara, where I saw the work that Gail is doing among the street children. At the end of week two I took all my remaining traveller's cheques to the bank, cashed them, bought everyone lunch, purchased a few presents to take home and gave the Evans family what I had left – all, that is, except for a small sum which I needed for my bus journey to the airport. When I got on the plane I had 8 pesos in my pocket – that's about 50p.

Mexico is a happy memory now and I'm rejoicing over a beautiful new kitchen extension. Both are signs of God's amazing faithfulness to me. But maybe the greatest highlight is hidden in a day when I passed another test of faith, the day when

God took me out of my comfort zone and said, 'Wouldn't it be fun to give more?' – and I believed him.

We in Brighton had been inspired by the Bracknell Family Church, which had gone ahead of us with a huge building project costing over £3m. Now we know of many other churches in NFI's ranks that are being led to purchase large buildings and face many financial challenges. God seems to be telling men to buy big barns for the coming harvest. But more of that later.

When we set out on this journey God told us that he would use our experience of raising the vast sum of money as an anvil. He'd shape us and refine us, building our faith in him. Once the final offering had been taken and the last bill paid (including the repayment of loans to other NFI churches who had generously stood with us) I reminded the people of this prophecy. We reflected together on some of the ways in which he had shaped us – faith, following leadership, generosity and sacrifice. We determined to continue in the strength of what we had learned.

Although the project was complete, the process was a rich experience. We have continued to take regular large offerings and in the year following completion of the building project were able to allocate over £200,000 to mission. We particularly focused on the homeless of Brighton and the needs of our brothers and sisters in some of the NFI churches in Africa, with contributions towards feeding programmes and start-up funds for micro-enterprise.

# 17

# A Bow and Arrow

With the closing of Downs we made two definite decisions. First, that we should continue to have a summer camp for young teens. About 1,000 gathered at Plumpton for the following two summers. It was a phenomenal success. At the second, in 1990, there was such a manifestation of God's presence that the young teenagers asked the leaders to cancel the sports programme in order to have further sessions. They wanted to hear about revival. Some were getting up especially early to seek God, others had extraordinary encounters with God where they felt that he called them to full-time service in the future. They lay on the grass overcome by the Holy Spirit, seeing visions and prophesying.

Second, we decided to arrange some weekends in major cities across the UK to teach specifically on the grace of God. It was proposed that I would travel with different teams to strategic centres, and in public meetings on Friday, Saturday and Sunday evenings, expound mainly from the Epistle to the Romans. Then, on Saturday mornings, I would take sessions on the church for leaders. On Sunday mornings, the various team members would scatter to churches in the location.

When I arrived home after the team meeting where the idea had been established, I found mail awaiting me which confirmed our thinking. There was a letter from a group of Assemblies of God pastors in the north-east, inviting me to speak at a weekend in Newcastle at Bethshan. They felt impressed to do this, although they knew that I rarely travelled to the north. A second letter similarly invited me to speak at a weekend in Bristol.

I wrote a book entitled *Enjoying God's Grace*, the title of the ministry weekends, and over about 18 months I travelled to some 16 cities in the UK, doing what became known affectionately as the EGG Tour. Thousands of tapes and books went out and I had the privilege of receiving many letters testifying to changed lives as people came to grasp the wonderful benefits of the grace of God. I also remember taking the programme to Cape Town and, at the conclusion of my talk, a woman wearing a navy suit, hat and gloves came to me alongside her huge Afrikaner husband. With tears running down her cheeks she asked, 'Is it really true? I can hardly believe it.' I assured her that I had simply been expounding the Scriptures and it was undoubtedly true. The following year I saw the same couple again and her husband told me proudly that it was like having a new wife! She stood next to him, delighted with her new-found acceptance in God's love. I am often approached by people who tell me that their lives were transformed when they first encountered the *Enjoying God's Grace* message and I am told that tapes are often passed to friends by people who have greatly benefited themselves.

The book *Enjoying God's Grace*, which was later translated into several languages, was actually prepared by Mary

Austin, who by that time was part of our NFI staff in Brighton. She took a series of my recorded messages and committed them to book form, as she did a number of other 'how to' books which we began to publish. Mary also did most of the work on my book *Weak People, Mighty God* (later published in the USA as *God Knows You're Human*) which followed *Men of Destiny*, books which encapsulated my teachings on Bible characters at six Downs Bible Weeks. These were followed by Oasis Bible study books, providing daily readings but again based on originally preached material. Several of the brothers within NFI who had developed helpful ministry were happy to find that their ministry could be transposed into book form with Mary's aid. A number of books followed, which enjoyed good distribution.

As planned, I invited Kriengsak to come and address all of our NFI leaders in the UK. He agreed and spoke for us at Ashburnham Place, a memorable day which had a profound effect on us. He shared his vision and also expanded on his values and style of working, especially in connection with church planting. The grace and warmth with which he spoke totally won our leaders, and his breadth of vision and passion for world evangelisation proved genuinely stimulating. God was clearly stirring us up.

As another year went by, we began to feel that God wanted us to re-launch the Bible weeks, but this time not in a tent at Plumpton Racecourse, but at a much better site in the centre of the nation. We had just heard about the Royal Agricultural Showground at Stoneleigh, near Coventry. It was a huge site, on level ground, with concrete roads and massive sheds, and had far more facilities than Plumpton. We began to make our enquiries and plans for the following year.

Meanwhile we planned a large leadership conference to be held at the Brighton Centre with the objective of exposing Kriengsak's ministry to a much wider group of leaders. I also took some sessions on the life and ministry of John the Baptist and we called the conference 'Making Ready a People Prepared'. In the final session, Kriengsak spoke with extraordinary authority and invited those who were willing to move to new areas to plant churches to come to the front of the meeting. Scores of people poured forward. As the years have passed I have been amazed at how many people have told me that in that moment they were not only expressing willingness to move house and to help plant a church, but were explicitly told where they would go. It was a very supernatural time, and I believe that something of Kriengsak's phenomenal apostolic anointing was in opera-tion and there was a genuine impartation of his passion to church plant.

As he was speaking, he suddenly stopped, and then elec-trified us by asking if we knew a town called 'C-O-V-E-N-T-R-Y'. He mispronounced it but spelt it out for us. He was being given a revelation of the word right there in the meet-ing and told us that he could see that God was going to gather us there and that over us God had placed a funnel through which he could see God's blessing being poured out in an extraordinary way. As you can imagine, we were con-siderably excited that God was confirming Stoneleigh just outside Coventry as the venue of the new Bible week. We made our plans for the following year anticipating a great time.

Meanwhile, I had an opportunity to see some of Kriengsak's work first-hand, since he invited me to speak at his annual conference in Thailand. Ross Paterson of Chinese Church Support Ministries had also invited me to speak at conferences in T'ai-pei in Taiwan, which resulted in *Restoration in the Church* being translated into Mandarin. I invited Steve Brading, who was currently based in Hastings, to accompany me. It was a very exciting privilege to speak there. Ross arranged an excellent programme and it was great to meet some of the key leaders from the nation as well as have a look at the extraordinary country (so different to Communist China, as I was to discover the following year).

We then travelled to Thailand, for Kriengsak's conference, where thousands were gathered at a vast camp. The heat was colossal and we met in a large area that had a roof but no walls. I wondered how we would cope with the temperature. The thousands of predominantly young people (at that time 80 per cent of Kriengsak's people were single) who attended were sitting in upright metal chairs. But they had arranged soft covered armchairs for Steve and me at the front of the crowd and then brought large buckets of ice and followed up with a large electric fan, which was placed so that it blew across the ice at us – a brilliant and effective cooling system! While there, I also enjoyed meeting Frank Damazio from Portland's Bible Temple in the USA, who was the other main speaker and who did a tremendous job preaching via translators on some great themes from the book of Daniel.

It was strange at last to hear Kriengsak address his people in his native tongue. I suddenly realised that I had now heard him preaching at two conferences in the UK, one in the USA and one in Canada, often using extremely wide vocabulary and handling Western concepts with extraordinary skill. Only now was I actually seeing him on his home ground and in his own language.

With our growing exposure to the challenge of world mission we began to consider what more NFI could be doing overseas and particularly within Europe. Still predominantly a group of churches limited to southern England, we began to consider our responsibilities for nations immediately across the Channel. Harold Owen and the Woking church had helped to serve and oversee a congregation in Berkel, Holland, for a long time and we also worked with a church in Basle on the Swiss/German border, but apart from that we had no substantial continental outreaches.

One weekend, when I was in north Kent at an NFI elders' and wives' retreat for that region, we were having a prayer session and suddenly I saw a vision of southern England with a bow superimposed over the coastline and an arrow pointing to the south. Gradually the string and arrow were pulled back across the heart of the nation until the bow was fully stretched and the arrow was ready to be shot out.

As I contemplated the vision, I understood that a bow-string has to be pulled back to its fullest extent to obtain maximum energy to shoot the arrow out. If it is drawn back only a little, there is not sufficient impetus for the arrow to travel far. God was showing me that if we were to have any impact overseas we needed to strengthen our base and multiply resources in England far beyond the south-east corner. We needed to pull back the bow string by planting more churches in our own nation, in order to reach out across the frontiers of other nations. This was a new strategy! We were no longer to confine ourselves to the south-east.

Apart from one or two anomalies, all our churches up to now were in that area. We regarded other parts of the country as being the responsibility of other teams. One notable exception had been a small church plant in Newcastle. Their leaders had regularly attended Downs Bible Week and repeatedly asked me if I would get involved with them. I refused, telling them that we only worked in the south-east and that they should seek help from another team doing similar work near them. Their reply rather surprised me when they insisted that our style was different, which I dismissed as incorrect, arguing that the apostolic teams in question were essentially the same.

Another year went by and they approached me again, once more encountering my refusal based on the fact that we only worked in the south-east. This time they argued further, 'Oh I see, only in the south-east of England and India!' We laughed at this rather gaping inconsistency and then I said that we served India differently to the churches in England. Teams visited them only three or four times a year. 'We'll settle for that!' was their immediate reply. I conceded and have never regretted being involved with what has since become the vibrant City Church in Newcastle.

With the vision of the bow and arrow, it was time for Newcastle to be an exception no longer. We felt that God was commissioning us to break out of the south-east and spread across the UK. Within the next year the economy in the UK came under considerable pressure, with the south-east being particularly affected. Many were losing their jobs and having to relocate to other parts of the country. Remembering Kriengsak's policy of following his church members when they moved from Bangkok across Thailand, I asked Colin Baron, who was currently leading a church in Swanley, Kent, if he would kindly do some research for me. Would he ask the churches where most of their people who had moved from the south-east for economic reasons were going? His research brought two towns to our attention. One was Swindon and the other was Manchester. But what proved even more significant was that, while making the enquiries for me, Colin and his wife Mary began to hear God speaking to them. They were themselves to go to Manchester. Not only that, God imparted faith to Colin that he was not simply to start a new church but rather to plant 20 churches in the Greater Manchester area. When Graham and Charlotte Webb heard about the bow and arrow vision, God also impressed Manchester on them. So Graham, who was an elder at the NFI church in Horsham, joined Colin and they started to pioneer a new stage in our development. Others began to follow as months and years slipped by, many testifying that they first had a particular town impressed upon them when walking forward at the Brighton conference at Dr Kriengsak's invitation.

Happily, at this time there was also a renewal of fellowship among a number of men who had formerly been together following Arthur Wallis's invitation to the original 'Magnificent Seven'. Arthur had himself worked quite hard behind the scenes to heal wounds and reconcile brothers. Gerald had also been very active in patiently and lovingly trying to re-gather men. Some of the 20 that I briefly joined those years earlier were scattered now. Some were no longer in full-time ministry but some were willing to reach out to one another in a renewed effort for friendship and fellowship. I certainly appreciated Gerald's friendly overtures and gladly attended informal get-togethers that he arranged.

These were markedly different from the earlier gatherings when differences of style and theology had eventually brought discord and produced tension. Although these differences were still acknowledged they now became secondary. The contrasting emphases were publicly known, but the object of the gatherings was not to debate them but to promote friendship, acceptance of one another and fellowship. The atmosphere was altogether more relaxed and there was no attempt to present one united prophetic voice. The renewed setting was a blessing for all involved and Gerald suggested that we arrange a joint leaders' conference.

'Together for the Kingdom' was held in Sheffield and brought many men together who had not seen one another for years.

However, a few days before the event, the sudden death of Arthur Wallis through a massive heart attack shocked us all. The news spread rapidly and, though now absent, he seemed to cast a powerful shadow over the whole conference. There were constant references to his life and his impact on many of the individuals present. Who could calculate our indebtedness to Arthur, a man of such prophetic vision backed by such godliness of life? We felt bereft of a true gentleman and a radical Christian.

Eighteen months later, we returned to Sheffield for 'Together for the Nation', followed subsequently by 'Apostles and Prophets for the Harvest', which ended the series. Our genuine mutual affection meant that we could happily meet for the occasional conference together. Our differences of emphasis meant that we could not at that stage actually build anything together. Nevertheless, behind the scenes fellowship continued and there was far more overlapping and interrelating than we had experienced for years.

One area of contact came through meetings arranged by John Wimber. By this time he had developed a friendship with Mike Bickle from Kansas City and the remarkably gifted prophet, Paul Cain. Mike Bickle gave a very powerful talk on unity at one of John Wimber's leaders' conferences and invited Roger Forster and me to come and pray over the many who responded in what looked like genuine humility and desire for oneness among leaders in the country.

Paul Cain also visited an NFI leaders' meeting in Brighton. He was at the end of a very demanding schedule of meetings, mostly with Church of England groups, and arrived exhausted. I don't think he had clear awareness of where he was or what sort of church we represented. He was rushed into the meeting and after some worship he began to speak. Then suddenly, he interrupted himself and proceeded to prophesy. His words were rather stumbling but included the following:

> Your ministry is more inclusive than I thought, not just an exclusive body of believers, which I thought I might find. There is such a beautiful thing that I see in a vision tonight. It's like there's no way of seeing the exact geographic location of this thing or of pinpointing the exact spot. It seems there are satellite beams arching in every conceivable direction, as it were, and I think even over the sea here south of us, and in every conceivable direction these things are going to be touching down. And Africa, of course, is already established, India, all of these things. It's a beautiful vision that I see for you. I don't know how many names you call yourself, World Frontiers, or whatever it is, but God is enlarging you and it is like he's calling out to you to lengthen your cords and strengthen your stakes. It seems like these things that are arching down are really strengthened. If they are satellite spots they're solid and are becoming more solid, and the Lord is establishing his outreaches and his witness stations here, there and everywhere. I just didn't know the magnitude of it until tonight until I just closed my eyes and began to see that this is no small matter, this is no gathering of 300 people. This is a matter of a sovereign work of apostolic character and nature and chemistry and the Lord is going to use it to change the expression of Christianity all over the world. And that's the word I came to bring. The Lord will use you here in a sovereign way to change the expression of Christianity throughout the world. You haven't even touched down on some of these places yet but it's a glorious work and it's of the Lord. It's the Lord, it's the Lord. I see that this is something that God has put together. It may be

despised by some who want to analyse it in a carnal way, but the Lord has shown me in a spiritual way what this is all about. I just know, and I know that I know, that the Lord is helping me discern what you are all about.

It was a memorable night. We had hoped that Paul Cain would bring detailed words of knowledge about individuals, as was often his style. In that sense we were disappointed, since there were no such words. Instead we received this extraordinary prophecy with its far-reaching implications. It has been an encouragement and provocation to us ever since.

# 18

# International Developments

Paul Cain was right. We were already working in Africa and India. By now Duncan and Vasanti Watkinson had made wonderful progress in Bombay. The original 'Living Word' church had prospered under Duncan's leadership and had planted a number of new churches, such as 'Living Light' and 'Living Hope', across the city, with excellent young pastors coming through their ranks and being discipled and trained by Duncan. Also, Rosemary Stapley, originally from Allerford Chapel in Catford, who had been a missionary in India for over 20 years, moved across the nation to Bombay to join the Living Word church and pioneer a clinic in the nearby slums.

As the number of churches grew, and conferences and training programmes multiplied, Arun Philip provided administrative skills in overseeing the office work. David Fernandes emerged quickly from being a fairly recent convert into a mature, wise and godly leader. With the leadership now well established in Bombay, Duncan and Vasanti were ready to respond to a small group from Goa who came seeking their help. To everybody's surprise, God led Duncan not simply to promise occasional visits to Goa to help support the group, but instead it became clear that, as a family, they should uproot and replant in Margao, Goa, and give hands-on apostolic oversight.

Leaving all their established friends in Bombay represented a huge sacrifice, but their guidance was clear. They joined Melvin Pereira and the small group in Margao and watched it begin to grow. They also realised it was an ideal location to establish a training centre. Churches in England were thrilled at the prospect of being involved in such a venture and funds were raised at the first Stoneleigh Bible Week to help with the building. More young men and women were trained and the churches continued to multiply both in Bombay and in Goa.

I and a growing number of NFI pastors from the UK became frequent visitors to the churches and provided lecturing skills to augment the training programme. It has been wonderful as the years have gone by to see men converted, added, trained and emerge as pastors in the growing number of new churches in India. The brothers and sisters there are our dear friends and demonstrate such an excellent serving spirit. In addition to our visits there, we bring the pastors and their wives across to the UK for our annual international leaders' conferences. They are known and loved among many of our UK-based churches, as we often host them locally and send teams to them. Two-way traffic over the years has built strong bonds of love.

Meanwhile in South Africa, our involvement with the church in Cape Town continued to develop to such a degree that Simon Pettit from Uckfield in Sussex was invited to join the eldership team to assist the pastor in leading the work. When Graham Ingram, the pastor, first asked me to suggest this possibility to Simon I was totally dismissive of the idea.

I had several alternative suggestions to bring to Simon. He was obviously a very gifted man and there were some situations developing in the UK which were beginning to need a leader such as him who could take them on to their full potential. I arranged an evening to meet with Simon and Lindsey and, having asked them how open they might be to moving from Uckfield, brought my list of possibilities. At the very end of the list, in a less than enthusiastic way, I told Simon and Lindsey of Graham's request, simply in order to fulfil my promise. To my surprise, they both lit up at the suggestion and told me that they had always believed that they would ultimately serve God overseas. I had forgotten that they had also been part of the first large team that came with me to Cape Town in 1987, at which time they had also felt that God was speaking to them.

I have frequently visited South Africa over the years and have often taken David Holden with me. In 1989 Simon had accompanied David on a visit and this had further stirred Simon's interest. Now he and Lindsey, who had never lived outside of Sussex, were ready to uproot and move to the southern hemisphere. They would be missed not only in the Sussex area, where their presence was such an encouragement to everybody who knew them, but also at prayer and fasting days and all the settings where NFI leaders gathered. Simon had become a real force to be reckoned with and his absence would be keenly felt.

There was a very unexpected last-minute hiccup on our next visit to Cape Town, which was planned to finalise details. Graham Ingram sensed that God was surprisingly calling him to move away from Cape Town, first to New Zealand and then perhaps on to the UK. He had actually made known his decision to resign as pastor and could therefore no longer invite Simon to be his assistant. It seemed that everything was cancelled. Indeed, he had even spoken to another local pastor about the possibility of being his replacement. The door appeared to be closed!

In my heart, I did not believe that the guidance we had recently received that Simon should go should now be abandoned, so on hearing the news, Simon and I simply prayed for God's perfect will to be done. My morning Bible reading had been Psalm 37, which gave me great encouragement with its command not to fret, but to trust in the Lord, with the added promise of inheriting the land. The following day the remaining elders of the church gave themselves to a day of prayer and fasting and, at its conclusion, approached Simon and invited him still to come and actually be the leader of the church. It was settled. So in 1990 Simon and Lindsey moved to Cape Town with their children, Emily, Charlie and Alice, a move which was to have huge ramifications not only for their future but also for the future of NFI.

After a while the church, which incidentally had previously been called 'Vineyard', though not part of John Wimber's group, was requested by the growing group of Vineyard churches in the area to consider changing its name, in order to avoid confusion. They agreed to do so and changed their title to 'Jubilee', reflecting their passion to see the people of Africa released in every way into the glorious liberty of the gospel.

Our involvement in South Africa not only became more firmly established, but God was also bringing other men into place. During several of our Downs Bible Week years we were visited by Edward and Fridah Buria from Kenya. They were keen to become associated with NFI, but we did not immediately respond since we could not see how we could really care for them and serve them effectively. Nevertheless, they continued to turn up every year with open hearts and excellent attitudes. (Now we are fully involved with them. They and the 42 churches they serve in Kenya are full members of the NFI family.)

Also, a young Ghanaian from Accra called John Kpikpi was at Sussex University for five years, doing his PhD in Zoology. During those years he had become part of the Clarendon Church and thoroughly immersed himself in our vision and values. He also married Alex, one of our church members, and ultimately returned to Ghana, where he became Professor of Zoology at Accra University. Having searched for a church, he discovered he could not find one anywhere which reflected the kind of church life he now so highly valued, so he began a small group in his home, a step which was to have far-reaching consequences. (Now he leads a thriving and growing church with hundreds of members. He has left his job at the university and is fully involved in church leadership and the planting of new churches in Ghana.)

One day out of the blue I had received a call from an Afrikaner couple from Pietermaritzburg, who informed me that God had impressed upon them to come and join themselves to Terry Virgo in Brighton for a season, in order to get to know our ways in Christ. They assured me that they would simply find secular work in the area and join us, which they promptly did. So we had the enormous pleasure and privilege of being introduced to Piet and Hettie Dreyer, who would later return to Pietermaritzburg and prove to be one of the most extraordinary pioneer couples I have ever known. On their return they would start one of our most trail-blazing social action programmes, called Project Gateway, in a former prison in Pietermaritzburg.

God was beginning to bring the pieces together across Africa, so that, having established his base in Cape Town,

Simon could later develop an apostolic work which would begin to spread across the continent.

Meanwhile, in Mexico, the number of churches we were touching began to grow. El Camino, our original church base in Guadalajara, had by now become fully associated with NFI and was now led by John Evans. Ray Lowe from Biggin Hill began to emerge as the key man for our contacts there, and later a network of churches would develop.

One more contact that was going to have more repercussions than I could ever have imagined came when Arthur Wallis told me of an impressive church in Columbia, Missouri. He enthused greatly about it and asked if I would be interested in their publishing my book *Restoration in the Church* in the USA. Unusually for a local church they had their own publishing house, called Cityhill, and had recently published a number of Arthur's books in the US, including *Living God's Way*, *On to Maturity* and *The Radical Christian*. I was definitely interested and they proceeded to publish my book.

Not only that, but they also invited me to speak in 1989 at their annual pastors' conference, together with Tony Morton. I was delighted to do this, since Arthur had told me what an exceptional and strategically significant church they were. They had built a church on restoration values and had developed an extraordinarily loving community which was well known in the Mid-West and had influence on a number of churches in nearby towns.

I enjoyed the conference enormously and was extremely well received. What was unique about it was that the conference was hosted within the church itself. Not only were all the meetings held in their premises, but all of the delegates were provided with accommodation in the homes of the church members. Also, all the meals were provided within the large church facility and were magnificently presented at a very high standard, with church members serving everybody. It was quite an experience simply to be there!

On the Sunday, the whole church gathered in their hundreds and a substantial band and modern-style choir led a phenomenal worship time. It was unlike any conference I had ever attended. Arthur was right: it was a wonderful church. Many of the members lived very close by and there was a great sense of community, as Christian neighbours were greatly in evidence greeting one another in the surrounding streets each day.

They held no pastors' conference the following year, but approached me again to see if I would speak for them in October 1991, to which I readily agreed. Tragically, in the June of 1991, they called me to say that the pastor's marriage was in severe disarray and they felt they would have to cancel the October conference. I was deeply saddened by the news but of course agreed to the decision. Shortly afterwards, I received a further call. They knew that I had the conference dates in my diary. Would I please still come to see if I could be of any assistance in the problem they were now facing? They would also like me to speak at a small 'in-house' conference with a few local pastors who were somewhat affected by the recent developments. I agreed that I would go in the October as planned.

Meanwhile, our first Stoneleigh would soon be upon us. I had once again invited C.J. and Larry to be our speakers. By now they had become very dear friends of ours and I had spoken several times at their PDI celebrations in the USA. Their largest was Celebration East, held in a university campus in Indiana, Pennsylvania. I also spoke at their West Coast Celebration in Flagstaff, Arizona (which for me included a visit to the magnificent Grand Canyon!). In addition, I had spoken at several of their churches across the nation, in such towns as Pasadena, California; Atlanta, Georgia; Orlando, Florida; Philadelphia, Pennsylvania and frequently at C.J.'s home base at Washington DC. I was always deeply impressed by the levels of enthusiasm and integrity in their ranks and over the years they have had a powerful effect on me, and indeed on NFI as a whole. It is extremely difficult to walk through the crowds of people at PDI churches without a great number of individuals personally greeting you and almost always with very specific expressions of appreciation for ministry. They are never vague and generalised! The sharp focus that they bring to all that they do is very stimulating.

C. J. Mahaney, who leads PDI, is one of the most impressive men of God it has been my privilege to know. He combines an extraordinary sense of humour with red hot passion for Christ and devotion to his church. The whole movement is filled with the fruits of his outstanding example. Although their personal warmth and humour is a great joy, they are passionate with zeal for God. Their attention to detail is (as the Americans would say) 'awesome', but their zeal comes with warmth, grace and evident affection. I love being around them!

At one particular Celebration East they decided to have a 'fun' evening. Mark Altrogge, their amazingly gifted songwriter, who has wonderfully served us all with so many great songs, had written one of their most popular songs at the time, namely 'I have a destiny I know I shall fulfil'. They decided at the celebration to perform the song in a variety of different ways, reflecting the different parts of the country from which the churches had gathered. They reckoned, for instance, that if it had come from California, it would have had a different sound altogether, and a group from one of their churches came up and presented the song with a Beach Boys feel. Others came, giving it a Bruce Springstein twist; a Mexican group gave it their treatment; a great black group went to town on it, and so on. It was a huge success, and everybody loved the fun.

The next morning I was sitting at breakfast when it occurred to me that the English should have been represented. I opened my paper napkin and began to write on it the words of Mark Altrogge's well-known song, but with a Liverpudlian twist!

> I have a destiny
> I know I shall fulfil.
> I have a destiny
> In that city on a hill.[1]

> I know he loves me
> And you know that can't be bad.
> I know he loves me
> And you know you should be glad.
> He loves me yeah, yeah, yeah . . .

It actually fitted the well-known Beatle melody, and I reckoned it would work, and so I secretly approached the extremely gifted Bob Kauflin, who led their musicians. Yes, they could play it without difficulty (and with style!). I then approached Simon Pettit, John Wheeler, Mike Frisby and John Groves, the team of English guys who were with me. We agreed it would be a great surprise to spring on the conference. The only American beyond the musicians to know

---

1. © 1986 People of Destiny Int. Adm. by Copycare, P.O. Box 77, Hailsham BN27 3EF. Used by permission.

anything was planned was the team administrator, my friend Bo Lotinsky.

So, on the last morning, just before I was to bring my final talk, I expressed my great appreciation to the thousands gathered at the conference for their warm reception and added that I would like my English friends to join me on the platform so that we could together thank them. At the pre-planned moment, guitars were quickly put into our hands and the powerful electric chord was struck (not by us, since we were only miming, but by their musicians!) and we rocked into our number! They absolutely loved it and Bo (adding a further note of authenticity) had spoken in advance to a group of teenage girls, who ran down the aisles screaming as we finished! Years later, people still remind me of the day the Beatles came to Celebration East!

It was great to anticipate starting our new venture at Stoneleigh with C.J. and Larry standing with us. My own theme of ministry for the Bible week was the City of God, seen first at a distance by Abraham, then captured and inhabited by David and his contemporaries, and finally prophetically described in all its glory in his eighth chapter by Zechariah. Lex Loizides wrote a great song that summed up our focus: 'I have seen the city of God coming down from heaven. I have seen the city of God and I cannot turn away.' As we gathered in our thousands (about 8,500 at this first Stoneleigh), we were like a small town – a city that God was building. As we entered the last decade of the millennium, more and more people were becoming captivated with the vision of the city to which we are called and about which God feels so passionately.

# 19

# A Memorable Sabbatical

Stoneleigh was a great success. The facilities were excellent, even if the main shed used for the great evening celebrations retained a certain agricultural fragrance! Undoubtedly, it was a huge improvement on Plumpton, with its very limited space and lack of solid ground and substantial buildings. Also, by being more central we could draw people from a wider circle across the nation. The wide, spacious areas of the agricultural showground gave more room for sports competitions and play areas for children.

The following year, we pressed on further and saw our numbers grow. We also added to our speaking team Kriengsak and Mahesh Chavda, while also retaining C.J., Larry and myself. We had never had such a large number of visiting speakers at a Bible week. Also, the number of over-seas guests was beginning to grow and our sphere was defi-nitely extending way beyond our experience at the Downs.

Meanwhile, I not only attended the smaller conference in Columbia, Missouri, as promised, but found that the crisis there was worse than we had feared. I was asked to return again within a few weeks and actually went on to visit the church seven times during the next two years. I became increasingly attached to the people, who were terribly distressed because of the collapse of the pastor's marriage and all the disappointment and disillusionment that accompanied that. Our hearts became knit together and I know that my visits brought them security and hope for the future.

Quite early on, I strongly recommended that Phil Schaefer, one of the existing team of full-time elders, should take the lead among them and be regarded as the church pastor from now on. Phil was originally very daunted at the task, but he rose to the challenge and the church essentially stayed together, losing only a few people through the crisis. Nevertheless, the church's wounds went deep and there was a corporate heavy-heartedness that was difficult to shake off. I urged them as a church to link up with a group of churches within the USA that they could respect and had some links with, such as Dick Iverson's MFI based at Portland, Oregon, and serving churches not only across the USA but among the nations. I also invited them to consider joining PDI and arranged for them to attend the PDI Celebration East in Pennsylvania, at which I was about to speak, but at that time PDI were not sensing that God wanted them to adopt existing churches and the Columbia elders were unsure of God's will. I know that my visits were increasingly appreciated and some began to drop hints that it would be great if I could move to be with them, an idea that I quickly dismissed as impossible.

Two pastors from the Kansas City area, who were loosely related to the Columbia church, actually decided to come to the UK to have a look at our church life and to attend one of our prayer and fasting conferences. Towards the end of our time together, Carl Herrington came to the microphone full of emotion and said publicly that whatever he had to do, he wanted to become a member of this group and he wanted his church to be part of NFI. He was just about to be planted out from a church in Raymore to an area called Lees Summit and he was clear that he wanted to be an NFI church. The Columbia church began to wonder if this was the way forward for them, too.

After the second Stoneleigh Bible Week, I had been strongly encouraged to take a sabbatical. The elders at Brighton had begun to take sabbaticals on a rota basis and returned refreshed and reinvigorated. The ingredients of the sabbaticals usually included some travel, to see what God was doing in other places, and also the study of particular topics or a Scripture theme that was arresting their attention at the time. The possibility became more and more attractive and finally I happily yielded to my brothers' advice. I had been in ministry for about 30 years and suddenly a sabbatical seemed like a great idea! Although I have found two- or three-day fasts helpful, I had never experienced an extended fast and reckoned that the sabbatical would provide an ideal opportunity. As I looked at my diary, I saw that the beginning of the sabbatical was the best time. My journal at that time records:

> I have been looking forward to this opportunity to seek the Lord in prayer and reading for a long time. Today I am starting what I believe will be a 21-day fast. I am excited and a little apprehensive about it. It has come at an important time of expansion in the work; international calls are multiplying and the number of churches in the UK is growing quite rapidly. I fear the danger of having my diary dictated to me by those who seek my involvement in their programmes. This may often be OK, but I must be doing the will of God. In all the business, my prayer and reading no longer holds the central role that it

should, or that it used to. My hope and prayer is that this sabbatical will prove a life-changing experience. My goals are firstly that through prayer I will gain a renewed intimacy with God, a quickening of faith, a sense of God's will for the future, and a new fellowship with the Holy Spirit. Through reading I will find a fresh stimulation for my mind, a rethink about discipling, some research on the cell church system, and enjoy working through Romans using John Murray's commentary. Thirdly, through rest, a chance to refresh my whole being. Fourthly, through absence from NFI and Clarendon Church, to provide opportunity for change. Fifthly, through time with my family, to bless them individually and together. Sixthly, through Bible meditation, to meet with Jesus in a new way.

Sadly, at the conclusion of the fast, I would have to say that I was disappointed, though I did feel that several of my objectives were fulfilled. I probably chose a bad time to start it. I had just completed an extremely busy time of ministry, so felt weary from the beginning. Not a clever way to start! I gradually felt a loss of energy (I also lost 28lb). My voice grew weak and I found it difficult to speak with any sense of urgency and enthusiasm. This actually affected my ability to intercede with energy as I so wanted to. In the end, I must content myself with the fact that God alone knows what is accomplished when we seek him in this kind of way. We are undoubtedly the least qualified to evaluate what takes place and I do not regret the experience. I enjoyed my opportunities to read and study and especially appreciated working through Murray's Romans, which of course continued throughout the whole sabbatical.

One unexpected development resulted in my obtaining a late booking for my first ever visit to Israel, which was very enjoyable. However, the most memorable part of the whole sabbatical break was the privilege of an extraordinary visit to the Far East, best communicated here by telling it in diary form, just as it happened:

**Saturday 7 November.** Flew through the night to Hong Kong. The plane comes in among huge skyscrapers which cling to the narrow coastal area surrounded by mountains. Met Rodney Kingstone at the airport. Hong Kong itself is amazing. Huge crowds of people everywhere. Met local team led by a New Zealander who hosted us overnight. First meal with chopsticks!

**Sunday 8 November.** Took a train to the Chinese border, then to the mainland. Impressed by some similarities to India (paddy fields). One of the differences is that nearly all the women wear trousers. Booked into a very nice hotel in Canton, designed particularly for international visitors. Rather a showpiece.

*Evening*: First introduction to the house churches. We took a taxi through packed streets and down a crowded alley. Went up narrow steps to a house where about 150 people were crammed into a large room watching a television screen. Mounted another flight of stairs to an almost identical scene (minus TV). Sat on planks of wood. The speaker, who had a closed circuit camera on him (which explained the scene downstairs), was about 70 years old. His congregation was 70 per cent young people.

Congregation gave him rapt attention. His subject was the place of tears in the Bible and he drew from the experiences of Jesus, Peter and Jeremiah, contrasting the tears of shame with those of compassion and intercession. We then broke bread together – very moving. Speaker showed no sign of weariness at the end of a busy day, but was happy to answer our questions as the congregation gradually drifted away from his home.

Three other identical-sized congregations meet on different days of the week. His whole church numbered about 1,200 and met each week in his home. He'd spent 21 years in prison including 15 years' hard labour in a coal mine. His face shone brightly as he spoke – evidently devoted to Christ and brimming with gratitude at the way Jesus had kept him throughout his imprisonment.

**Monday 9 November.** Wandered around sightseeing. Was particularly thrilled when a young man at the hotel asked if he could practise his English on me. He later agreed to be our guide and showed us around the nearby park – great opportunity to tell him about Jesus. After conversation, Nigel Lloyd gave him some literature and swapped addresses.

**Tuesday 10 November.** Travelled on to Beijing, where it had snowed the previous day.

**Wednesday 11 November.** Visited Tiananmen Square, scene of the student uprising. Vast crowds of people everywhere, many queuing at Mao's Mausoleum. Also visited the Forbidden City, made famous by the film *The Last Emperor*. Fascinating place where former emperors of the Ming Dynasty lived.

*Evening*: Met Allen Yuan, another pastor from the house church, who told us that in 1958, at the age of 44, he had been imprisoned for the sake of Christ. His wife had to raise their six children, aged from six to seventeen, and care for an elderly mother. Throughout his 21-year sentence, he never saw his family, or had any Christian fellowship, or saw a Bible. He remembered two Christian songs; 'The Old Rugged Cross' and Psalm 27 set to music. He told us that sometimes the temperature dropped to –29°C, but added that he had never been ill.

Was very moved as I listened to him. Could not help thinking of my own children of similar age range. What a terrible sacrifice not to see them grow to adulthood. When we commented on the high price he'd paid, he replied, 'Nothing compares with the cross.' He was released in 1979 when he was in his mid 60s. Now, at 79, he and his wife are still very active. He left us late at night, carrying bags full of books that we had brought him.

When we asked him if he could sum up his goal for ministry, he said, 'Back to the book of Acts and follow the apostles' footsteps.' He also told us that persecution was the growing pains of the church. The meetings he leads are based on 1 Corinthians 14:26 and he reported many miracles to us. What a privilege it was to listen to such a thoroughgoing charismatic! Couldn't get his face out of my mind for a long time afterwards. Couldn't erase from my memory the tremendous joy that flowed from him, either.

**Thursday 12 November.** Went by bus to the Great Wall of China. Extraordinary phenomenon! Bitingly cold, fierce wind tore at us as we climbed the steep wall. Staggering view. Also visited the ancient Ming Tombs many metres below ground level. China is an amazing place.

**Friday 13 November.** Flew to Shanghai – home to twelve million Chinese. A 70-year-old 'Bible woman', who likes to be called 'Auntie', told us her story. Her family were poor and she, the tenth child, had often been sick and left to die. But God had taken care of her. In her teens, she was powerfully influenced by an elderly missionary lady and became a Christian. She told us that she had experienced dreams, visions and encounters with angels. On one occasion, her soul went out of her body. She saw bright clouds in the sky and was told to take the Bible into the countryside. Initially, she resisted the call to be a humble preacher. Instead, she spent two years in seminary and took a teaching job in a local school – which resulted in the salvation of many young people. Then the Communists came and imprisoned her with her three-year-old son. While she was in prison, her hair was shaved and she was beaten and kicked. She was also taken to places where the temperature was –25°C.

One day, she was so sick and close to death that she wanted to die. Then God told her in a dream, 'Your work is not finished.' That night, the fever left her. Sometime later, her son heard God sing him a song saying, 'Follow Me.' Like Samuel, he asked his mother what he should do. She told him he must give his life to God. Now he is being trained for the ministry.

At one time she asked the Lord if she could respond to the 'peace treatment' that her captors were offering her. 'Can I write them a positive response?' she asked. 'No,' the Lord replied, 'you are married to Christ.' Her guards told her, 'You have deep poison in your mind. You need Mao's thoughts. We will set you free if you judge the Bible.' In the night, God told her not to fear.

In 1980, after 25 years in prison, she was released. She now travels widely, serving the Lord. She told us that she was sometimes reluctant to make long journeys – particularly in the icy winter. But God's love melted her heart on one journey. She stood on a train all night and much blessing followed her obedience. She told us that sometimes up to 8,000 people would gather in the mountains for open-air meetings. She also said that two weeks previously, three men had been beaten to death by the Communists. Recently, the Communists had beaten three pastors, one of whom died. When the Communists left, the remaining believers gathered around the man and God raised him from the dead.

When we asked what we in the West could do for her, she said 'Don't send Western money. It corrupts. We don't buy meat; we eat vegetables so that we can send money to one another. We wear fewer clothes so that we can give clothing away. Just pray for us.' At the end of the evening 'Auntie' slipped away into the darkness of the streets and was gone. A totally unforgettable experience. Great to pass on to her (and the other leaders) copies of my book, *Restoration in the Church*, in the Chinese translation!

**Saturday 14 November.** Spent much of the day in prayer and fellowship.

**Sunday 15 November.** *Morning*: Visited a very crowded official 'Three Self' church – very formal and entirely without inspiration. Subsequently met with some of the leaders who gave us the official line, assuring us that there was no persecution of Christians in China!

*Afternoon*: Walked among the vast crowds, hoping for some personal contact. Met one man who wanted to practise his English. Had tea with him. Have never seen such crowds as on the streets of Shanghai. Couldn't take more than two steps without having to stop and negotiate the volume of people. Most people take Sunday off and visit the shops. Many were walking by the riverside. Saw many hundreds of family trios (husband, wife and one child). It's government policy that you have only one child (by law).

**Monday 16 November.** Spent time in prayer. Also chatted to a young man who took literature from us.

**Tuesday 17 November.** Flew to Hong Kong and were met at the airport by Jackie Pullinger (now Jackie To). Taken to Hang Fook Camp, where ex-drug addicts live together during the second stage of their rehabilitation.

**Wednesday 18 November.** *Morning*: Met with Jackie, her delightful husband and her staff and heard the history and vision of this extraordinary ministry. It was rooted in Jackie's pioneering commitment to see Hong Kong's drug addicts delivered from their terrible bondage. Many have been totally set free and given new life. What excellent fruit has followed her courageous obedience to Christ! Because she obeyed the Lord in faith, all this has happened!

*Afternoon*: Were driven around Hong Kong to several of the houses where people first go to be set free from their addiction. Heard wonderful testimonies from two young men formerly destroyed by drugs. They've been transformed by Christ and are now leaders in Jackie's work. Throughout the first ten days, each 'new boy' is prayed and cared for non-stop for 24 hours a day. They are never left alone. What a 'follow-up' system!

*Evening*: Enjoyed a barbecue with the men whose lives are being rebuilt and who are living on the camp. Met Fiona Morrison (member of Clarendon Church). She's been working with Jackie for two years. Thrilling to see her speaking fluent Chinese and working well with a team. Obviously incredibly fulfilled and happy in God, in spite of the very real challenges that each day brings.

**Thursday 19 November.** Took Underground to see Dennis Balcombe, who leads the Revival Christian Church in Hong Kong and who has an extensive ministry serving the church in China. Excellent fellowship. He spoke about recent visits to China, where persecution is rife. On one occasion he was speaking at a meeting when the police raided the church. He had to hide in a cart disguised as a corpse. He showed me a video of 'house church' meetings of up to 1,000 people. Full worship band. Very enthusiastic worship.

*Evening*: Attended one of Jackie's 'down town' meetings, where men and women are brought in from the streets, some under the influence of drugs. Very moving to see ex-addicts praying with and laying hands on those who needed to be set free. Great to see Jackie in action too. Amazing ministry. Unique approach to people. They obviously love her very much.

**Friday 20 November.** Flew to Bangkok to spend the weekend with Dr Kriengsak at his Hope of Bangkok Church.

**Saturday 21 November.** Kriengsak had booked some rooms in a hotel away from town. Spent time there with him, his wife, Rojana, their two sons, Paul and Peter, and two members of his staff. Excellent fellowship together. Thrilling to be unrushed and to share many things concerning God's purpose in the worldwide church today.

**Sunday 22 November.** Up at 5.30 a.m., ready for the journey back into central Bangkok. Spoke at the first three of the four main meetings in the Hope of Bangkok Church. Another pastor took the fourth and Kriengsak ministered to his international congregation.

Thousands of Christians poured in and out of the meetings and over 120 were counselled for conversion throughout the day (which is the normal Sunday experience). Everything done excellently in the services. Enthusiastic, heartfelt praise and worship. Many university students and young professionals are building their lives on gospel truth. Wonderful investment into the future. Incredibly moving experience to see the huge building filled over and over again.

Kriengsak's day did not finish until after 10.00 p.m. because, after all the multiple services of the day, he gathers all his house group leaders every Sunday night for training and instruction. Now there are over 160 church plantings from the centre – a growing number worldwide, as well as in Thailand.

**Monday 23 November.** Spent the day with Kriengsak, visiting some of the Bangkok tourist spots. Also saw the building where the first church meeting took place 13 years ago, when only about 15 were present. Flew from Bangkok Airport at 1.00 a.m. bound for Heathrow.

The teeming millions of South-East Asia certainly had their impact on me! The vitality of the church, its willingness to persevere in suffering and its zealous commitment to Jesus Christ stirred my heart.

I felt incredibly privileged at having some exposure to China's house churches – surely the most authentic New Testament churches in the world today. What stories they can tell! Also, Jackie's work demonstrates the power of the gospel and the compassion of Christ beyond anything I have ever seen. As for Kriengsak and the Hope of Bangkok, what can I say? It was magnificent seeing scores of people pouring forward for conversion at the end of each of the services – and to realise this is happening every week!

# 20

# Come Over and Help Us

'I think you should come and live in Columbia for two years.' Dan Barraco, one of the elders, was once again making the suggestion, but this time he was more specific and more pressing. I was again inclined simply to dismiss an idea that had been expressed to me by several people in Missouri. To my surprise, the very next morning in my reading I came to Acts 19, where it says that Paul remained in Ephesus for two years. The idea at last found an unexpected crack in my defences.

It would be true to say that in my repeated visits to Columbia over the two years, I knew I had been able to be of genuine assistance to the church in coming through the crisis. Some said that my involvement held the work together. On my arrival, I would often find that the difficulties of the situation had depressed the church and heads were down, but after my being there for a few days, having fellowship with the elders and speaking publicly and privately to the church and its members, hearts appeared to be lifted. Phil, the pastor, and his wife Debbie agreed that it would be wonderful if I could possibly go. He had never had the responsibility of leading a large church before and faced genuine challenges.

For the first time, I gave the idea a chance. I wondered if it would be possible to be away from the UK for two years. Certainly my home base in Brighton was very secure, with a great team of full-time elders, now headed up on my behalf by John Hosier. Although deeply committed to my home base and particularly giving the lead regarding our purchase of the new building and its transformation to a worship centre, I was increasingly away on Sundays, fulfilling my wider responsibilities. In May 1993 we moved our Sunday meetings from Clarendon Villas in Hove to the new centre in Brighton. The building work was not yet complete, but we used the first floor space while the top floor was being constructed.

We had clearly reached a significant stage in the building programme. NFI across the UK was increasingly being organised on a regional basis and David Holden, based in Sidcup, Kent, had emerged as a true 'Joshua', had my full confidence and was already carrying a growing amount of responsibility among the NFI churches.

We had been working with a flexible team of itinerant men for several years. When Bryn Jones had first suggested that I gather a team, I could see the pragmatic wisdom of sharing the load. I could also see the biblical example of Paul and the men who travelled with him. But I did notice that Paul started with Barnabas. Later, he was accompanied by Silas. Subsequently Timothy or Titus was with him. In Acts 20:4 his team included Sopater, Aristarchus, Secundus, Gaius, Timothy, Tychicus and Trophimus. Several other men are also mentioned from time to time as travelling either with Paul or to and from him. It was impressed on me that this was not a static 'team'. Indeed the phrase 'apostolic team' does not actually appear in Scripture. Given a grow-ing number of very gifted men in our ranks, I was concerned that being a member of the team might be seen as a measure of status and have negative connotations. I would rather have settled for the total flexibility of Paul's example in Scripture.

Our team has changed several times over the years, start-ing with Richard Haydon-Knowell, Alan Vincent, David Holden, Henry Tyler, Ray Lowe and Ben Davies, with Nigel Ring administrating. It gradually grew over the years, as gifted men took on more regional responsibility. So, if a man's gifting meant that I could ask him to oversee some churches, the outcome was that he also came onto the ever-increasing team. Gradually it became unworkable, as team meetings became not only the focal point for men travelling among the churches, but also inevitably became the admin-istrative hub of all our activity, where a growing number of decisions were being made. It became an increasingly large cabinet office and was far too unwieldy, so we eventually reduced its number back to a central hub for decision-making and administrative purposes, though the travelling men and regional overseers retained their responsibilities.

As time went by, we also began to recognise the obvious fact that different men had very diverse gifts. They were not simply regional overseers helping us care for the growing number of NFI churches; they had evident grace from God and gifts that differed. Some were increasingly skilful church builders, while others had more incisive and inspirational prophetic gifts. Some were obviously extremely gifted pas-tor/teachers, who could bring wisdom and security and evi-dent blessing to a local group of churches and their pastors, but lacked the spiritual clout that the emerging apostles and prophets were displaying. We also saw the real value of recognising and releasing evangelistic men to serve among the churches and also to be particularly involved in helping to get new churches started.

So, for instance, when I originally met Don Smith in Hastings he was gathering about a dozen people in a basement flat. I began to visit him on a monthly basis and helped him settle foundational matters, and for some years continued visiting and encouraging him and his growing church. He is a highly skilled church builder and gradually the church and his leadership team grew, repeatedly having to change locations until the church is now the largest in Hastings, meeting in a huge former indoor sports facility.

I asked Don how many of his members travelled to Eastbourne for their employment. He told me that about two dozen made the daily journey. 'Why don't you invite them to move to Eastbourne with you and start a new church?' To Don's own amazement, the idea immediately resonated deep inside him. He handed over the now strong King's Church to the capable leadership of one of his co-elders, John Groves, who has continued to see the work grow from strength to strength. Meanwhile, Don and his two dozen moved to Eastbourne (not without difficulty, Don having to accept offers on his home seven times from seven different people before a contract was actually signed and the sale was completed). He hired a schoolroom and got started. We immediately released Lex Loizides, a gifted evangelist, to be with him from the start and helped by providing the funds from our central resources to cover his costs.

Indeed, all the churches in NFI are invited to give a tenth of their income to a central fund precisely to help us do things together that we would not be able to do alone, as John Groves' prophecy had said to us those years before.

Many of our new church plants have been started with assisted funding over a two-year period. The amount donated in the first year is halved in the second so that faith for the local growth in numbers and resources is not undermined. We never intend simply to prop up works financially in an extended way. We reckon that if a church is alive and God is blessing it, it will grow and especially with the aid of an evangelist like Lex.

This indeed proved to be the case in Eastbourne, where Lex's evangelistic presence not only resulted in additions to the church, but also helped give the church an evangelistic ethos among its membership from the beginning. The church has grown and prospered and now meets in a beautifully renovated and massive warehouse, gathering hundreds of members. After a couple of years Don came to me and said that he believed Lex's evangelistic work had been accomplished and that, if I wanted to move him on elsewhere, I should feel free to initiate a fresh move for him. After prayer and consultation, Lex moved to Newcastle, where once again he did a magnificent job. Other evangelists have been similarly involved in planting new works and more recently in serving whole new developing areas, but more of that later.

Men were becoming more open to the possibility of moving house to plant new churches. We had developed a fairly strong support base and also found that the offerings at Stoneleigh could help release more finance to undergird our growing mission within the UK and overseas.

David Holden now had a strong home church in Sidcup based on the original small house fellowship that I first encountered but now meeting in a large church building. He had also planted out congregations into Bexleyheath and Orpington. His influence particularly over the London and north Kent churches had been established and he was clearly seen as my right-hand man in the work, taking on increasing responsibility not only among the churches but also on the platforms, initially of youth events and subsequently at the Downs Bible Week and other high profile settings.

Several years earlier, when I had the privilege of meeting Dick Iverson at the Bible Temple, Portland, Oregon in the USA and spending time with this very experienced and godly man, he confided in me that he was eagerly seeking God that he might soon 'get his Joshua in place'. Since he was about ten years older than I, I felt highly privileged and blessed that in David I clearly already had my Joshua and, thank God, behind him a growing army of incredibly gifted men and women. Over many years, we had gradually gathered a great team of church leaders. Some had purely local responsibility while others were both local and itinerant. All those who travelled among the churches were also rooted in their own local church. Although the network was not very large and by no means perfect, it was essentially secure, healthy and growing.

I shared with the elders in Brighton the request that Dan Barraco had put to me, that I should consider relocating in Columbia, Missouri for two years. To my amazement Alan Preston, one of the more prophetic elders in our team, said that he felt God had recently told him that I would go to Columbia for two years. His was the first confirmation to follow my own reading in Acts 19. Others followed and what could never have been predicted six months earlier began to settle in our minds and hearts and take shape in our plans. We would leave after Stoneleigh '93 and return in time for Stoneleigh '95, though of course just as I had visited Columbia seven times over the last two years, I would similarly aim to visit the UK frequently and others would come to visit me from time to time. We arranged for six young men from the Brighton church, recently renamed Church of Christ the King, to live in our home during our time away and details began to fall into place.

As a family, this represented our greatest ever upheaval. Our five children had essentially stayed at home until this time and ranged in ages: Ben 22, Anna 20, Joel 18, Simon 14 and Tim 11. Now we would be scattered. Ben planned to spend the first year working with Jackie Pullinger in Hong Kong. He had spent a few months with John Wimber in Anaheim at John's invitation and had also travelled within the US with a band called Violet Burning, who toured the country from their Anaheim base. He had returned full of faith and now wanted to give a year to get among the drug addicts that Jackie was helping so magnificently. Joel decided that he wanted to spend a year in Africa, nine months with Simon Pettit in Cape Town and three months with Michael Eaton and the vibrant Chrisco Church in Nairobi, Kenya. Anna, Simon and Timothy would accompany us, though Anna would spend roughly half of our two years working as secretary to Carl Herrington at his Lees Summit church near Kansas City.

The day before we left, I found Simon, my 14-year-old, crying and saying that life would never be the same. We had been blessed with a wonderfully happy family life and he knew how deeply he was going to miss it. I assured him that it would be OK and that we would all return in two years and be back together again. He, of course, proved to be more insightful than I: Ben married Rachel within two weeks of our return and moved to London; shortly after that, Joel moved to Newcastle for four years of university and teacher training, then married Kate and never lived at home again; while in the USA, Anna would meet Stephen van Rhyn, a South African from Simon Pettit's church in Cape Town, doing a Frontier Year in Columbia. Life was certainly never going to be the same again.

Just before I left the UK I was sent an extraordinary written prophecy. Robyn Lowe, a woman from the church in Canterbury, had seen a vision of me with a machete in hand, striding up a hill and cutting through undergrowth. My temptation would be to look back to ensure that all was OK behind me, but God urged me not to do that but to be fully assured that, as I moved forward in obedience, behind me and fanning out in ever-widening ranks would be workers and rows of people. In her vision, Robyn saw the first ranks behind me were clearing tree trunks, roots and foliage from the path where I had trod. Behind those were others, who were ploughing the ground and, behind those, yet others were sowing seed. Beyond them, still more were tending orchards and crops and further still were those who were gathering a harvest. She said that in the picture she saw me watching all this activity with interest and wanting to offer advice to those working behind me, but that God spoke to me again and said, 'Turn, go forward and clear the way.' The word continued and said, 'I know that you have a heart for those people. You will not be forsaking them by going forward – rather you will be helping, as it is important that you clear more ground so that in turn, all can move forward.' Evidently, as I moved on in obedience, God would cause those behind me to move up the hill and grow in increasing responsibility, experience and maturity. We were heading for a significant time of growth in our ranks at home, and under David Holden's excellent leadership this certainly proved to be the case.

As I stood on the Stoneleigh platform with Wendy for our final evening, thousands were praying. Hands were being laid upon us and there was a great spirit of adventure and excitement added to the now customary last night mixture of celebration and jamboree. A lady slipped through the crowds and told me that while we were praying she had seen a vision of a cushion that was being repeatedly punched, but because it absorbed the punches and didn't retaliate it would ultimately be hugged and embraced. She felt that it had to do with my going to the USA. Having delivered her word, she disappeared into the huge crowds. I wondered what that meant.

Many tears were shed as we said our goodbyes to Joel and Ben at Heathrow and Gatwick. Now it was our time to go so we handed our house over to the young men of the church and flew to Columbia, Missouri, for what would prove to be two phenomenal years.

# 21
# There's a River!

We landed at St Louis airport just as the extraordinary Mid-West floods of 1993 were coming to an end. At first we had some vacation time at the Lake of the Ozarks and then arrived at Columbia. I had prayed that the house we were to live in would be one that Wendy could really appreciate and would help her with the huge transition that she would be making in living in the States. She had prayed fervently for a sense of guidance about the move but had not heard anything from God. One day, when Nigel called at our home, he had asked in his loving and gentle way how she was feeling about the move and was surprised to encounter a flood of tears. She had no guidance at all! She longed for some kind of personal confirmation that such a far-reaching step was indeed right. She was actually quite unsettled. Why hadn't God spoken? Nigel asked her what she felt originally called to, and after some time of reflection she replied, 'I was called to marry Terry and be with him.' 'Sounds like you have your guidance, then,' he replied. Wendy later testified publicly that she immediately knew complete peace and never looked back after hearing Nigel's word.

Nevertheless, I wanted the home in Columbia to be a blessing and prayed that she would love it. I had seen the selected house empty on a recent visit and liked it very much but I was absolutely delighted when, after our holiday break at the Lake of the Ozarks, we arrived to find it magnificently furnished. Everything in the house had been given or loaned by members of the church. It was absolutely fantastic and the furniture and furnishings even matched, as though one person with a clear design and intention had purchased it all. Wendy was delighted with it and again shed tears, but this time in a sense of wonder and gratitude that such love and sensitivity had been demonstrated by the church. What an extraordinary loving community they were, and many of them literally lived all around us in the local sub-division. Even the names of the streets reflected the Christian commitment of the local believers who had earlier erected the church building and church school and developed the whole area. We, for instance, lived in a street called Bright Star, which was joined by Mount Carmel. Nearby were Dayspring, Cornerstone and, the street leading to the church facility, Christian Fellowship Road.

We were received with incredible love and excitement and couldn't wait to get down to work and hopefully be a blessing to them and to the other churches in the area. We had our first elders' meeting and I was surprised by the atmosphere being rather less than enthusiastic. I had always been received so warmly by the elders when I visited before, so I was totally unaccustomed to this different mood. I wondered what had happened and they quickly told me that they had been quite hurt by a prayer letter that I had distributed just before leaving the UK. It had referred to the church's strengths but had also listed what I regarded as its weaknesses, which I saw as my responsibility to address.

The Columbia elders were not impressed with my style of making these things public. They regarded it as insensitive to their feelings and disagreed with some of my appraisal anyway.

We talked it out, I apologised and we put it behind us. I then came to the subsequent elders' meetings with enthusiasm, raising suggestions for future developments and again met with what seemed a defensive stance. Gradually, I realised how deeply the eldership had been wounded by all that had happened in the church in the recent past. They were in no mood to respond to my desire to make instant adjustments and plans. I had to learn to back off and move at a slower pace. Formerly, decisions had been imposed upon them in an arbitrary way and they had felt very abused by that form of leadership. I had to learn to apply the brakes.

After a while, Clay, one of the elders, came to my office and thanked me for my willingness to adjust. He expressed real appreciation that I had been responsive to their need to move slowly. I must confess that I found the pace difficult. In Brighton over the years, with many NFI responsibilities as well as the local church, I had been accustomed to a fast and demanding pace of life, but I tried to learn my lesson and not impose my will in an inappropriate way. The previous leadership style they had experienced had clearly damaged trust, understandably leading to insecurity and caution.

Nevertheless, we began to pray together and on Thursday mornings we invited the other pastors from around Missouri to gather with us for prayer. I also made it clear that I would be very happy to develop clear relationships with any of these pastors and their churches, but that I was not very interested in having a fraternal simply to chat about things. Some were keen to press in immediately but some drew back to watch how things would develop. Happily, most of the original group of pastors that had for years enjoyed good fellowship eventually came to appreciate what I was trying to do and asked me to help them apostolically.

I began to travel among the small group of churches and when in Columbia on Sundays I began a series on Nehemiah. Several of the church members had testified to me that they felt they had been 'burned' in the past. I was happy to preach that Nehemiah had faith to rebuild a city even with burnt stones (Nehemiah 4:2).

The previous leadership model had not been based on an expositional approach to teaching Scripture, but rather on the previous pastor's extraordinary inspirational leadership gift. This would not be uncommon in the USA. I know that early on in my relationship with C. J. Mahaney, he said to me, 'You preach the Bible.' I replied by asking him, 'What else is there to preach?' He clarified his point by adding that he always preached truth from the Bible but not working as it were from a text and expounding it. He had not been exposed to that kind of preaching. It is hard to believe that about C. J. Mahaney now, as he has for some years become one of the most articulate and powerful Bible expositors I know, painstakingly working his way through the text with great insight and effectiveness. Similarly, Phil, the new pastor at Columbia, has become a Bible teacher of real skill and is now an avid Dr Martyn Lloyd-Jones fan, devouring every book of his that he can lay his hands on. So the previous preaching and leadership style has been replaced by something much healthier and more enduring.

The church was already a very loving community. Their worship, though different in style to most in the UK, was wonderful. As a church, they knew how to give themselves to God in unrushed, heart-felt praise and adoration. Nevertheless, behind the scenes there were a lot of hurting people. I think that the depth of commitment being expected from the people and expressed by the people made them feel even more hurt and betrayed by the previous pastor's failure. Because he had led them into such a high level of commitment to community, many felt personally wounded and disillusioned when things went wrong. I have never counselled so many individual men of mature years in one church who have shed tears while talking out their pain and disappointment.

Nevertheless, heads were gradually coming up, and church and elders' prayer meetings began to experience God's presence in a powerful way. A visit early in the New Year from Steve Brading from England brought a breath of fresh air, particularly at a men's meeting, when Steve prayed over a number of the men present and the Holy Spirit began to move powerfully. Hope was clearly rising and we sensed the promise that better days were just around the corner. We could never have predicted just how good those days were going to be.

Missouri has four very distinct seasons (though some who live there say that you can experience all four of them in one day!). The summer can be extremely hot, with people rushing from air-conditioned homes and air-conditioned cars to air-conditioned shops, malls and offices. I don't know how the pioneer settlers survived the colossal heat! The autumn is magnificent: the climate is delightful and the trees are unspeakably beautiful, their colours in late October almost defying description. The winter is intensely cold, often falling way below freezing. I encountered my coldest ever weather conditions. On my brief walk of less than half a mile from home to church, not only would my face freeze, but my head would ache with the cold! When the temperature rose again to one or two degrees below freezing it felt positively mild! Nor have I ever encountered such deep snow (or such quick and efficient removal of it from the roads!). But the spring in Missouri is truly memorable. Whereas England's green and pleasant land displays a deeper green in winter, Missouri turns to a dusty brown as the grass fades. The spring is heralded by the arrival of green shoots that gradually transform the colour of the fields and hills. Somehow, as spring broke through in 1994, my hopes were rising that God was going to come in a refreshing way, but I could never have predicted how that was going to happen.

I was due to visit the churches in South Africa and had a full and excellent programme in Durban and Cape Town. At that time we were approaching a frightening climax in connection with the political situation in South Africa. Nelson Mandella had been released from prison, emerging with extraordinary statesmanship, but it seemed that Chief Buthelesi's people were not going to play ball with Mandella's ANC. Around the world, many were interceding and when I left Durban to fly home to Missouri the situation looked critical. Many were forecasting a blood bath.

When I arrived at St Louis and walked down the concourse of the airport, I noticed that all the television screens in the bars and cafés were showing smiling and happy black South African faces. The historic turnaround had taken place while I was travelling the long journey home and the famously peaceful elections took place. God had shown wonderful mercy to South Africa so that they could have the opportunity to build a multi-cultural society in the future.

Wendy met the incoming flight and unexpectedly suggested we attend a meeting taking place at St Louis. She told me that a South African evangelist had been taking meetings for a month and dozens from the church had been attending. Some amazing things were happening!

It was midday and I suggested that any morning meeting would be finished by now. She assured me that it would not and sure enough, as we arrived at the crowded church, we were just in time to see Rodney Howard-Browne invite all the pastors to come to the front. There were about 2,000 people present, and some hundreds went forward. Two large video screens clearly showed some of my friends and co-elders from Columbia were responding! When prayed for, they fell to the ground, as did hundreds of others. I had seen this sort of thing before on a smaller scale, and so was not particularly impressed. Then I noticed something else taking place. Several people scattered round the building were laughing loudly and in a manner that seemed unusual for a church service. I thought it was rather strange. At this point, several friends noticed I had arrived and warmly welcomed me back from South Africa. Happy to see me, they were obviously in a bright and enthusiastic frame of mind. Eventually, we left and completed the journey home.

On the following Sunday, after an excellent sermon on 'Suddenly from heaven' from David Holden, who, together with his wife, Liz, was visiting at this highly significant time, a number of people were invited to give testimony to what had been happening in their lives. To my surprise, a man came forward immediately who had not been in a happy mood for some months. He had repeatedly indicated that he would probably leave the church and had seemed 'under a cloud' for ages. Mounting the platform, he amazed me by saying that on the previous Sunday morning he had been present and that at the conclusion of the service Phil Schaefer, the pastor, had invited the Holy Spirit to come. He then described how he had fallen to the ground and how God had come to him powerfully. He concluded with warmth and enthusiasm, saying that he was sorry for his previous attitude and that he would be different from now on and be enthusiastically committed to the church.

Next, a greatly respected church member and a teacher of Latin at the local public school, told how she had similarly been overwhelmed by the Spirit on the previous Sunday and how she had fallen to the floor laughing, but had received a powerful longing to see her students converted and a fresh commission to give herself to witness and intercession. She was radiant. Later, she told me of the first converts beginning to come.

Thirdly, a very faithful church member, committed with her husband to the youth work of the church, told how on the previous Sunday she had fallen under the power of the Holy Spirit at the conclusion of the 8.30 morning service and had ultimately surfaced halfway through the second (10.30 a.m.) service wondering where she was. She then related in magnificent terms not only how she had met with God in an awesome and almost fearful way, which had rendered her unable to move physically for some time, but also how her relationship with her husband had been so enriched since the experience.

I was staggered at the outstanding quality of the testimonies and became aware that something new and wonderful was beginning to take place among us. The events of the following weeks continued to amaze me. A fresh and exciting dimension had entered our church life.

Two weeks later, a special weekend with a guest speaker was planned. On the Friday evening, he spoke to a packed church and, on the Saturday morning, to an enthusiastic leaders' seminar. None of the recent phenomena had taken place, for which I was somewhat grateful, since I did not know how my visiting friend would feel about such things. On the Saturday evening, a packed church waited eagerly for more of his inspiring ministry. We had enjoyed an exhilarating time of worship; now it was time for him to speak. He took the podium, opened his Bible, read a passage from Chronicles and began speaking to a hushed congregation. 'The story of Solomon is the most tragic in the whole Bible.' To everybody's amazement, this sober introduction was greeted by uncontrolled guffaws of laughter from about 30 people. For five or ten minutes, various attempts were made to continue, but the overwhelmed and overjoyed simply couldn't contain themselves. Finally, those who were being so affected were invited to come from their seats, scattered around the congregation, to stand together at the front, where they might be prayed for.

Directly the relevant individuals arrived at the front of the church, they all, without anyone praying for them, fell to the floor, overwhelmed in paroxysms of joy and hilarious laughter. None of us had seen anything like it. The whole experience was totally unrehearsed and unsought. Several were trying to stop laughing, but could not. Others tried to stand up and were similarly unsuccessful. All hope of preaching was abandoned and gradually people began to lay hands on one another to pass on the extraordinary blessing that had so sovereignly invaded the evening. Many were still present at midnight. Several had to be carried home, quite incapable of walking unaided and apparently totally 'drunk'. This all took place in April and May of 1994. In over 30 years of Christian ministry, I had never seen anything like it.

The following week, I flew to England for a previously arranged series of meetings. On my arrival, I heard that

Alan Preston, one of the elders of my home church in Brighton, had recently returned from the Airport Vineyard in Toronto, where extraordinary things were also happening. He had had a dramatic experience and had begun to pass on the blessing in the church.

My first meeting was a day with the elders. God broke in powerfully as we laid hands on one another. Several fell to the floor and prophecies of far-reaching significance began to flow. Next, I had two days with a group of 15 men who held senior responsibility in NFI. Leaders from India and Africa were present, in addition to the British leaders. David Holden and I began to relate what God had been doing with us in recent weeks. Almost immediately we were once again in the midst of an extraordinary outpouring of Holy Spirit joy, delight and, in some cases, a kind of drunkenness. Magnificent prophetic utterances began to flow. Our two days together brought deeper intensity, joy and anticipation.

The following Sunday in Brighton saw further outpourings and amazing scenes of joy and excitement. Meanwhile, news was spreading fast among the churches that something was happening.

The following week, about 250 men arrived at Stoneleigh for our regular days of prayer and fasting – some totally ignorant that anything new was happening, others longing to hear the news first-hand and have opportunity to be prayed for. We had a time of praise and then once again David and I told our stories. While I was still speaking, one man fell from his chair and lay on the floor, then another. Others began to show evidence of being similarly affected. We invited all to stand while we began to pray. Soon, these 250 full-time ministers were in total disarray. Many had fallen to the ground. Others were laughing uncontrollably. Some were singing in a style normally associated with a drunken state. Normally on these occasions we pray for two hours, pause for one, and then pray for two, and so on throughout the two days. This time you could say that the programme became flexible! Again, extraordinary prophecies began to be given, promising 'a monsoon of blessing' at the coming Stoneleigh Bible Week, due to take place ten weeks later at the same location, where there would be not 250 but 14,000 people.

Duncan Watkinson, who leads our works in India, described what true monsoon conditions were like and how the torrential rains would unavoidably dominate life throughout the monsoon season. We were filled with expectation. Another described a vision that he could see of someone who had recently laid concrete foundations, seeing the rains come and beginning to panic. He was rushing to cover them with tarpaulin for protection lest they be washed away, but the word came strong and clear that there was no need of protection, since we had been laying good foundations of doctrine and practice for years. They were strong and secure and would stand well in the monsoon season that would certainly come upon us at the Bible week and beyond. Joy knew no bounds!

I asked the keyboard player 'Do you know "Singing in the rain"?' Praise God, he did! The familiar introductory chords broke out and 250 men began to dance and sing. Gene Kelly certainly never knew such joy and abandonment! Was this really 250 Englishmen?

After two days we returned to our homes and churches scattered around the nation and, indeed, the nations. Duncan Watkinson stopped off at Dubai in the Gulf on his way back to India. He gathered the churches there with which we work, told the story, and once again the Holy Spirit came in devastating power. A planned three-day stop had to be extended to two weeks. Then on to Bombay and Goa, where the same experiences followed. The pastor of the church in Bangalore was visiting Goa and in turn 'took the blessing' back with him to his amazed and rejoicing congregation. Simon Pettit returned to South Africa and, once again, the same glorious demonstration of the power and presence of the Holy Spirit followed in church after church.

Soon, we began to hear that similar things were happening all around the UK. Many churches from various denominations and groups were enjoying identical phenomena. After two weeks, I returned to the United States where we had planned a leaders' conference. About 500 leaders attended from churches we serve there and once again God broke through in glorious ways. Prayer meetings and services repeatedly experienced these extraordinary phenomena and lives were being radically changed. The whole atmosphere of the church was transformed. Morale, which had been low, was at an all-time high. New prayer meetings were started, services were extended for prolonged times and God turned our mourning into dancing. The church in Columbia was totally transformed, as were the others I worked with in Missouri. Pastors' conferences were arranged and many pastors began to press in from several different states to enjoy the blessing.

We started our NFI/USA Family Camp on the campus of Warrensburg University, not far from Kansas City, where we enjoyed a wonderful outpouring of God's blessing and set the pattern for an annual conference that gathers the NFI/USA churches for fellowship and ministry every Memorial Weekend.

Stoneleigh '94 came around with 14,000 in attendance from 30 nations. We were not disappointed. The power of God came flooding in. We gave full explanation as to why we were open to the new extraordinary breakthrough of God's presence and I preached on Acts 10, pointing out the many strange phenomena associated with that story of Peter's visit to Cornelius's home, which included a dream, a vision, a trance, angelic visitations and an outpouring of the Holy Spirit, which interrupted Peter's sermon long before he had finished it. Indeed, according to his own report to the other apostles given in Acts 11, he had only just begun to speak when the Spirit fell in such a way that it was impossible for him to continue preaching. We felt we undoubtedly had scriptural warrant for being open to a God who could interrupt our programme supernaturally if he so desired. He seemed to be doing it quite often in those days.

Literally thousands of stories can be told of lives touched and transformed, people saved, bodies healed, and people falling in love with God in a way that they had never known before.

# 22

# Back to the UK

The so-called 'Toronto blessing' swept the UK and touched down in many other places around the world. It was said that more visitors attended Toronto from the UK than from any other nation and undoubtedly the effects were very marked in many churches.

As with the initial outbreak of 'tongues-speaking' in the 1960s, there was a strong backlash from many quarters. Many regarded the manifestations associated with the outpouring as bizarre and dishonouring to God. Even the secular press covered the phenomenon, since it was so widespread and included the kind of sensational aspects that attract the media.

Undoubtedly, there was often excessive preoccupation with the phenomena associated with the blessing, but I am grateful to God that my first exposure to it was with people I knew at Columbia, whose lives were so radically changed. The fruit was excellent in their lives and though we made a lot of space for the Holy Spirit to come among us, I never saw the kind of so-called 'animal noises' and other related distractions that were grabbing the headlines elsewhere. In fact, all the elders in Columbia were affected in a profound way and led the church excellently. Phil, in particular, pastored the people with skill and sensitivity. He constantly applied illustrations from Scripture and from church history to the situation and repeatedly urged the people to receive all that they could from God. He was clearly full of faith and wisdom and the church made transition in a context of great security. The Columbia pastors' conferences were very well attended and scores of pastors and their wives travelled in from various states and had powerful encounters with God.

I am so grateful that during those extremely heady days of the outpouring of the Holy Spirit, my friend C. J. Mahaney introduced me to the writings of John Piper and Gordon Fee. I devoured John Piper's *Desiring God* and was even more stirred by his *The Pleasures of God*. Then I worked from cover to cover through Gordon Fee's weighty and magnificent *God's Empowering Presence*. John Piper's emphasis on the fact that God is most glorified in us when we are most satisfied with him was a superb eye-opener. His appeal for us to find all our joys in Christ and his love for us provided intoxicating reading. I have read and repeatedly re-read his excellent writings; they proved an ideal accompaniment to the exhilarating experience of the Holy Spirit that we were so enjoying.

Gordon Fee's *God's Empowering Presence* is a masterly treatment of every one of Paul's references to the person and work of the Holy Spirit in all his epistles. His teaching creates a fresh longing for more of God's presence in his church through the coming of the Holy Spirit. He emphasises that the command to 'be filled with the Spirit' is the ultimate imperative, but goes on to show that the command is actually directed not so much to the individual Christian but to the gathered church. We are to be a Spirit-filled community, drenched in God's presence and overflowing with his gifts. We are a people of the presence of God, tasting in advance the power of the age to come and fully enjoying the 'Abba, Father' cry of true sons. I cannot thank God enough for the magnificent insights that I have gained from the writings of these two men. In addition, we have wholeheartedly recommended them among our people, so that their experience can genuinely be a mixture of enjoying the Spirit and understanding the word of God. Our passion is to be a people of both word and Spirit, both knowledge and experience, both doctrine and power!

I was personally invited to speak at Randy Clarke's Vineyard Church in St Louis, where I enjoyed excellent fellowship with Randy, and also spoke at the Airport Vineyard in Toronto, where I had the joy of meeting John and Carol Arnott. I subsequently invited them to Brighton (and later Bombay, where they were a great blessing to a crowd of about 4,000 people at the Joy in the City conference).

The Toronto blessing has been well documented elsewhere and does not need to occupy us any further here, except simply to testify that when John and Carol attended a small NFI leaders' event in Brighton they prayed for all of those present with great love and power and with extraordinary results. When they had prayed for everybody else they finally came to me. As I lay on the floor John was at my head and Carol at my feet as they continued to pray. The sensation of raw power was such as I have never known before or since. It gradually grew in intensity, like waves of an electric current, until it reached a point where I was literally scared. I was not sure how much more I could stand before I would have to ask them to stop praying. I was in a serious dilemma. Did I really want God to stop blessing me?

Surely not. But how could I take this extraordinary shock of power through my whole head and body any longer? I was scared for them to go on but I was scared to tell them to stop! Eventually it seemed to pass its frightening peak and I lay alone on the floor trembling for ages after everybody had left, eventually returning to my study in a fuzzy kind of daze. There was no accompanying word from God, or any sense of fresh commissioning, but it remains an experience of power that is extremely difficult to describe.

Shortly after that brief visit to the UK, I returned for our final months in the USA. I made a couple of visits to Mexico, where things continued to progress well and the Holy Spirit was poured out very freely on the churches we served there. I also visited South Africa once more and, at a very memorable leaders' conference, we specifically commissioned Simon Pettit as the apostolic leader of all our NFI work in South Africa. This was greeted with great enthusiasm and established a clear base for our future work in the country. The presence of God in some of the meetings was breathtaking. In fact, I would say that I personally witnessed some of the greatest outpourings of joy and power on that occasion, particularly in KwaZulu Natal, where a number of churches were looking for a relationship with us.

Just before our final return to the UK, Mike Bickle invited me to speak at a conference at Metro Vineyard in Kansas City, where Paul Cain was another of the speakers. From the platform Paul gave some of the most dramatic personal prophecies that I have ever heard. For over half an hour he called out people's names and shocked them with extraordinary lists of personal details. Some people gasped out loud, others squealed with delight. Occasionally, ripples of applause would run through sections of the congregation (which numbered about 2,000 people) as they particularly recognised and identified with the phenomenal accuracy of the supernatural knowledge he was making known through his prophecies to their particular friends or associates. After each word, he would ask if his prophecies were meaningful and could be identified with. Each time, he received a positive response. Many were plainly shaken by the supernatural element of the experience. Several were in tears as they received such loving words of encouragement from God. Paul's manner was always beautifully sensitive, tender and encouraging. He exhorted people to receive God's love and the promises that were being brought through his prophetic gift.

Suddenly Wendy and I heard our names being spoken. We were asked to stand. Paul, who knew me and had met my eldest son, Ben, knew nothing more of the rest of my family. Nevertheless, he proceeded to name all five of my children accurately. He told my daughter Anna that she had a South African in her heart. He gave words to Joel, associated with his time spent in Africa. He even gave a word concerning my third son, Simon, who was 16 years old and had drifted far from God. Paul's tone of voice changed (we often listen to the tape of the whole prophecy) and he quoted Jesus' famous words to Peter, 'Simon, Simon, Satan has desired to have you that he might sift you as wheat.' He spoke with great gentleness words of extraordinary encouragement that carried the promise of Simon's recovery. He went on to assure us that all of our five children were in God's 'safety box' and that all my sons would make their father's heart glad. As you can imagine, it was a profoundly moving time. The mixture of tender love and supernatural knowledge made a heady cocktail.

To Wendy and me he spoke words of great encouragement. First, he affirmed Wendy as being of equal anointing with her husband. He then continued that God was sending us back to the UK with his grace upon us. His next words were, 'You have finished what he called you here to do in the USA.' He then went on once again to describe the laser beams and 'golden arches' that would go out from the UK (to my great delight repeating the motif of his prophecy in Hove five years earlier!). He said that they would be ever increasing and non-stop as they circled the earth. He then told me that I was returning to the UK with a commission that involved 'apostolic evangelism'. It was a memorable night. Anna, whose romantic attachment to her South African friend was in its very early stages, has since become very happily married to Stephen van Rhyn and lives in Cape Town. Simon, our wayward 16-year-old, later came back to God after five years of backsliding and 'hit the ground running'. He cannot get over God's grace towards him and, along with the others, he certainly 'makes his father's heart glad'!

For Wendy and me, it was so encouraging to hear that God's word included, 'You have finished what he called you to do in the USA.' I had often felt my own great weakness and ineffectiveness in serving God there. I wasn't quite sure what I had expected to happen in measurable terms through the two-year visit. It had been such an unexpected development, but we were quite sure that God had sent us and we counted it a great privilege not only to serve the churches there but also to be present when the great outpouring of the Holy Spirit came. One of the prophets associated with Mike Bickle's Kansas City church had said some years earlier that when the Mississippi flowed backwards there would be a major fresh outpouring of the Holy Spirit. A few days before we had arrived in the USA in 1993 the flood in the Mid-West resulted in precisely that effect and the city of St

Louis itself was in considerable danger of serious flooding.

I am so glad that we had the joy of being there when it happened and could be part of a group of churches that so wholeheartedly responded to God's coming. At one meeting, Bill Penkethman, one of the gifted prophetic men in the Columbia church, saw a vision of an empty suitcase and brought a prophecy that God had not come for a fleeting visit but had, as it were, completely unpacked his case as a demonstration of his commitment to stay. This was such a meaningful vision to me since I often travel, visiting towns and churches briefly and, since I am not staying, don't completely unpack. God was certainly not paying them a fleeting visit!

Now, however, it was time for Wendy and me to pack up and go home, but the Holy Spirit would be staying with full commitment to the people there. We had a great farewell party and were presented with a treasured photo album of the church family in Columbia, page after page of dear friends whose fellowship we had come to love over those two years and whose faces we still enjoy as we turn the pages. The church had not fallen apart after its crisis, as some had feared or forecast, but was in a healthy state and continuing to grow. Now, through ministry such as Alpha and special door-to-door outreaches to some of the poorer sections of town, people dramatically transformed by the coming of the Holy Spirit are reaching more people than ever before, including evangelistic outreach to international students at the very large local Missouri University campus.

We also needed to make sure there was a team in place to provide ongoing care for the churches in the USA that had come into the NFI family. John Lanferman, who was pastoring one of the NFI churches at the Lake of the Ozarks, responded to my invitation to him and his wife Linda to move to St Louis. It was a challenging and costly move but he was clearly the brother gifted to serve the group of churches in the USA on my behalf and St Louis seemed to be the ideal centre from which he could work. Now John has pioneered and leads the Jubilee Community Church in St Louis and has developed an excellent team and travels among the churches from that base. New churches have been added under his oversight. They have developed a successful Frontier Year Project programme and run annual camps for young people from the NFI churches in addition to the popular Warrensburg Family Camp. At the latter, they have raised wonderful offerings to help with overseas work in Mexico, Africa and Haiti. Annual men's and women's conferences gather hundreds from all of the NFI churches and provide further encouragement, inspiration and sense of unity of mission. Their commitment to our mission together has also been expressed in very practical ways. Teams of men have travelled not only to Guadalajara and Los Mochis in Mexico, where work has been done on church buildings, but also to Haiti, where work on a pastor's home has been deeply appreciated among the poor Christians there. So although Wendy and I and the family have uprooted from the States, the work continues in good hands and John has become a very valued member of our international team.

We arrived back in England a few weeks before Stoneleigh '95 where, for the first time, we had to overflow into two weeks to cope with the growing numbers. The previous year's worship tape, *Ruach,* had somehow captured the extraordinary atmosphere of the occasion and songs introduced there, written by David Fellingham, Stuart Townend, Paul Oakley and Lex Loizides, were being sung everywhere. Stoneleigh Bible Week was growing into a major international conference. Around 20,000 people from 40 nations attended. In the light of many people having fresh encounters with God, I took Joshua as the main theme for my evening sessions. After years of training under Moses' shadow, he had his own life-changing encounter with the captain of the host of the Lord and was commanded to take the land. In the leaders' session I felt God's authority as I spoke on 'Moses is dead; arise, therefore!'. Many testified afterwards to a fresh sense of commissioning from God.

Once again, God came in power. Every age group was affected, including children who had powerful experiences with God and many teenagers who knew that God was setting them apart to serve him among the nations. On some evenings in the teenagers' meetings, the programme was abandoned as young people gave themselves to deep intercession for God to send revival, and many offered themselves with tears to God, aware that he was calling them and thrilled at the privilege. Many leaders who were present said it was the most awesome experience of their Christian lives.

We had thoroughly enjoyed our time in the USA but it was good not simply to return home but also to know that we were being freshly sent to the UK by God. Prophecies – not only from Paul Cain, but also from John Arnott, Marc Dupont and Stacey Campbell, given over us at a large conference in St Louis hosted by Randy Clarke – sent us on our way with a great sense of renewed commissioning for exciting and fulfilling days ahead.

Some years earlier, I had received an unexpected visit from Teddy Saunders, a godly evangelical Anglican, a true 'older statesman' and former close associate of David Watson. I had never met him before, so I was shocked by his coming to tell me that in the last few months he had heard me speak at John Wimber's conference in Brighton and at

Spring Harvest. He felt that God had sent him to urge me to make sure that I fulfilled my destiny in God. He then went on to describe something of what he felt that to be.

Upon our return to England, three different people in three separate places brought strong reminders to me of that word. God was certainly catching my attention that we had not merely come back home. We had a calling to fulfil and a fresh sense of commissioning to the task. Much more was yet to be accomplished in God's wonderful purposes.

# 23
# Cells for Life

On our return to the UK, we discovered that cell church had become the preoccupation of many. My fellow elders suddenly seemed to be speaking a language unfamiliar to me. '*Oikos* Groups', 'Equipping Tracks', 'Arrival Stations' and 'Shepherds' Guides' were being discussed. In many ways, the recently popularised cell church principles were consistent with our values. They underlined the vital place of discipling, accountability, community, commitment to small groups, evangelistic motivation and yet also incorporated the meeting of the whole church in weekly celebration.

It would be true to say that we were beginning to meet some problems regarding our longstanding house group structures. Generally speaking, they had been rather inward looking, mostly focused on mutual care and providing a place for intimacy and fellowship. When they first started, they were revolutionary and extremely helpful. They released many people into a context of responsibility and gave opportunity for genuine spiritual growth.

In my early Baptist church experience, only the official full-time pastor had genuine pastoral responsibility for the flock. All came to him for counsel. The church deacons were not seen as having personal spiritual care for people in the church. They tended to form a committee that organised the general running and administration of the church. There was little discipling taking place and many church members were comparative strangers to one another. Opportunities were rare for forming close friendships within the church membership. When I broke out of my backsliding and started attending church prayer meetings, Bible studies and working with the youth, one of my biggest shocks was that I very rapidly became part of quite a small nucleus carrying that large church.

House groups not only created a great context for fellowship and care but also provided a setting in which leadership gifts could be developed and recognised and potential church elders could 'cut their teeth'. They also gave opportunity for a large group of people within the church to develop, with genuine responsibility for its spiritual life and progress. Nevertheless, our structures were beginning to creak.

Successful house group leaders tended to develop quite large house groups that were greatly appreciated by those who attended. As time passed, however, we had not developed a strong expectation of multiplication leading one large successful group to become two, with the process starting again. Sometimes the level of growth in a group demanded such multiplication, but it was not in the ethos of our churches to expect one group frequently to become two and then repeat the process. Indeed, elders could encounter quite entrenched resistance to breaking up a group which enjoyed its present identity. In contrast, cell churches build in the hope and expectation of multiplication, and the apprenticeship of the trainee leader, or 'intern', in preparation for leading the next group, is one of the main responsibilities of the cell leader. The hope is that growth and multiplication might take place fairly soon.

Furthermore, very few church elders provided detailed instruction to their house group leaders regarding the running of their groups. This often resulted in different groups within one church gradually taking on quite a different style from the others and simply reflecting the emphasis of the particular leader. It would be possible to be in one group that began with an hour of praise and prayer, followed by an hour of teaching prepared by the house group leader – or to be in another, where people sat on the floor chatting over coffee and biscuits for much of the evening. The programme of the cell church brings far more consistency across the whole church by providing significant input from the elders. Notes from each Sunday's preaching are distributed, with suggested questions for application associated with that particular sermon. This results in the cells having far more focus and purpose.

As years slipped by, it was not unusual to notice that some of our best house group leaders were asking to be released from their role. Their ability to lead had resulted in growing numbers being attracted to their groups. However, many were carrying increasing responsibility in their workplace and also had growing families. Their lives were becoming overcrowded. Something had to go. Some had reluctantly decided that house group leadership was the proverbial straw in danger of breaking the camel's back and needed to be dropped.

Although cell church principles coincided with our previous values, they introduced excellent fresh practices that would sharpen up effectiveness and solve some of our present problems. It was important, however, that a totally fresh start was made. This presented quite a challenge! How do you transform an existing church already built on a small group system into a cell church? Many NFI churches that wanted to embrace the cell church philosophy faced a dilemma. The temptation was simply to make minor adjustments, incorporate some principles and change some words here and there, such as starting to call previous house groups 'cells'. In Brighton we introduced transition but began to falter. We had embraced a far too superficial approach.

After a while we invited Bill Beckham to visit and teach us. His book *The Second Reformation* had already proved really helpful. He was genuinely provocative and incisive. He also had great pastoral grace and excellent answers to pragmatic questions. He pointed out that it was easier for a church that had never worked with small groups to be transformed into a cell church, since the contrasts were clearer. He told us we should also make the transition slowly by starting with a prototype cell in which we would model the values. Then, having spent time with that nucleus, we should multiply its members slowly and gradually into more cells, incorporating more people, making sure that the initial values embraced would not be diluted in the new groups. This second tier phase should also take time, so that the three or four new cells would really gel before further multiplication took place and the whole church would gradually be drawn in. Indeed, the model cell should become a provocation to the rest of the church.

Such a transformation would be easier with a church not already committed to an existing house group programme. When we asked Bill Beckham and others how long the process would take they suggested four or five years to make the full transition! This was a very unattractive prospect and the temptation to take shortcuts to speed up the process was very great. However, we eventually realised that we must start again with a prototype cell made up of some of the couples on our eldership team and knuckle down for the long term. We had recently released John Hosier to a vital international teaching ministry within NFI and had appointed Peter Brooks, a dynamic young Australian, to be the leading elder at Christ the King. He had served first among our youth and then become one of the elders, but his inspirational team leading skills soon became apparent and, although he is our youngest elder, I asked him to take the lead and bring the church into this full transition. Bill Beckham suggested that we made sure that our prototype cell modelled the values we wanted. He warned us not merely to embrace other people's emphases but to reflect our own. Nevertheless, he argued for the value of structured programmes built around the now famous 'four Ws' – Welcome (with the notorious 'Ice Breaker'), Worship, Word and Works (including witness).

We happily embraced the skeleton structure and saw the value of our cells spending their corporate time of Bible study and its application being based on the previous Sunday's preaching. The cells created a really helpful context for reflection on the Sunday sermon, which could lead to practical application and outworking of the message. We felt that this was genuinely preferable to house group leaders feeling that theirs was the responsibility to prepare another 'mini sermon' for the mid-week meeting. Now their responsibility was to oversee and provoke discussion, facilitate debate and action. Experienced cell group leaders have been invited to oversee three or four cells and provide backup to cell leaders and a link to the elders who carry final responsibility.

Building biblically implies building intimately. We are not

mere 'meeting attenders'. We are a fellowship of disciples who share our lives. The word *koinonia*, often translated 'fellowship' in the New Testament, suggests partnership. Peter, James and John were fishermen 'partners' (same root Greek word). If one of them had a torn net, the others would rush to his aid. Partnership implies shared responsibility and shared rewards.

The root of sinfulness is independence – everyone turning to his own way (Isaiah 53:6) and doing what is right in his own eyes (Judges 21:25). The church is God's antidote to independence. It gives you the opportunity to open up to others, with all the pains and pleasures that accompany that process. The moment you believe in Christ you are saved and thoroughly justified in God's sight. But from that time a process of sanctification begins to take place. You were a sinner; now God wants to make you holy. You had huge areas of selfishness, thoughtlessness, pride, fear, anger and so on. Many of these things can be overcome by personal application of the truth of God's word and the inner work of the Holy Spirit. But much of your character will change only through close fellowship with other Christians and discipleship accountability. Jesus discipled twelve men. Their experiences included wonderful encouragements: 'Blessed are you, Simon, son of Jonah!' and fearful confrontations: 'You are thinking from men's point of view, not God's.' Impetuous Simon was discipled and became Peter, the Rock.

Cell churches discourage 'hiding in the crowd' and promote the need to be discipled – in character, in gifting and in spheres of service.

Jesus gave the agenda to the church in the Great Commission: 'Go and make disciples of all nations' (Matthew 28:19). Disciple-making is the foundation for church life. A church is a body of disciples. If a church has no disciple-making activity we must question whether it is a biblical church. If there is no disciple-making going on in your church, you need to do something about it. Christians are born, but disciples are made. We are commanded to make disciples; not bully people into submission, but lovingly encourage them into wholeness and meaningful relationships. Paul wanted to present every person mature (Colossians 1:18) and was sad when he had to address Christians of many years' standing as 'babes in Christ'. He knew they were being robbed of their full inheritance, both now and in eternity, and wanted them to receive rewards for their well-spent and fruitful lives. Paul always had a long-term view, wanting what was best for his spiritual children in the light of eternity.

In an increasingly heartless and lonely world, the church should provide a contrast of intimate love and trust. We must learn to bear one another's burdens and weep with those who weep. As God enlarges churches to impact society, we must never lose the crucial place of the small group network. As John Stott says, 'I do not think it is an exaggeration to say that small groups, Christian family or fellowship groups, are indispensable for our growth into spiritual maturity' (John R. W. Stott, *One People*, Falcon books, 1969).

Discipleship was modelled for us by Jesus in a small group setting. He took twelve men and apprenticed them, promising that he would make them fishers of men. His purpose was not to entertain them but to train and transform them. Sadly, over the centuries our expectation of church life has been drastically changed. Now our church services have developed an 'audience' mentality where observation has replaced participation and platform performances can replace training.

was once preaching at Covenant Life Church in the ashington DC area. It had been a good meeting and the large congregation applauded generously at the end of my sermon. Their leader, my great friend C. J. Mahaney, then asked, 'How many have been blessed this morning?' Hundreds shouted enthusiastically that they had. He then amazed the congregation by telling them that they were totally deceived.

Everybody was taken aback. What had I said to deceive them? Thankfully he quickly explained that Jesus said, 'If you know these things, you are blessed if you *do* them' (John 13:17).

He then pinpointed the great danger of thinking you have been blessed merely by hearing. Hearing is a stepping stone. It opens the way to doing and to the blessing that follows doing. Our danger is that instead of being trained and equipped for works of service (Ephesians 4:12), we become mere consumers who evaluate church life by the wrong criteria. Discipleship is crucial if we are going to produce the real thing, and small cell groups are surely the best context for this process so that openness and accountability can develop and training can take place.

Without these principles in place we may still become a large congregation, but people may gather for the wrong reason, be trained to do nothing and leave when they feel like it. In real terms such attenders add nothing to the resources of the local church. They have not been partakers in any kind of discipling and are bearing no fruit that counts.

The church described in Ephesians 4 is a many-membered body where each part is working properly. Children tossed to and fro by every wind of doctrine are contrasted with a mature man. As Andrew Lincoln argues, 'Not only do silly infants contrast with the mature adult, but the plural of "children" also contrasts with "the mature person", individualism being a sign of childishness, unity a sign of maturity' (Andrew T. Lincoln, *Ephesians*, Word Biblical Commentary, Word Incorporated, 1990).

As new converts are discipled systematically and lovingly through 'equipping tracks' prepared by church elders, they can be trained for works of service and ready to take their place in a functioning body.

This is not the place for a full discussion of the strengths and weaknesses of cell church principles, but perhaps the most marked change of emphasis for us involved a fresh preoccupation with evangelism. Previously, our house groups did not include prayer and planning about reaching our neighbours and friends with the gospel. Now there is regular prayer and planning in connection with evangelism, including corporate responsibility for our church sowing and harvesting events. In the past, it has been all too possible for elders to arrange a special evangelistic endeavour, only to discover that when the dates come round for the event, few people in the church have made adequate contact with their neighbours and friends. Tragically, evangelists often visit churches only to discover very few unsaved people present. The new emphasis on evangelism in the cells has really addressed that problem and brought about substantial change, though we certainly cannot boast anything like the exponential growth that some cell churches particularly in Asia, South America and elsewhere are experiencing.

Cell church principles have been very widely embraced in South Africa, and Simon Pettit had made the transition in Cape Town ahead of any NFI church in the UK. He spoke to us with real enthusiasm about the progress being made there. He underlined the value of evangelism being more integrated into the life of the cell groups by illustrating from the example of 'family fishing', which is particularly seen in some developing nations. When in Goa, India, for instance, I have watched an 'extended family' taking a small boat across a shallow bay and drawing a net behind it. Gradually they draw the net up onto the beach with family members involved at both ends of the net and women and children taking part. The family fishes together. This is not fishing of the single rod and line style but a concerted team effort. So with cell church evangelism we recognise our evangelistic responsibilities more corporately and make every endeavour to draw our contacts into the net of church fellowship and even cell attendance, rather than making it exclusively the burden of the individual to do his isolated 'personal evangelism'.

For ourselves in Brighton, under Peter's leadership we have added all kinds of 'sowing' and 'harvesting' events, with varying degrees of evangelistic confrontation. Some occasions, such as quiz nights, classical concerts, or jazz evenings, for example, are designed simply to draw people into our sphere of friendship, where the events contain no gospel presentation whatsoever. These are with a view to preparing them for a further stage of involvement at our next programme, where we have drawn upon the evangelistic skills of Rosemary Conley, Steve Chalke, Jennifer Rees-Larcombe, Alan Mullery, Ben Castle and others, whose testimonies are interesting in themselves but also provocative to the invited guests.

In addition, we have had very forthright 'in your face' evangelistic proclamation through the ministry of an Indian healing evangelist, Rambabu, who has proved very effective in both healing ministry and winning the lost. All this is punctuated by monthly evangelistic baptismal services, where the gospel is proclaimed clearly in testimony and sermon.

Finally, and endorsing everything else, we continually run the wonderful Alpha programme, for which we are so grateful to God. We see people regularly converted there and many of our contacts through other forms of outreach are channelled into Alpha. Broadly speaking, NFI churches not only in the UK but also from Mexico to Russia, have embraced Alpha and cell principles to a greater or lesser degree. We have greatly benefited not only from Bill Beckham's teaching on cell church but also ran a large conference, where Lawrence Khong from Singapore proved to be an excellent and helpful exponent of cell church principles. In addition, we have twice had the joy of receiving ministry from Nicky Gumbel at our leadership conferences, where his passion for evangelism and enthusiasm for Alpha have been imparted very effectively.

Indeed, 1996 concluded with our first large leadership conference held at the Brighton Conference Centre. We gathered about 2,500 leaders from approximately 30 nations under the title 'Brighton 96', with the stated theme 'Receiving the Spirit, Restoring the Church and Reaching the Nations'. It was good to have John Arnott with us again with his emphasis on receiving the Spirit, but we were also glad to underline the crucial place of church restoration and world mission. Other speakers included Nicky Gumbel, Paul Reid, Wesley Richards, Stuart Bell, Rob Warner, Greg Haslam, Simon Pettit, David Devenish, David Holden, John Lanferman and myself. I had never had so much enthusiastic comeback following any previous conference we have organised.

It was at that conference that our friends in Mexico and Russia were first introduced to Nicky Gumbel and Alpha, and both nations have taken it on board extremely effectively. Indeed our friends Pavel and Marina Saveliev, from Moscow's Rosa Church, have become Nicky's main Alpha channel of influence into Russia.

# 24

# Church Planting

During 1995, David Devenish of Woodside Church, Bedford, began to get a few enquiries from people in the Midlands about church planting or adopting churches in that area. A small group from Coventry started travelling to Woodside once a month, even though it was about a 50-mile journey, and people from Woodside visited this small group to teach them from time to time.

David and his wife, Scilla, went on holiday with their family in Turkey during that summer. They visited both the ruins of Ephesus and the hot springs at Pamukkale. When they got there, David noticed that this was the site of Hierapolis, and Colosse and Laodicea were nearby. That reminded him that these were all churches planted from Ephesus, where Paul taught daily in the Hall of Tyrannus, with the result that the whole of the Province of Asia heard the word of God. As he was travelling home on the coach, he decided to try and work out how long it took by coach from Hierapolis to Ephesus, bearing in mind that in Paul's day he and his companions would not have had that mode of transport available to them! As he was contemplating this, he felt the Holy Spirit began to speak to him about planting a whole region of churches.

David had previously been involved in planting two churches out from Woodside into other parts of Bedford but had not contemplated planting a whole region of churches. He sensed the Spirit of God saying to him, 'Ask me for 50 churches in the Midlands area of Britain by the end of the year 2000.' When he got home, he met with David Stroud, who was leading one of the other churches in Bedford that had been planted from Woodside; he had also felt a growing interest in the Midlands. As a result of this, the Midlands Initiative was launched and David Devenish felt that he should start on the 'Hall of Tyrannus' principle and gather together people in the Midlands for days of teaching once a month. He would first share our basic core values, rather than immediately start planting or adopting churches. He therefore gathered between 100 and 150 people each month in Solihull during 1996. These were leaders of churches in the Midlands who were enquiring about being adopted into the NFI family, people who were considering moving to the Midlands and other small groups who were already in the Midlands but wanted to have a church planted around them where they lived.

Church planting soon proceeded out of this initiative. In September 1996, Jonathan and Helen Bell moved from Odiham in Hampshire to Birmingham to plant a church there. Subsequently, George and Gill Tee moved from Bishop's Stortford to Coventry, Anthony and Gill Henson from Orpington to Leicester and David and Marion Dominy from East Grinstead in Sussex to Stafford. Still following the Hall of Tyrannus principle, David used to gather these church planters once a month for specific coaching in their church planting work. Each of these churches has now been well established and is also sending out church planting cells into neighbouring towns and districts. Other churches were adopted.

A further milestone was reached in summer 1998, when David Stroud was asked to move up to Birmingham. He would be able to oversee the work there better than he could from Bedford. He and his wife Philippa moved in November 1998 and planted a new church in the southern part of the city. Subsequently, Martin and Louise White have moved from Bedford and are in the process of planting a church in the multi-ethnic part of the city. Another key event, which helped to further develop the Midlands vision and encourage those involved, was the conference entitled 'Heart of the Nation'. This was held in February 1998, March 1999 and September 2000 and helped give strategic focus to the whole enterprise.

David Devenish and his team had been praying for 50 churches in the Midlands area by the end of the year 2000. They had not seen that as an objective to strive towards but rather something to guide their prayers and encourage them in a church planting initiative. Although there are not 50 established churches as yet, the team is working in over 50 different situations, including churches and church planting cells. Currently, there are 70 people on the Midlands three-year Church Planting Training Course, which is involving some who are already actively planting and others who are training for the future.

Meanwhile, Colin Baron's pioneering work in the Manchester area continued to develop and draw others from the south, including Rob and Helen Coleman from Crawley to Bolton, Andy and Liz Davies from Putney to Oldham, Geoff and Mandy Green from Storrington to Warrington, Steve and Caroline Alliston from Horsham to

Oldham, Howard and Naomi Kellett from Catford to north Manchester, and Keith Gamon from Brighton with his wife Esther (née Watkinson from India) to south Manchester. Small church plants have gradually prospered and grown, each new church having within its DNA the expectation of further church plants growing from them at quite an early stage. Colin carries the philosophy that just as comparatively young people give birth to children, so young churches are the best fitted and most flexible to give birth to further churches. They must not first be allowed to grow old, when giving birth becomes an unattractive idea. Towns that are now being affected by Colin's sphere of church planting in the Greater Manchester area include Bolton, Blackburn, Blackpool, Macclesfield, Burnage, Salford, Oldham, Warrington and Tameside, while Graham and Charlotte Webb, who joined Colin when he first moved to Manchester, have moved on again to plant afresh in Liverpool.

Others who have moved from the south include Arnold and Mary Bell from Odiham and Mike and Kay Sprenger from Brighton. They moved together to Sheffield, with a view to joining the congregation from Walkley and lead them into an exciting purchase of a former synagogue. This magnificent structure in the heart of Sheffield, with a seating capacity of 1,000, is immediately adjacent to the student centre of the town. Repairs and renovations are now well under way. Also, Christian and Amanda Selvaratnam from Bishop's Stortford, and Steve and Ruth Hurd from Bedford moved to York, while Tony and Kay Smith left Bedford to pioneer in Leeds. Jeremy and Ann Simpkins similarly left Eastbourne to head up a new work in Teesside.

With only 22 established NFI congregations in our capital, we hope to plant many more churches in an endeavour to reach London's millions. Whereas in the past our style had been to aim to plant a nucleus of between 30 and 40 people (enough with the help from NFI resources to support a pastor and be a viable small church), we have latterly been breaking with our tradition by planting some very small cells, hoping to see them develop through growth and multiplication into authentic church plants. These begin in homes with hardly any public profile, rather like the house churches that I helped to get started in Sussex in the very early days.

With hundreds of young people pressing through our ranks, many of whom participate in the Frontier Year Project, we hope to see growing numbers in our future leadership programme so that pastors and teachers can be raised up to lead the new churches.

We have not only been challenged and stimulated by such men as Kriengsak, but also especially by our own dear friends in India. Duncan Watkinson has given an excellent and provocative lead in training new converts into taking early responsibility and then gradually bringing them into eldership and full-time ministry. One of my great joys has been to see men in India, whom I remember meeting soon after their conversion, develop in godliness and maturity and trained in skills at the Indian Training College, and now leading churches. Duncan and Vasanti started with one existing church in Bombay in 1981. Having moved on first to Goa in 1988 and subsequently uprooting a second time and moving to Bangalore in 1997, they have seen steady growth in the number of the churches they serve from 6 in 1991, and 15 in 1995, to 24 in 2000, with the work extending not only to different parts of India but also into the United Arab Emirates and Pakistan.

Similarly in South Africa, three of the elders who were formerly alongside Simon Pettit at the Jubilee Church are now leading new NFI churches. Jeff and Viv Kidwell were the first to move out and start the very successful Bay Community Church in Muizenberg, which is now over 350 strong. François and Liz Heunis then moved to Somerset West to establish the Helderberg Christian Fellowship. Under François' leadership (more recently joined by Gary and Nicky Welsh from the UK), a small nucleus has become a thriving congregation that has recently built a magnificent new church building seating hundreds.

Craig and Shannon Botha, with 50 others from Jubilee, planted Uzuko Lwakhe Church in Khayelitsha, the nearby township, and then, having seen that established under the leadership of Emmanuel Chanda, they moved on to Pietermaritzburg.

Steve and Heather Oliver from the Bay Community Church moved to Clarens in the Freestate in 1996, as a result of which the Dihlabeng Christian Church was planted with extraordinary success. Hundreds of local people were converted and now three churches exist in Dihlabeng, Golden Gate and Mahohweng in Lesotho. The Beacon Church in Langebaan was planted under the leadership of Jacques Adamo in 1998, followed in 1999 by the Coastlands Church in Kleinmond, launched with a leadership team headed up by Philip Verwey. In February of 2000, Jubilee Church planted out Khanyisa in Guguletu, another Cape township, led by Nigel Measures, who moved from Chertsey and has married Lisa, a South African.

Other churches have been started and adopted so that the work goes on developing not only in South Africa but also in other African nations. In Kenya, Edward and Fridah Buria oversee a growing number of churches across the country. In Ghana, John and Alex Kpikpi are developing a wonderful growing church in Accra and are already planting out into the nation, while in Sierra Leone Kai and Catherine Manyeh have planted several churches in Freetown and the rural areas.

The more people we can disciple, train and send, the more churches we can plant across the UK and the nations. Our goal is that all in our ranks will identify with this ever-increasing responsibility and that we do not regard 'missionary' work as the sphere of specialists but of the whole church. Certainly, we acknowledge the vital place of God's call and anointing for leaders but we want to encourage the whole church to see that we are all on a mission. A possible job change or house move should not be regarded as merely the secular part of your life, not related to church, but instead it might be the very thing that God himself has arranged in order to get another church started. We are all on a mission and the so-called sacred/secular divide has to be forgotten. God is interested in your house move. He may well have initiated it for his purpose. Formerly when people moved, they hoped that they might possibly be able to find a church in the area that they could join. Often in the past people who moved found that there was no church that reflected the kind of values and lifestyle that they held dear. Praise God, it is much easier to find lively churches in an increasing number of towns in the UK. This may well involve joining another so-called 'stream' that works in a similar style, and numbers of our people have made that switch successfully.

In our early days, we appealed to people not to move away simply because of job opportunities but to see the building of the local church as of more eternal worth and significance for their lives. Many made the choice to stay and turned down promotions for the sake of building a strong church where they currently lived. Now the number of strong-based churches has grown and the climate has changed. Though some will rightly retain the earlier stance of continuing to fulfil the role they hold in their present church, others will move into a new area and recognise that as part of God's strategy.

It would be wrong to underestimate the personal cost involved in planting a new church in a new town. Often people move from larger, more established churches to areas where they have no family, friends or contacts. Often, because the nucleus is comparatively small, they can find that at first there is little or no children's ministry in the church or very few skilled musicians. Perhaps there are hardly any other teenagers in the group. Hence a family may move to the new town and face a considerable challenge in their family life. Their children feel lonely or their teenagers seriously miss home base or like-minded Christian contemporaries. The sort of difficulties that missionary families have faced for years are encountered by the pioneering planting team, so there has to be a real counting of the cost before embarking on the new adventure. The call to evangelise the nation must grip people's hearts with real fervour so that they are willing to face all the discomforts involved.

As the years have gone by, it has become easier to discover people from the sending congregation who are willing to go with the church planter. For instance, some went with David and Margaret Coak when they moved from Haywards Heath to Cambridge. Similarly Al and Judy Shaw, when they moved to Bristol from Brighton, and Marshall and Chris Schaitel, moving also from Brighton to Exmouth, found that there were people who were keen to move with them. They were happy to uproot and find new jobs in a new town in order to provide a nucleus for the church plant.

Students, in particular, have caught the bug. When my son Joel was choosing his intended university town he was typical of many of our students in that high on his list of priorities was the possibility of being with a church that he could identify with and support. When speaking at one of our Midlands Initiative meetings I found that at the conclusion of the meeting I was surrounded by a circle of university students. I asked them all to introduce themselves and found that they had come from NFI churches across the country to study at Warwick University. When I asked them where they hoped to go at the conclusion of their courses, they all said that they wanted to stay in nearby Coventry for the foreseeable future to help establish the new church that we had planted under George Tee's leadership.

Though I would have to say that we have nowhere near the depth of corporate commitment that I saw among the churches led by Kriengsak in Thailand, we have definitely changed and young people and older people in our ranks are increasingly seeing themselves as potential church planters. Some taking early retirement are also joining the army of workers so that, for instance, the church plant in Cyprus has benefited from being joined by excellent, experienced people from the ranks of UK churches as they pioneer in that tough island.

At Stoneleigh '99 we were taken by surprise when John Kpikpi from Accra, Ghana, came to the microphone on the final night with a powerful prophetic call from God that we, in the UK, should plant 1,000 churches. John is himself a great man of faith and leads his people in Ghana with faith. His word stirred faith in our hearts and our aim is, with God helping us, to rise to the challenge.

Another development in recent years has been the unexpected purchase of very large facilities by a number of our churches. Don Smith, having used a number of school halls and other meeting places for his Eastbourne congregation, was looking for a building in the town suitable for about 500. To his great surprise and dismay he found that God seemed to be drawing him to buy a huge warehouse that would never have been his choice. It has potential for seating thousands and, although thousands do not yet meet there, hundreds do. Similarly, in Hastings, the church under John Groves' leadership was led to purchase a former indoor sports centre of vast proportions.

The church in Norwich led by Goff Hope has bought a huge facility. The church in Winchester led by Greg Haslam has bought and is renovating a former cinema of very great proportions in the town centre. The Sheffield synagogue, referred to earlier, seats a possible 1,000 people. Similarly, the Bracknell church has built its 1,000-seater Kerith Centre as we have our 1,000-seater Clarendon Centre in Brighton. The City Church, Newcastle, now owns a massive building and the Kings Church, Catford, has recently renovated and extended its building so that it can now seat hundreds. The Sidcup Community Church has now bought the freehold of its substantial premises and has plans for renovation and extension. Even in some of the smaller towns, such as Heathfield in Sussex, the church now owns the largest public meeting place in the town.

I was thrilled when I heard the *Re.vive* worship CD from Stoneleigh 2000. It not only recorded enthusiastic praise and worship from thousands of teenagers packed into the great meetings that they were enjoying together, it also included a clarion call from Matt Hosier from Sidcup, who was leading the gathered crowds as they shouted together, 'A thousand churches and churches of thousands.' At the moment, it is a shout from the mouths of teenagers. I pray it will increasingly become the dream of their hearts and then have its outworking in concrete commitment to God through the establishing of hundreds of churches based on good solid decisions made in their lives to put first the kingdom of God and see Christ's church raised up across the nations.

At Brighton 2000, our leaders' conference, Nicky Gumbel told the 1,800 delegates that NFI is like an army. The sad fact is that we are not, and no self-respecting sergeant major would ever consider calling us such (Nicky is a very gracious man!). We have miles to go in making transition. But it is true to say that we are moving in the right direction and are more like an army than we used to be. With God helping us, we hope to continue the transformation.

When I look back to what Wesley accomplished in his generation, when the nation was probably more deeply entrenched in ungodliness than it is even now, I realise that nothing is impossible to God. But when I look at our inner cities and our suburban estates and face the challenge, I realise that a very demanding task awaits us.

The cause of the gospel has lost so much ground. So many areas are without a vibrant New Testament witness. The fact is that, as we move out, there are certainly no well-worn paths before us.

# 25

# Remembering the Poor

Brighton '98, a leaders' conference attended by about 2,500 people from approximately 30 nations, was memorable in many ways. We shall not forget Claudio Freidzon's extraordinary contribution. What a live wire, exuding love and spiritual energy. Dave Devenish gave what Barney Coombs called 'the best teaching on spiritual warfare I have ever heard'! (now encapsulated in his excellent book *Demolishing Strongholds*, Word Publications, 2000). Many of us had been waiting for a long time for a more measured and biblical teaching on that important theme and we are greatly indebted to David for his thorough approach.

Most significant of all, however, was undoubtedly Simon Pettit's urgent and insistent appeal that we remember the poor. Greeted as it was by an immediate standing ovation from the gathered crowd, it has resulted in measurable and thoroughgoing action. This has included a significant influence in the release of over £2 million in the following two Stoneleigh Bible Weeks, and in the launching of Act 2000, an initiative to 'kick start' many works through NFI churches among the poor and disadvantaged in the UK.

Without overloading us with statistics about the unequal distribution of world resources, Simon insisted on the biblical centrality of God's compassion for the poor and our responsibility to give high place to caring for them as an outworking of our commitment to the gospel of the kingdom. He demonstrated to us that this is an integral part of God's apostolic commission to the church.

God's compassion for the poor is well documented throughout the Old Testament. The nation of Israel was given clear instruction to build into their culture a generosity factor, which should have resulted in their needs being met. Although Scripture makes it plain that hard work, with its accompanying rewards, is regarded as the norm for life, nevertheless the poor, for one reason or another, will always be with us and we have a God-given responsibility to care for them. In the Old Testament, the regular year of jubilee celebrated every 50 years meant that in most people's lifetime debts should have been written off, slaves set free and properties restored to their original owners. Other factors, such as gleaning, were built into the national (mostly rural) economy, so that fields were deliberately not to be thoroughly harvested, but the poor were encouraged to legally enter other people's fields and take advantage by gathering what remained, as exemplified in the biblical story of Ruth.

God spoke in the Old Testament through three main channels – the law (clear rules and instructions for building not only religious life but the whole of society), the prophets (immediately inspired utterances addressing the people in their present situation) and wisdom literature (nuggets of truth to live by encapsulated in such books as Proverbs). All three – law, prophets and wisdom literature – included clear, authoritative instruction regarding how the poor should receive compassionate priority. Such priority is at the heart of God's character and his great work of redemption. Sadly, in their backslidden state, Israel as a nation often omitted to fulfil their responsibilities to the poor and earned scathing denunciation from such prophets as Amos and Isaiah for the way that their greedy property acquisition resulted in the grinding of the faces of the poor in the dust.

God's judgements on Israel often came as a direct result of their failure to obey him in these crucial areas of national responsibility. Such failures, together with their adulterous lusting after other gods, even earned them the name 'not my people' (Hosea 1:9). As Christopher Wright points out, 'The primary ethical thrust of the Old Testament is, in fact, social.' Without this dimension of holiness, Israel's worship would never be acceptable. He continues, 'Failure to honour God in the material realm cannot be compensated for by religiosity in the spiritual realm' (Christopher Wright, *Deuteronomy*, NIBC, Hendrikson/Paternoster, 1996).

The coming of the gospel did not mark the end of God's interest in the poor but released it on a mammoth scale, no longer simply to Israel's poor, but to the poor and needy of the nations. When the good news of Jesus came to town, God's values of grace, kindness and compassion came with it. The birth of the church on the Day of Pentecost was swiftly followed by an explosion of lavish kindness shared among the saints. Many Jews who embraced Jesus as their Messiah would have been immediately disinherited by those who rejected Jesus of Nazareth. The saved would have suddenly become, overnight, poor and even homeless. But great grace was on them all and no one regarded anything he possessed as his own but they shared their possessions. Some even sold land and property and laid the proceeds at the apostles' feet for distribution among the poor.

Pentecost gave birth to an immediate Holy Spirit-inspired

...lee of caring and sharing. Such were the proportions of this huge welfare work that the apostles were in danger of becoming overwhelmed with it, so they appointed excellent men full of the Holy Spirit and faith who could handle such vital work. It is important for us to see, as Simon insisted, that this was not the apostles' way of washing their hands of an unimportant and secondary preoccupation, but rather the outworking of their responsible attitude to ensure that it was very well handled as a priority in the emerging kingdom of God.

Pure religion is described by James in terms that we can often forget in our passion to extend the kingdom and win the lost. His definition is simple and clear-cut, namely 'Religion that God our Father accepts as pure and faultless is this; to look after orphans and widows in their distress and keep oneself from being polluted by the world' (James 1:27 NIV). The gospel, put simply, is good news to the poor. James adds, 'What good is it, my brothers, if a man claims to have faith but has no deeds? Can such faith save him? Suppose a brother or sister is without clothes and daily food. If one of you says to him, "Go, I wish you well; keep warm and well fed," but does nothing about his physical needs, what good is it?' (James 2:14–16 NIV).

Jesus taught more about handling money than any other single subject, declaring that it was impossible to serve God and money. When Zacchaeus said that he would give half his money to the poor and repay those he had cheated, Jesus did not merely say that he had made a noble decision. He said, 'Today salvation has come to this house' (Luke 19:9). Zacchaeus, formerly dominated by greed, was now a free man. He had experienced salvation not simply in terms of going to heaven when he died, but in terms of an emancipated lifestyle. His bondage to money was broken.

It must be pointed out, however, that Jesus invited no one to embrace a life of asceticism and gave not the slightest hint that asceticism was inherently virtuous. His promise was that as we give it would be given back to us 'pressed down, shaken together and running over' (Luke 6:38). Paul added that as we sow our seed God will multiply it and increase our ability to give more (see 2 Corinthians 9:6–11). Poverty is, therefore, not to be seen as piety, and asceticism wins no points with God but rather holds the danger of leading us into a self-conscious endeavour to gain merit. Jesus lived simply but was free to attend a wedding celebration and even earn the title of a glutton and a winebibber. He accepted material support from wealthy women (Luke 8:2–3) and he even scandalised some by accepting the extravagant anointing with extremely costly ointment when according to the disciples' perspective it would have been better used by selling it and distributing the proceeds to the poor (Matthew 26:9).

Though Jesus did not withdraw from the world, he made it clear that our investment and our confidence should not be in the passing pleasures of this world where moth and rust can destroy. He encouraged his followers instead to lay up treasure in heaven. Paul advised Timothy similarly, telling him to instruct the rich in this present world not to fix their hope on the uncertainty of riches, but on God. They were to be rich in good works, to be generous and ready to share, storing up for themselves the treasure of a good foundation for the future (see 1 Timothy 6:17–19). It is said that when John D. Rockefeller died, his accountant was asked, 'How much did Rockefeller leave?' His reply was classic: 'He left it all!' Though it is impossible for us to 'take it with us', Jesus gave us the alternative of sending it on ahead! He made it very clear that clinging tenaciously to money in this life is futile and shortsighted.

Simon Pettit, coming as he now does from the continent of Africa, with all its stresses and strains, surrounded by millions of poor people, spoke with passion and power. He reminded us of the very clear commitment of the early apostles to this crucial ministry and mentioned that in the several books on apostolic ministry that he had read in recent days, not one of them had any teaching on caring for the poor. But poverty is a spiritual issue and clearly preoccupied the apostles, as demonstrated by Peter, James and John's words to Paul, urging him to remember the poor, something he was eager to do (Galatians 2:10). It is not to be regarded simply as the responsibility of aid agencies and governments. In the early church there was a clear connection between their care for the poor and dramatic growth. Today, the vast majority of people in the world are poor. If we are to change the expression of Christianity around the world, then we must remember the poor.

With Simon's impassioned appeal ringing in our ears, we felt we must respond beyond simply standing to applaud his excellent message. Action had to follow. It's not that we were not at all involved in such work. Rosemary Stapley had already been pioneering in Bombay's slums through the Asha Project, which we had supported. Piet and Hettie Dreyer had opened Project Gateway in Pietermaritzburg, South Africa. Gail Diani was working among the street children in Guadalajara, Mexico. Even within the UK Philippa Stroud, having worked alongside Jackie Pullinger in Hong Kong, returned to Bedford to start what became known as the Clarendon Street Project. Here the homeless could find shelter and renewed hope and, if they so desired, progress to a discipleship house for training in life skills and the rebuilding of fruitful lives. (The full story is told in Philippa's book,

*God's Heart for the Poor*, Kingsway, 1999.)The project has since been handed over to the Kings Arms Church in Bedford and further properties have been acquired. Over 3,500 people have stayed in the project's houses, which are established as the largest provider of supported accommodation in the town.

'Act 2000' was our response to Simon's powerful word and was established as an initiative to encourage local churches in the UK to serve people in need within their communities. We felt that by working together we could have far greater impact across the nation and create a context for networking by setting up a database of community involvement and linking churches with similar vision. We did not want simply to set up a department within NFI for helping the poor, but to stimulate and encourage one another to embrace ministry to the poor in church life in an integrated way and to awaken each believer to his or her individual responsibility.

Through Act 2000 we were able to give specific support to help strengthen and multiply some key areas of ministry through identifying some of the main challenges that churches face and help to kick-start smaller projects and initiatives. Within a short space of time pioneering work among the disadvantaged has been helped by Act 2000 in Bedford, Birmingham, Norwich, Bishop's Stortford, south Manchester, Newcastle, Burgess Hill, Christchurch, Cockermouth, Hastings, Maidstone, New Addington, Poole, Ringwood, Oxhey and Sheffield.

While there is no shortage of need in the UK, much of it can shrink when compared to the challenges faced by churches overseas. We will therefore continue to focus on supporting relief and development projects being implemented by churches with whom we relate in the Third

World. Current involvement includes agricultural work in Sierra Leone, feeding and irrigation in Kenya, and agricultural training and seed planting in Zimbabwe. Our goal is to help local churches fulfil the specific vision that God has given them, overseen by local church elders and apostolic teams.

We have really enjoyed developing relationships with national organisations in order to facilitate the sharing of resources and expertise. We have particularly appreciated encouragement from Tearfund, the Evangelical Alliance, Shaftesbury Society and CARE as well as the new Re-build initiative. Input from such groups has been of great benefit. We were also pleased to sponsor CARE for Life to produce a new post-abortion leaflet for use in Pregnancy Crisis Centres. This has been of real benefit not only to the 14 NFI churches currently involved in such centres but also many others nationwide affiliated to CARE for Life.

Our goal in working together has been to make some of the expertise, which already exists among our churches, more widely accessible. As a result we commissioned a series of introductory guides giving brief overviews of what is involved in different areas of community involvement. Subjects have included supporting homeless people, running furniture projects, serving asylum seekers and refugees, and fund-raising for church-based projects.

In many ways we feel we are only scratching the surface, but at least it is a surface that we are now scratching with far more wholehearted commitment. We have definitely been changed by Simon's stirring appeal and realise that God has brought this central aspect of Christ's kingdom much more strongly to our attention. We have also released Nigel Ring to give himself as a top priority to the work of Act International, which we believe will bring wonderful help to those in the greatest need across the many nations in which we serve, so that our gospel outreach is not in word only but endorsed by a message far more holistic than ever before expressed through NFI.

When we first considered what we would like to accomplish and arrived at a proposed budget, we were amazed to see that we would be looking for an offering from Stoneleigh of £1 million, which represented a huge challenge. The previous year's Stoneleigh offering had amounted to approximately £587,000 so this would require a major breakthrough. My theme for Stoneleigh '99 was the grace of God. I spoke first on the grace of God teaching us to say 'no' to ungodliness (Titus 2:12 NIV) which was a serious call to holiness, and on the final night I spoke on 'By the grace of God I am what I am', which focused on grace to live by. On the Wednesday night of each week, which was the offering night, I spoke on the grace of giving, based on passages of Scripture in 2 Corinthians 8 and 9. I felt God's powerful help in the presentation and we took up our great offering. When we eventually heard the total, it came to £1.3 million, more than double our previous year's. We were overjoyed at the people's wholehearted response and their willingness to embrace the message in such a practical expression of commitment.

At Stoneleigh 2000, I did not spend a whole evening's message addressing the theme but simply referred to the challenges we faced if we were to continue to follow through with our commitments. Once again the offering topped £1 million. Praise God for the generous and sacrificial giving of God's people. May he inspire us to continue to love not only in word but in deed and in truth, so that through our thoroughgoing obedience to Christ, the gospel of the kingdom continues to be good news to the poor.

# 26

# Who Are We?

So, is NFI a cell church movement, or a Toronto blessing movement? Neither! We have been greatly helped by receiving from many sources in the dynamic and multi-coloured body of Christ. God has blessed us by bringing many wonderful people and influences across our path and we have been affected and changed by their contribution. But we have never left, nor intend leaving, our fundamental passion to see Christ glorified through local churches restored to New Testament norms and making disciples of all the nations.

We remain convinced that foundational issues must be dealt with. We have to dig down as well as build up. Indeed, like Jeremiah we often have to tear down and uproot before we can build and plant. The great folly is to build on a wrong foundation. Dentists know that, however unpleasant the process, they must remove the offending decay before they start applying the filling. Without authentic preparatory work they have not solved the problem, but guarantee later pain and distress.

I am glad that from my earliest days as a Christian I was

taught to honour the final authority of the Bible as the word of God. E. G. Rudman, my Baptist pastor, established that principle in my life and it was fully endorsed by such early influences as John Stott and J. I. Packer. We have been very willing to receive help, inspiration and blessing from a wide variety of backgrounds as our history demonstrates, but always having been satisfied that we can at the same time honour biblical truth. We give great place to training based on the Bible and were happy to call our great summer family camp at Stoneleigh a 'Bible week', spending about an hour in every session on Bible exposition.

Though I was very impressed with the spiritual life and charismatic vitality of the leaders of the early 'house church movement' I was nervous of the emphasis of some who seemed to belittle the significance of the Bible, arguing that the earliest Christians did not carry a 'big black Bible' under their arms. Though this is obviously true, and they were undoubtedly enjoying the personal leading of the Holy Spirit as the Bible itself argues (Romans 8:14; Galatians 5:16; Ephesians 5:15–20), nevertheless the earliest Christians also devoted themselves to the apostles' doctrine (Acts 2:42) and were, for instance, taught by such men as the apostle Paul day and night, publicly and from house to house. Paul did not only tell them to 'live from their spirit', but continually taught them truth – continuing all night if necessary (Acts 20:11)! When leaving the Ephesian elders with the promise that they would never see him again, he committed them not only to God, but also to the word of his grace which could build them up (Acts 20:32).

His letters continually endorse the importance of truth and doctrine and make plain that there is a God-given wisdom that must be taught among the saints which stands in stark contrast to the wisdom of this world. Some of my charismatic friends urge me not to be so 'narrow', but to be open to what they call 'the prophets of the media or of the business world'. Whereas I read the *Economist* with interest and often observe what I regard as helpful insights, I still take note that God has said, 'I will destroy the wisdom of the wise and the intelligence of the intelligent I will frustrate' (1 Corinthians 1:19 NIV).

God has spoken in his word. The apostles were stewards of God-given mysteries. They received revelation about Christ and what was accomplished in his life, death, resurrection and ascension that is completely life-changing, releasing and fulfilling. I see it as our joy and privilege to keep digging ever deeper into that revelation and to build churches that are open to the Spirit and the prophetic word but regard the Scripture as providing their final authority. Such churches tend not to be open to short-term experiments and popular fads that sometimes enjoy fleeting popularity in the body of Christ. One of the features of Stoneleigh Bible Week was always the recommendation of books that really help establish people in their faith. For instance, when Wayne Grudem's *Systematic Theology* was first published we strongly encouraged people to buy and read it. Literally thousands of pounds' worth of copies were sold! Books by such authors as John Stott, Alec Motyer, J. I. Packer, Dr Lloyd-Jones, D. A. Carson, Douglas Moo, Gordon Fee, John Piper and Peter Lewis were strongly recommended and eagerly purchased at Stoneleigh Bible Week by thousands of enthusiastic campers.

The new birth changed my life and brought me a hunger for the word of God, but being baptised in the Holy Spirit changed my expectation of church life. God has come to dwell in me by his Spirit. He brought with him gifts that must be manifested. The manifestation of the Spirit is given for the common good (1 Corinthians 12:7). So we cannot merely internalise the gifts; they work by being shared in and through the gathered church. God demonstrates his presence in the church by gifts that he has distributed. Church life, therefore, must be fundamentally changed to provide space and opportunity for the presence and power of God through the gifts that he has been pleased to give. A fresh wineskin is fundamental to our success. We cannot merely bolt on to our faulty foundations some of the so-called new charismatic trends. We cannot merely add guitars and overhead projectors.

Going to the roots involves rethinking the very nature and calling of the church as the people of God. It involves corporate obedience to the revelation of Scripture. It seems pointless to me for devout men of God to preach to their congregations on matters of personal and individual obedience to Christ while at the same time ignoring issues of obedience related to church structure and style. How can we ask individual Christians to obey the Christ of the New Testament while we maintain churches that in no way resemble the church of the New Testament?

We who live in Europe, in particular, must freshly evaluate our church models, many of which are built on centuries of traditions of men and are far removed from the simplicity of Scripture. They clutter up the church with antiquated and unscriptural practices and obscure the gospel from our twenty-first-century contemporaries. This is no appeal to be merely modern but rather to discover authentic New Testament church life and adapt it with integrity for our own generation.

If we are the dwelling place of God in the Spirit (Ephesians 2:22) our church life must expect the Spirit's presence to be of paramount importance. We must therefore

arrange our church meetings to allow adequate op[ ]
for him to manifest his presence among us, no[ ]
through one gift, such as the wonderful gift of pr......g,
but through multiplied gifts as God may direct. Moses was
very clear about this issue. It was God's presence that made
his people distinct. Without his presence what are we?
Moses was passionate about the matter and refused to go
forward without God's guarantee.

Even modern charismatics must seriously be on their
guard that music does not replace the actual manifestation
of the Spirit's presence. In the 1960s, as a young charismatic, I attended the Royal Albert Hall Easter Monday
Pentecostal Celebration. Huge crowds gathered. Great
choirs were singing and the atmosphere was lively. But I will
never forget one elderly gentleman who was sitting next to
me. He turned and said sadly, 'We used to have power, now
we have choirs!' The growing popularity of new worship
songs and the developing skill of excellent music groups can
actually mislead us. We can think that singing new songs as
opposed to old hymns, using guitars and electronic key-
boards instead of church organs, and overhead projectors
instead of hymn books demonstrates that we are charismatic. A sad and serious delusion!

When I started leading the Seaford church many years
ago we gradually abandoned the 'hymn sandwich' (including the hymn board with its previously selected list of
hymns). We replaced it with a dynamic meeting where many
gifts of the Holy Spirit were in evidence and songs were
spontaneously sung by the congregation. In more recent
years it has become alarmingly observable that in many so-
called charismatic churches (including NFI churches) the use
of spiritual gifts seems to have declined rather than
increased. A sad lack of expectation of the manifestation of

the presence of God has led to some passivity and pre-dictability. Many seem to have abdicated their privileges regarding the priesthood and participation of all believers and allowed what used to be the hymn board's choice of hymns to be replaced by the pre-selected list of acetates for the overhead. The sense of wonder that we used to experience in charismatic meetings is rare today. Passivity and predictability are gaining ground to our peril.

Large celebrations, such as those held at Stoneleigh Bible Week, inevitably depend on being platform led. Congregational participation is barely possible. In spite of our frequent warnings that local church meetings should not be modelled on such large celebrations I find comparatively small congregations embracing exactly that style. It is of vital importance that we stop this drift and structure our meetings in such a way that the Holy Spirit has full freedom to manifest his presence and do his will among us. Spiritual gifts, particularly the gift of prophecy, are to be zealously sought and play a full part in our gatherings, so that it becomes self-evident that God himself is among us (see 1 Corinthians 14:25).

The Spirit not only manifests his presence in meetings but also confirms our individual sonship and brings us fully into the enjoyment of the new covenant. As sons we no longer live in bondage to law. Christ came to live and die under the law in order to deliver us from its slavery and bring us into full rights as sons. For freedom Christ has set us free; therefore legalism and the bondage it brings is to be withstood. We live as sons free from the law.

I was once preaching on the truth that Christians are not under law when a man in the congregation could take it no longer. He stood up and interrupted me, saying it was the most outrageous thing he had ever heard! I was thrilled. I spoke to him very respectfully and told him that he had *almost* understood everything that I was saying. Yes, grace is scandalous! I asked him to take his seat again while I went on further to explain the scandal of grace and the wonder of righteousness as a gift.

Our churches enjoy freedom from legalism and from the atmosphere that legalism brings. Jesus battled with the legalists of his day, with all their preoccupation over rules and regulations. Legalism robs us of our sense of acceptance in God's love and the joy that follows. Many Christians today have not fully grasped their freedom from law, and sadly, in the name of holiness, spend their time majoring on minors. We will never live holy lives until we see our death to the law and our freedom from legalistic religion.

But we must not misunderstand God's grace. I was once asked by a pastor if he should apply grace or righteousness in a certain situation. His question provided a real shock to my system. He went on to explain that an unmarried couple who were living together were asking about the possibility of being baptised at his church. The pastor clearly saw grace and righteousness as alternatives!

When God declared the old covenant obsolete (Hebrews 8:13) and introduced a new covenant he wasn't throwing in the towel in the battle against sin; he was revealing a new and better way of overcoming it. In the coming of Christ, grace suddenly 'shone out' (Titus 2:11, literally an 'Epiphany'). Grace 'appeared', according to the apostle Paul, not to lower the standards but to equip believers to rise to unprecedented heights.

Not that God had not always been gracious. When Moses asked for a revelation of God he was told that God's presence would pass before him and that he would reveal his name. So Moses heard 'the Lord, the Lord, compassionate and gracious, slow to anger' (Exodus 34:6). God has always been gracious. However, grace was particularly displayed in Christ's coming. The Law came by Moses. Grace and truth came through Jesus Christ, and of his fullness we have all received grace upon grace (John 1:16–17).

Grace certainly shone out in the coming of Christ but grace doesn't come to lower the standard; it comes to motivate and enable us to live a totally new life. Paul told Titus that the grace of God 'appeared' instructing us to say 'no' (Titus 2:11–12). The vivid NIV translation arrests our attention.

Saying 'no' is a vital part of holy living. The downward gravitational pull of human society is so all-pervasive that if we don't learn to say 'no' we will soon be in trouble. If young people don't learn to say 'no' they will be quickly compromised by the opposite sex. If they don't learn to say 'no' they will soon be experimenting with drugs and alcohol. 'No' is a word we must be instructed to say. It is an anti-social word. It goes against the tide. It takes courage and commitment to say it. It needs strong motivation, and grace motivates powerfully.

How does grace teach us? It begins by telling us that we are totally acceptable to God through our faith in Christ. We are justified freely as a gift. So I am a winner before I start. I am accepted before I have done anything. What a relief! How magnificent! Some would argue 'How dangerous!' But they don't understand. God starts by totally qualifying us. He will test us later but he qualifies us first. We start accepted, qualified, justified as a gift. The righteousness of Christ is freely given to me not only to start my Christian life but every day of my life, and he is the same yesterday, today and for ever. His totally righteous life of magnificent decisions, perfect holy choices and steadfast

purity in the face of fierce temptation is freely cr
my account.

This is so encouraging that it is almost too good
true. When I first heard the grace of God I felt like the early
witnesses of the Resurrection. It says of them, 'They could
not believe for joy.' I had lived in a school of tough and zealous commitment for quite a while. Condemnation was often
overshadowing me. Trying harder was the way to succeed!
School reports, with their oft-repeated 'could do better' and
'should try harder', had a similar ring to my understanding
of how to live the Christian life.

Suddenly I saw it! God's grace covers my failure and sin,
and justifies me freely as a gift. What a revelation! What
joy! What thanksgiving and praise! Grace instructs me first
by telling me I am a winner before I start. This revelation of
grace pervades NFI as a movement.

Here's some more good news! Grace tells you that Jesus
wants you for his very own possession, his special treasure
(Titus 2:14). God has a particular and personal delight in
you. He chose you from before the foundation of the world.
He foreknew you and predestined you to be his own. He
says of his church 'My delight is in her' (Isaiah 62:4). God
actually delights in you. He didn't save you by mistake. He
didn't have to take you in a 'job lot'. You were not born of
human will but by the will of God. He will always love and
cherish you.

> Not your own but his by right
> His peculiar treasure now.
> Fair and precious in his sight
> Purchased jewel for his brow.
> He will keep what thus he sought
> Safely guard the dearly bought,

Cherish that which he did choose
Always love and never lose.

F. R. Havergal

Next, grace teaches us about the terrible price that was paid for our salvation. Those three simple words are so unfathomable in their depth: 'He gave himself.' Some, motivated by kindness, might give a gift, or even a fortune, but he gave himself. He gave himself to the human race. He gave himself to a motley band of followers who would deny him in his hour of need. He gave himself to Satan's hour. He gave his cheek to those who tore out the beard. He didn't hide his face from spitting. He gave himself to the full wrath of God, the total curse of the Law. He gave himself without reserve, though he was appalled in Gethsemane, though he shuddered at the shocking revelation of the bitterness of the cup. He sweated, as it were, great drops of blood, pleading with his Father that if it were possible it might be taken from him. Yet he prevailed, determined to save us and for the joy set before him endured the cross, despising the shame. He became the centre of mocking and shame from men and demons. He gave himself to the sheer fury of a holy God who hates sin with a perfect loathing, and fierce anger. The Son of God loved me and gave himself for me!

Here is the crux of the matter ('*crux*' is the Latin for 'cross'). From the cross came the excruciating cry (excruciating is derived from *ex-crux*): 'My God, my God, why have you forsaken me?' Grace teaches me by telling me about the price that was paid.

Grace also teaches me what a glorious goal he had in mind. He wanted a people 'zealous for good deeds' (Titus 2:14). He wants zealots. He hates lukewarmness. He would rather we were cold or hot. Lukewarmness makes him vomit (Revelation 3:16). He wants passionate people burning with motivation and wholehearted in commitment. He gave his own life as our example. Zeal for his Father's house consumed him. Beware the 'hang loose' mentality. Don't get squeezed into today's preoccupation with being 'cool'. I will never forget the early video testimony of the girl from Pensacola. Powerfully impacted by the breakout of the Holy Spirit there, where she had formerly been backslidden, reluctant and indifferent, the Holy Spirit suddenly overwhelmed her. She ended her testimony with a radiant smile and the unforgettable words 'I am hot now!'

God wants us red hot for the works that he foreordained for us. He doesn't want mere busyness or hectic activity. He has prepared handpicked works for us. Grace teaches me that he chose the works in advance and he wants me excitedly committed to doing them so that he can finally and enthusiastically receive me to his eternal kingdom with the glorious words, 'Well done, good and faithful servant.'

Finally, grace teaches me that this world can be viewed as 'the present age' (Titus 2:12). It is not permanent; it is just what's taking place now for a short while. We live only briefly, like a flower that buds, opens, fades and quickly falls. So the very world itself is short-lived. This age is passing away. Grace opens my eyes to that reality. If I thought this life was going to last for ever I might live differently, but I know it's brief. Eternity awaits. The new heavens and the new earth are ahead.

I often travel internationally and stay briefly in other countries. Often I don't fully unpack my case. I don't learn the language. Sometimes, if it's a particularly brief visit to Europe, I don't even change any money, or even adjust my watch. Walking down the street I probably look like anyone else, but actually I don't belong! I don't fully identify. In a few days or hours I won't be there; I'll be flying home again. I belong elsewhere! Grace teaches me not to get my roots down too deeply in this temporary scene. Grace teaches me that it's easy to say 'no' when I am not really part of the culture; I am a visiting alien; my citizenship is elsewhere.

Not only do I not belong, I am eagerly anticipating another 'appearing'. Grace has 'appeared' (Titus 2:11) but soon the glorious 'appearing of our God and Saviour' will take place (Titus 2:13). This full revelation will soon burst upon the world. He will come to be glorified in his saints and to be marvelled at among all who have believed (2 Thessalonians 1:10).

Saying 'no' to the world, the flesh and the devil seems to make good sense when grace instructs me about all these things. When I am told that actually I am an heir of eternal life (Titus 3:7) I tend to lose interest in the 'here today and gone tomorrow'. I feel like fixing my hope on the grace that's coming to me at the revelation of Jesus Christ. Jim Elliott said, 'He is no fool who gives up what he cannot keep to gain what he cannot lose.' In real terms this will mean that house moves for the sake of the kingdom take priority over house moves that are merely for the sake of career advancement. However, kingdom and career can be involved in the same move, since God is happy to promote and bless his children as they put first the kingdom.

Steve Whittington, the full-time youth worker from our church in Brighton, suddenly felt that God had called him to Middlesbrough. Though there was no promise of a job, he and his wife Jo received this sense of calling with such certainty and peace that they immediately began to take action, having already discipled Steve Horne, a replacement leader in our ranks. The church in the area is led by Jeremy Simpkins, a former elder from the church in Eastbourne who, together with his wife Ann, obeyed God's prompting to move north and lead a small but growing church. Jesus did not invite fishermen to leave their nets simply to study systematic theology, but to accompany him immediately on his mission to establish his kingdom in the world. He taught them truth as they went with him. So devotion to Christ is in the context of mission and teamwork among churches that help to open doors and create contexts for service as God leads. There are many who have received training into leadership in our church in Brighton who have moved on in this way. People formerly in Brighton now have leadership responsibilities in such places as Bristol, Sheffield, Sidcup, Exmouth, Torquay, Leicester, London, Wolverhampton, Manchester, Cape Town, Accra and Guadalajara.

Devotion to Christ is not to be measured purely in personal piety, but also in identification with Christ in his mission to reach and disciple the nations. We received a prophecy several years ago telling us as leaders that if, like pillars, we would stand upright in terms of righteousness and in a straight line in terms of good fellowship with one another, the Lord would cause shoots to grow around us that he would cut and use as arrows and send out into his service. We constantly pray for this process to continue. Other churches, such as Sidcup and Biggin Hill, have similar testimonies, having sent out numbers of leaders and people. In sending them on their way, we do not say a final goodbye, but endorse them and supply Ephesians 4 ministries to serve and encourage them as noted earlier (see Chapter 24).

We are committed to the development of 'apostolic teams', creating a context for gifted people to discover and develop gifts which might best be fulfilled not simply within one local church but in an itinerant way, serving among the churches. Our TIM (Training Itinerant Ministries) programme is one of the most fulfilling in which I am involved, where David Holden and I regularly meet with approximately three dozen men who have increasing responsibilities in travelling among the churches, like Timothy, Titus and others did on Paul's behalf. Our longing is that they might serve, like Timothy, as beloved and faithful sons. The whole atmosphere of the New Testament church is not one of an institution but of a family. Paul wrote to the Corinthian church, for example, as his beloved children. He often used such language and spoke openly of his love and affection. When he could not himself visit his beloved children at Corinth he sent not only epistles but also his 'beloved and faithful child in the Lord' (1 Corinthians 4:17). As with our heavenly Father, he found that the best way to communicate was by sending a beloved and faithful son. Family, friendship, love and loyalty are the very stuff of the kingdom of God. Biblical correctness alone will never build churches or a family of churches such as Paul served. His apostolic relationship, often expressed through such men as Timothy, Epaphras, Epaphroditus and others, was crucial to their growth and success.

We are committed to the autonomy of local churches, each under the oversight of their own eldership, but we do not believe in the ultimate independence of the local church as an isolated unit. We are in a team, part of an armada, on a mission together, as were the Pauline churches in the New Testament. They received and sent Paul and his companions into their apostolic sphere. Paul could say to the Corinthians, 'Your growing faith will mean the expansion of our sphere of action' (2 Corinthians 10:15, J. B. PHILLIPS). He knew that the health of local churches affected the extension of his apostolic work. The health of local churches and the success of apostolic labours being able to extend to regions beyond were interrelated. Sickly churches overwhelmed by long-term internal problems frustrated Paul's desire to move into new territory.

Paul's constant goal was expansion. I am sure that he was convinced that there will be no end to the increase of Christ's government (Isaiah 9:7) and that God has promised his Son the nations as his inheritance and the ends of the earth as his possession (Psalm 2:8). He did not embrace the eschatology of doom that some of us were taught in our early days, but anticipated that the gospel would run through the nations. As Jesus said, 'This gospel of the kingdom shall be preached in the whole world for a witness to all the nations, and then the end shall come' (Matthew 24:14). We therefore have a clear goal and objective. I am deeply grateful for the impact of Iain Murray's magnificent *The Puritan Hope* (Banner of Truth), which finally freed me from my former exposure to an eschatology of despair and confirmed me in my expectation of the ultimate triumph of the gospel among the nations.

Some of the robust worship heard in our churches and at the Bible weeks is deeply rooted in this theology, which was embraced by a previous generation of believers. Now it is gradually being rediscovered in the modern church, albeit against the backdrop of popular dispensationalism. Famous old hymns of the past sound a note of the inevitable triumph of the gospel.

> Jesus shall reign where'er the sun
> Doth his successive journeys run;
> His kingdom stretch from shore to shore,
> Till moons shall wax and wane no more.

> Isaac Watts

Such men as Carey, the so-called 'father of modern missions', were motivated and sustained by that kind of theology. They believed in a sovereign God who had covenanted to cause Christ's reign to fill the earth and invade every nation, tongue and tribe before the end comes. In looking for restoration we do not triumphalistically anticipate perfection this side of the Lord's return. Only then will the perfect come (1 Corinthians 13). Our longing is for a church like the one in the Bible that grew empowered by the Spirit in the face of entrenched hostility. People often long for angelic appearances but in the New Testament most seemed to take place when pioneering saints were suffering in prison. We look for the recovery of a militant, believing church. This will not herald a day of ease but will almost certainly involve the recovery of opposition of New Testament proportions. As Dr Martyn Lloyd-Jones used to say, we are more likely to share the fellowship of his sufferings after we have known more of the power of his resurrection (Philippians 3:10). At the moment, the world sees little in us to persecute. The worst we endure is the indifference, dismissal and mockery of an unimpressed generation. Our longing is for the recovery of the kind of churches we see demonstrated in the Bible, enjoying the presence and power of the Holy Spirit, realising that they are on a mission, celebrating the grace of God and being joined together with arms of love. In addition we need the help of travelling Ephesians 4 ministries that constantly serve us and remind us of the bigger picture to which we are all called.

# 27

# Turning up the Contrast

I was once described in *Renewal* magazine as 'the acceptable face of Restoration', a tag which, though pleasant – who doesn't want to be accepted? – may prove a real snare to any servant of God! I felt that as I draw to a close I should include a chapter that might put that pleasant description in some jeopardy. Some years ago, a preacher friend challenged me that I was in danger of not sufficiently highlighting my case by also stating why I reject opposite views, thereby demonstrating the contrast. He told me that you get a much clearer TV picture when the contrast is correctly adjusted. The picture is less bland. In an endeavour, therefore, to say goodbye to blandness I offer a chapter of contrasts that you will find in this particular TV! Goodbye, acceptable face!

Against the trend, you will not find women in governmental leadership in NFI churches. Though the gospel clearly brought a revolutionary breakthrough in attitudes to women and their full acceptance and equal value to men in the churches, we believe that male headship was also clearly taught and practised. Jesus, who, as a rock of offence and a stone of stumbling, fearlessly cut through the traditions of

301

his day and attacked all mere conformity to established norms, nevertheless chose twelve *men* to be apostles. A tax collector, who would not only have been hated but also socially and religiously unacceptable and outcast, plus a member of the extremist Zealots, was invited, demonstrating that Jesus was not simply keeping within what was politically correct in his day, but he included no women among the twelve. Women were welcomed in the apostolic travelling band (Luke 8:2–3) but even here it is clear that their role in the group was different from that of the men who were being trained for apostleship.

Obviously, I cannot handle this issue thoroughly here. A whole book would be required and this is a small section of one chapter, but I simply state our stance (which is identical to the well-argued chapter in Barney Coombs' book *Apostles Today*, Sovereign World, 1996).

Women are actively involved in many diverse aspects of life and ministry in our churches. My own wife, who embraces our stance wholeheartedly, helps to lead a cell, speaks at women's conferences, writes books, leads an Alpha table, prophesies freely, lays hands on the sick and casts out demons. Kate Simmonds has regularly led the thousands in worship at Stoneleigh Bible Week and in our church in Brighton. Women baptise. Women break bread in our communion services. (We have no problem with 'priesthood' as such, since we are all priests.) Women lead works associated with crisis pregnancy and reaching out to the poor. We are more than happy, furthermore, to endorse and celebrate the awesome mercy ministry and evangelistic labours of Jackie Pullinger in Hong Kong. I have visited her work and arranged for her to speak to all our leaders, sharing testimony of her evangelistic passion and faith for wholeness among ruined drug users. The caricature that we have sometimes been given in NFI (No Females Included!) of frustrated women in our ranks with no space to serve God is completely inaccurate. We encourage women to emulate the challenging and multi-faceted example set out in Proverbs 31 with maturity and security.

Our specific areas of concern are church government, headship and the authoritative teaching and leading of men. We would regard these as territory forbidden to women by Scripture, not simply through what some people are pleased to interpret as the supposed caprice of a hard-faced, anti-woman, ex-Pharisee like Paul, but through the whole tenor of Scripture from beginning to end. In heaven it seems there will be neither male nor female; this is true of us in Christ now, in terms of our value and standing in his sight! But the New Testament, in dealing with gender-related issues, tends to take its standards by looking back to creation rather than forward to our ultimate heavenly state (see 1 Corinthians 11:8; Ephesians 5:31; 1 Timothy 2:13). God has made us different and has given us different roles. We are happy to celebrate the difference and genuinely honour what the Bible calls the weaker vessel.

Let me emphasise at this point that we don't maintain our position out of a desire to see women boxed in, shut up and shut out. Our desire has never been to belittle or underestimate over 50 per cent of God's created humanity and we don't aim to perpetuate a historic Victorian stance, dictating that women should be 'seen and not heard'. We simply and honestly believe that the Bible shows us that there are roles in the church that are gender-specific and that if these principles are correctly observed we shall see women blossom and flourish into the beautiful potential God has for them. I hold this stance without hostility or lack of love and with genuine respect for many who I know hold a different view.

With crunching gear change, I will highlight another contrast. Broadly speaking, we are not very enthusiastic about so-called 'parachurch' activity, though from the outset let me say that I realise people often find themselves in such settings motivated by red-hot zeal for Christ and his mission, sometimes mixed with frustration regarding the apparent impotence of local churches.

It would also be true to say that some work seems to be best done by specialists in a context other than the local church. Wycliffe Bible Translators would appear to be an excellent example of such work, though perhaps it could be mentioned that William Carey did major Bible translation work and also planted 17 churches in India. The Missionary Aviation Fellowship again supplies a unique service to the body of Christ in our mission to reach the world. Others, such as Care Campaign, could similarly be identified and honoured.

My concern regarding so-called 'parachurch' organisations is where they plainly have taken on work that should have been done within the province of normal healthy church life. As a result, many individual Christians have the impression that church is a boring, inward-looking place fully entrenched in maintenance mode. If you really love Jesus, therefore, and want to make him known you will not hang around church very long but you will go and join another organisation that is vibrantly getting the work done. Such a concept is foreign to Scripture and sadly helps us leave local churches in their moribund state while creative and zealous Christians put their energies elsewhere.

The apostolic strategy of the New Testament was obviously one of vigorous church-based mission, rooted in the local church and planting new churches with all the safeguards and strength provided by God-ordained eldership and the normal disciplines and privileges of church membership.

For instance, if we particularly want to reach business-men, let local churches do so from their church base, using their church people. I have met zealous Christians whose whole energies are committed to reaching businessmen and whose chief loyalty is outworked in that sphere. Their actual local church involvement is limited and often displays atti-tudes somewhat critical and dismissive of church life. They argue pragmatically that businessmen are getting saved and love the fellowship. But often new converts are then sadly drawn into this context as their main sphere of fellowship and outreach. Other aspects of church life are thereby for-feited. Relationships with the elderly, the young, and the poor are not developed. The normal processes of church life, which are ordained by God to help us in our corporate maturity and sanctification, are bypassed. Perhaps evangelis-tic gains are made but serious losses are also sustained. Specialist outreach among students unrelated to local churches develops similar weaknesses. Evangelism is best done reaching out from the local church and feeding into the local church. Conversion should result in people being added to communities of vibrant Christians drawn from all spectrums of society and demonstrating the church as God's multi-coloured work of art (Ephesians 2:10).

Sometimes, parachurch organisations achieve a position of high visibility and are seen as the pacesetters in the nation. Local churches are then encouraged to endorse their initiatives and are often expected to supply manpower and financial backing. For example, some years ago a Christian friend who sometimes finds himself involved in the 'para-church world' was attending a committee meeting convened for discussing details of a proposed evangelistic endeavour.

He was somewhat scandalised when he found that their pre-planned programme included an agenda item which cynically stated: 'Getting the backing of the local churches and helping them to believe it is their vision.'

Sometimes literature making financial appeals from parachurch organisations suggests that they are on the exciting cutting edge of Christian outreach and activity and therefore would really appreciate local church funds. The implication is that they are where the action is, while the local church is simply a resource base in maintenance mode, a concept foreign to the New Testament. Paul could say of the Thessalonian church, for instance, that from them the Lord's message rang out not only throughout Macedonia and Achaia but their faith in God was known everywhere (1 Thessalonians 1:8).

I acknowledge that much of this parachurch activity started in order to fill a vacuum left by the church. But my appeal would be that our energies are better spent in restoring local churches to their originally intended strength and God-given role, rather than multiplying specialist ministries and littering the Christian scene with multiplied parachurch works while deploring the local church's ineptitude.

Some would plead that in this twenty-first-century world we must redefine church and argue that church does not consist of simply gathering at 10 o'clock on Sunday mornings in a specially sanctified building. I respond to that point with the assurance that I would never dream of seeing the church as a mere Sunday meeting. (We work in some Muslim nations where believers meet when they can and where they can and if they can.) Church is not static, nor is it identifiable simply in terms of special buildings and special services. Nevertheless, there are clear biblical building blocks which we discard at our peril. People may have to gather at different times in all sorts of different places, as no doubt they did in the New Testament church, which was born in extreme pressure, hostility and persecution. Nevertheless, even in the midst of such challenges there was an undergirding order in those communities so that, for instance, Paul could write 'to all the saints in Christ Jesus who are in Philippi, including the overseers and deacons' (Philippians 1:1). Local church order was clearly honoured, even when churches existed in very flexible settings.

Another recent development enjoying some popularity, but not embraced by us, would be so-called 'Youth churches'. Motivated by the fact that youth attracts youth and perhaps acknowledging that normal church life can seem archaic and irrelevant to the modern generation, some have put all their eggs in the one basket of exclusively gathering youth and building 'Youth churches'. As a pragmatic answer to the problem of our modern youth culture, it may well experience some success, but in terms of building the kind of church described in the New Testament it falls far short of the stated goal, where the various age groups and classes are expected to come together, slaves and free, Jews and Greeks, male and female – all one in Christ. God's alternative new society is meant to demonstrate its unique ability to unite the formerly un-unitable. 'Specialist group' churches fail to embrace that great purpose for the church in terms not only of impacting the nations but also demonstrating to principalities and powers the amazing manifold wisdom of God (Ephesians 3:10).

You will notice that this united people also includes Jew and Gentile. This was the great mystery revealed to the apostles, namely that the Gentiles are fellow heirs and fellow members of the body and fellow partakers of the promises of Christ Jesus (Ephesians 3:6). The dividing wall of hostility between Jew and Gentile has come down through the cross. He has made the two into one new man (Ephesians 2:14). We Gentiles have happily abandoned our former gods in order to submit ourselves to Israel's God, as Isaiah and other Old Testament prophets said we would. We have been fully incorporated into the promises made to Abraham. We are part of his family. If we belong to Christ then we are automatically Abraham's offspring, heirs according to promise (Galatians 3:29). The New Testament then goes on to contrast the 'present Jerusalem' (that is, the physical one found in the Middle East) with 'Jerusalem above' (a spiritual city which is to come). Paul clearly states that it is because of 'the hope of Israel' that he is bound in chains (Acts 28:20 NIV). In Christ, the Messiah, he sees the hope of Israel fulfilled. According to Paul, Christ is the promised seed of Abraham (Galatians 3:16). He is the fulfilment of what was promised. Paul does not see himself as abandoning his Jewish hopes and roots and replacing them with Christian values. Rather, he sees the coming of Christ as the fulfilment of all his Jewish hopes and longings.

Paul says that this is a mystery previously hidden but now revealed to God's holy apostles and prophets. It is a biblical principle that we interpret the Old Testament through the eyes of the New. The apostles were specially commissioned by Christ and were given special revelation of all that happened in the cross, death, Resurrection and ascension of Christ. Without the revelation they have given us we would have no understanding of the cross. If they had not told us, for instance, that we were also crucified when Christ was crucified, we would never have known it! They received revelation of mysteries bound up with Christ. Now their goal and ours is to know Christ, be married to Christ, have fellowship with him and be the temple of the Holy Spirit. Our inheritance is now a spiritual one, not a physical and natural one.

The old order is over. The Samaritan woman at the well asked Jesus which was the most important worship centre: Jerusalem or Samaria. In his reply, Jesus ignored any particular physical location and told her that God is looking for worshippers who worship in spirit and truth. When the apostles looked in wonder at the glorious Temple, Jesus told them it was coming down! Now we are his temple (Ephesians 2:19–22). Hebrew Christians were told (perhaps to their total amazement after all of the Old Testament emphasis on Jerusalem) that here we have no lasting city but are looking for the city which is to come.

The earliest Christian believers, who of course were almost exclusively Jews, were no longer preoccupied with the land or the Temple. They came to understand that these former physical symbols had no continuing significance. When a rich young Jewish ruler came asking Jesus what he must do to inherit eternal life, Jesus' reply included the invitation to sell his possessions, leave all, and follow him. The Jewish Christian Barnabas, who was famously a good man and full of the Holy Spirit, no longer regarded his land of any importance but sold it, gave away the proceeds and went on international mission, looking for a better inheritance. He was a true child of Abraham who was heir of the whole world, not just of a few square miles in the Middle East (Romans 4:13).

As John Stott says in his excellent commentary on the book of Acts,

In the exposition of these verses I am following what may justly be termed the 'Reformed' perspective, namely that the New Testament authors understood the Old Testament prophecies concerning the seed of Abraham, the promised land and the kingdom as having been fulfilled in Christ. Although Paul does predict a widespread turning of Jews to Christ before the end (Romans 11:25ff), he does not link it with the land. Indeed, the New Testament contains no clear promise of a Jewish return to the land. I fully recognise that the 'dispensational' view is different. (John R. W. Stott, *The Message of Acts,* IVP, 1990)

In agreement with great orthodox evangelical Bible teachers, such as John Stott and Dr Martyn Lloyd-Jones, we therefore withstand the currently popular dispensationalism that has so affected modern church thought. Originally developed by J. N. Darby and popularised by the Scofield Bible, this stance has become further endorsed by multiplied paperbacks and magazines so that many Christians have no idea that there is an alternative to this widely held view. In my early Christian experience, I was taught that the church was a parenthetic interruption in God's ultimate plans and would soon be removed so that God could once again get on with his plan, which would be centred in the Jewish nation.

In contrast, Dr Martyn Lloyd-Jones taught,

How terribly wrong it is for those who call themselves Dispensationalists to say that the Christian church was a mere afterthought in the mind of God, that he had never really intended it in eternity. The greatest thing in the universe, the greatest manifestation of God's own wisdom an afterthought! The church, far from being an afterthought, is the brightest shining of the wisdom of God. It is equally wrong to say that the church is only temporary, and that a time will come when she will be removed and the gospel of the kingdom will again be preached to the Jews! There is nothing beyond the church. She is the highest and the most supreme manifestation of the wisdom of God; and to look forward to something beyond the church is to deny not only this verse but many another verse in the Scriptures. The church is the final expression of the wisdom of God, the thing above all others that enables even the angels to comprehend the wisdom of God. (Dr Martyn Lloyd-Jones, *The Unsearchable Riches of Christ*, Banner of Truth, 1979)

Sadly in today's climate, when one honestly holds this straightforward orthodox biblical stance, one is sometimes accused of anti-Semitism, which is a grossly emotive and unfair charge. The truth is that we honour the God of Israel, Isaac and Jacob, believing him to be the only true God. We abandon any English gods and submit exclusively to him. Like Paul, we also long for the natural children of Israel to turn and embrace their Messiah, as we believe they ultimately will in vast numbers according to Romans 9–11. We believe in an end time awakening and regrafting back into the olive tree, as promised, which will be as life from the dead and will result in the blessing of the world.

One further area of contrast relates to the theme of spiritual warfare. In recent years, paperbacks and magazine articles have multiplied, with various emphases in connection with the church's conflict with Satan, principalities and powers. Special forms of prayer, prefaced by research of historical developments in an area, have become the norm for some. People climb up to 'high places' overlooking towns in order to do warfare. Others urge us to express repentance for the sins of bygone generations in an attempt to spiritually 'clear the air'.

In contrast, Paul's attacks on the demon-infested cities of his day seem very simple and uncomplicated. He preached the gospel of Christ, healed the sick and cast out demons when they manifested their presence. He then instructed the new converts and formed a church. The whole operation was spiritual warfare. Preaching the gospel of the kingdom, proclaiming that Jesus is Lord and calling for repentance is a declaration of war against the kingdom of darkness. Planting a church is the establishment of a counter culture and its very existence, maintenance and growth is a continual expression of war; the action of an invasive army determined not to succumb to the prevailing lifestyle, but using the weapons of righteousness for the right hand and the left to establish the reign of their King (2 Corinthians 6:7).

Time and space forbid a thorough appraisal of this theme. Suffice it to say I am unimpressed by the fanciful techniques and methodology often being embraced in recent years, for which I can find no basis either in Scripture or in the well-documented historic revivals of the past.

Again, I do not question the zeal and passion of those who promote these developments. Their longings for God to move in power and revival may well exceed my own and for this I genuinely respect them, but I cannot embrace the unbiblical practices that many seem to be promoting. When I recently challenged one zealous exponent of what he called 'identificational repentance' and appealed to him to show me an example in Scripture of what he was promoting, his simple reply to me was, 'Not everything is in Scripture.' When we consider emails, cell phones and 747s, this is manifestly true, but when we also consider the unchanging grounds of effective world evangelisation, we must surely look to Scripture for the vindication of all our activity.

Perhaps these few comments will once and for ever destroy the 'acceptable face of Restoration' tag. I raise them not merely to be controversial but rather in order to bring some clarity by way of contrast and make my appeal for ongoing love and discussion that we might come ultimately to the unity of the faith, not simply by burying our distinctives, nor even merely agreeing to differ, but with the hope that ultimately unity might be attained, with our eyes fully open to the light of Scripture.

Unity is no small thing to be regarded as a pious but impossible hope. It is our Christian duty to do all in our power to honestly strive for it. Therefore we must handle our perceived differences not with arrogance but in the fear of God, always asking for his help and respecting one another's integrity.

# 28
# Unity and Revival

In recent years, New Testament scholars have challenged their contemporary believers with the charge that we tend to read the book of Romans almost entirely through the eyes of the sixteenth-century Reformers and regard the whole letter as being centred in justification by faith. We tend to regard the meat of the letter as being almost exclusively in the first eight chapters. These are followed by teachings on Israel in chapters 9–11 and conclude with various practical remarks in the remaining chapters.

In contrast, some modern scholars have provoked us to ask: what was the main purpose of the letter? What is its chief preoccupation? Their conclusion is that Paul's greatest concern was that Rome, the strategic capital of the Empire, should have a united church, not one that was painfully split between ex-Jews and ex-Gentiles. He, therefore, restates the basis of our standing before God which requires a full treatment of justification by faith and life in the Spirit. His goal is to demonstrate to former Jew and former Gentile that they have both been freely justified by what Christ has done in the cross and thereby are all the true people of God. His argument concludes with the appeal of Romans 15:5–7: 'Now may the God who gives perseverance and encouragement grant you to be of the same mind with one another according to Christ Jesus; that with one accord you may with one voice glorify the God and Father of our Lord Jesus Christ. Wherefore, accept one another, just as Christ also accepted us to the glory of God.'

Paul's urgent appeal was that they would accept one another. Surely we, with all our historic distinctives, must respond to that appeal and make mutual acceptance our chosen policy. One of the tragedies of church history that survives today is that people regard those brothers and sisters who differ from them as worthy of scorn, hostility and character assassination, instead of respect and brotherly love. For instance, as regards the gender debate, it is all too easy to hurl abuse from either side of the debate, dismissing one another as either narrow-minded misogynists or alternatively mere trend followers shaped by modern feminism.

It is not impossible to stop the heated words and cold shoulders, and learn to respect opponents as simply brothers and sisters who have searched the Scripture and (amazingly to you or me, no doubt) honestly reached a different conclusion from us. I am told that when Martyn Lloyd-Jones was urged not to allow Arminians into a group for which he was responsible and essentially consisted of Reformed men, he refused that stance, and argued that though he held his own well-known convictions, he fellowshipped with all who submitted honestly to Scripture.

I once heard him preach an unforgettable sermon on Acts 7:2, 'Brothers and fathers, listen to me!' (Only Dr Lloyd-Jones could face a 60-verse chapter and spend an hour preaching on six words at its beginning!) He gave the most impassioned teaching on the horrors of prejudice, saying that before Stephen even began his great sermon in that chapter, he paused to urge his brethren to hear him through. Sadly, the chapter ends with them literally covering their ears (see verse 57). The Doctor pointed out that prejudice is literally pre-judging an issue and making your mind up before you have heard the case. With a portrait of Dr Martyn Lloyd-Jones looking down over my shoulder on the day that I spoke at the Westminster Fellowship those years ago (see Chapter 12), I began by using that illustration. Regretfully, I still received the Stephen treatment, though thankfully without stones.

Surely we can accept and respect one another as a first step to unity. Rejection is a painful part of modern society: rejection between races, between age groups ('old fools', 'young thugs'), between genders and even invading the womb to reject unwanted babies. In our age of escalating divorce figures, let's beware of the danger of being shaped by the spirit of the age and allowing personal rejection to affect our ability to hear one another with honesty and humility. Paul knew how hard it would be, for instance, for Jewish Christians from their historical perspective of godliness to receive recently saved pagans who had no respect for Sabbath or food laws. The offence caused would sometimes have cut deep into their consciences. Rejection would be the easy knee-jerk reaction. Paul appealed for a better way, 'forgiving each other, just as in Christ God forgave you' (Ephesians 4:32).

God helping us, we must also try to abandon any complacency about our differences. Disunity is not to be regarded like the poor as 'always with us'. We must not allow cynicism and hopelessness to prevail but must regard our disunity with sadness and see it as it surely is, namely our failure to hear God and one another.

The fact remains that ultimately there must be one truth. Division in the church is hateful to God and so it is our duty to make every effort both to maintain the unity of the Spirit and attain to the unity of the faith (Ephesians 4). When we make our goal simply 'agreeing to differ' we are still not aiming high enough. The fact remains that the most difficult doctrine must have a true interpretation – even eschatology! Unity of faith and practice is a tough objective to strive for, but we must not approach the theme by passing through a door over which is written 'Abandon hope, all you who enter here'. God will surely ultimately bring us there.

How can we make progress? Surely with honesty and humility, remembering how we received any spiritual insight in the first place, namely through God's gift of revelation. Doctrine is not our own opinion and preference; it is revealed truth. When Peter suddenly realised that he knew that Jesus was the Christ, his Lord quickly pointed out to him that flesh and blood did not reveal that to him (he hadn't worked it out for himself) but 'my Father who is in heaven' (Matthew 16:17). Jesus actually rejoiced in this arrangement saying, 'I praise you, Father, Lord of heaven and earth, because you have hidden these things from the wise and learned, and revealed them to little children' (Matthew 11:25 NIV). Paul tells us that God has set himself to destroy the wisdom of the wise and make foolish the wisdom of the world, pointing out that the world through its wisdom did not come to know God. Praise God that we have received his Spirit so that we may know the things freely given to us by God through the apparent foolishness of the preaching of the cross (see 1 Corinthians 1:18–21 and 2:6ff.).

God has revealed his gospel to us. We could never have worked it out on our own. He has to bring it to us. Now that it has been delivered to us by God, we must not become speculators or inventors of new doctrines not found in the Bible, but 'contend earnestly for the faith which was *once for all delivered to the saints*' (Jude 3). Our responsibility is to handle it correctly. As Paul reminded Timothy, 'be diligent to present yourself approved to God as a workman who does not need to be ashamed, handling accurately the word of truth' (2 Timothy 2:15). We must also heed Peter's warning, '. . . just as also our beloved brother Paul, according to the wisdom given to him, wrote to you, as also in all his letters, speaking in them of these things, in which are some things hard to understand, which the untaught and unstable distort, as they do also the rest of the scriptures, to their own destruction' (2 Peter 3:15–16). Yes, even Peter regarded Paul's letters as hard, but we distort them at our peril!

Jude therefore tells us to contend for this once-and-for-all delivered gospel. But isn't that our problem? We are not meant to be contentious! The fact is that God wants us to arrive at sufficient Christian maturity that we can embrace a positive attitude to healthy confrontation. Having told the Roman Christians to accept one another (Romans 15:7) Paul goes on in the same chapter to remind them that they are 'full of goodness, filled with knowledge and also able to *admonish one another*' (Romans 15:14, my italics).

Rather than withdraw from Peter, Paul withstood him to his face (Galatians 2:11). It was not sudden pique on Paul's part, but an impassioned plea to Peter to be consistent for the sake of the ultimate unity of the church based on a correct embracing of gospel truth. Withdrawal results in isolation and separation. Honest and loving confrontation has got to be the better way, though we know it is much harder to accomplish and easier to avoid.

Furthermore, for unity to succeed there must come an uncompromising desire on everybody's part to submit to biblical revelation when you clearly receive it. So, when you receive a truth, don't duck its implications for your life! Sadly, it is possible to reject a doctrine, not because you are convinced from the Bible about your stance, but because of the dangerous implications for your life if you accept and obey fresh revelation from the word.

Jesus posed his opponents a teasing question regarding John's baptism. Was it from heaven or from man? The Bible then records not only the answer that his opponents gave, but the reason they gave it! Their approach was not straightforward. They were totally preoccupied with the implications of their answer. 'If we say, "From heaven," he will say to us, "Then why did you not believe him?" But if we say, "From men," we fear the multitude; for they hold John to be a prophet.' And so they gave an astute and dishonest answer, 'We do not know' (Matthew 21:25–26). We cannot afford that kind of dishonesty in the church today if we are going to fear God and arrive at unity. Many issues are fudged because of the price that might have to be paid if individuals own up to what they truly believe and follow through the consequences.

Paul's appeal in Romans 14 is that we should demonstrate patience and love and not judge one another. He would rather have some lack of uniformity in the church than contempt and judgement. One person might regard one day above another, while others regarded every day alike. Or one might have faith to eat all things while others, whose faith was weak, ate only vegetables. His appeal was that in the light of revealed truth each person must be convinced in his own mind with the awareness that ultimately each one of us will give account of himself to God (Romans 14:1–12).

I am sure that Paul would not be impressed with us being convinced of one thing in our mind, but actually living out another lifestyle because of the immediate consequences of consistency with Scripture. I know of pastors, for instance, who have told me that of course they believe in certain doctrines and practices but that if they taught them they would be in terrible trouble and may lose their job. I am not belittling the seriousness of such a challenge for a married man with wife and children to consider, but I believe that ultimately there is more peace to be derived from simple and honest obedience. I know of a pastor who when confronted with fresh revelation which he knew threatened his ministry and therefore his home and security (which included job, salary and supplied house) said, 'I will become a milkman and start again.' Actually, God had other plans for him and his radical obedience to the truth that he had received from God opened a fresh door to far more fruitful service in a different sphere.

We must not close our ears to the prayer of Jesus that we be brought to perfect unity (John 17). We know his will. We must aim to live in the light of it. Unity must therefore be one of our earnestly sought goals.

Some, of course, will try to push the theme further than we can possibly go, appealing for reconciliation without reference to Christ or his cross. I was recently anonymously sent a tape that appealed for reconciliation among religious people of every type. The passage 2 Corinthians 5:18 was quoted at the outset – God who reconciled us to himself and gave us the ministry of reconciliation. The remainder of the tape was an appeal for reconciliation between many diverse groups in the name of unity. However, the passage of Scripture from which the phrase was taken was never expounded and the unity appealed for on the tape made no reference to Christ and his cross as the only basis for unity that Christianity provides.

It is possible to approach the subject, therefore, in a sentimental and unreal way. If we are not careful we can find ourselves in John Lennon's slipstream, seizing his beautiful and nostalgic theme, 'Imagine . . . if there were no religion too'. Many of us would happily see ourselves as the enemies of 'religion' as such, but we dare not think of ourselves as enemies of truth and doctrine. We dare not regard doctrine simply as something that divides. The fact is that Jesus claimed to be the truth and told us that the truth would set us free. He claimed that man lives by every word that proceeds from the mouth of God. It is fantasy to think we can arrive at a unity in any way other than by submitting to him who is the truth and the truth that he provides.

Recently, someone also brought to my attention that, as a perceived apostolic leader, my main responsibility was to lead my so-called 'tribe' into full unity with all the other 'tribes' for the sake of revival. The argument proceeded along the following lines. All the so-called apostolic groups of churches (he later added to his argument all the historic denominations) should be regarded like all the Old Testament tribes. Their duty was to come together as 'one nation' and only when this happened would God be able to send revival, blessing and powerful spiritual authority to the church. I am afraid that I would have to say that I differ on every point made and, since this concept in one form or another can easily become popularised, I want to address it here.

It is totally fanciful to regard the various groupings of churches like Old Testament tribes. Paul certainly had a sphere of responsibility for what theologians call the Pauline churches and saw himself as their father, but the thought of tribalism never surfaced. He gave short shrift to those in the church he fathered in Corinth who wanted to claim that they were exclusively of Paul or that in any sense the churches that he served represented anything that could be compared to a tribe.

If, on the other hand, we had said to Paul that in the name of unity and for the sake of revival he should bury his differences with the legalistic Judaisers and let them carry on with their practices in the churches, I think you would have met with, to put it mildly, a firm refusal! He would have seen his apostolic responsibility as being the exact opposite!

Furthermore, the whole imagery of tribal unity being the prerequisite for spiritual blessing doesn't even bear investigation within the Old Testament itself! Spiritual breakthrough in the Old Testament usually arose not when somehow all the tribes got together, but when God sovereignly raised up a Joseph or a Moses, a Gideon or a David and gave them his powerful anointing. Often that God-given authority led first to backlash and division rather than unity, as in the case of Joseph and David. Unity tended to follow after the fruit of their individual anointing and obedience and after they paid the price of hostility and isolation.

Finally, church history is littered with the stories of revival that are not the fruit of organised unity, but rather the opposite. Men like Wesley and Whitefield were ostracised and hated by the existing church. Evan Roberts and the Welsh Revival were severely persecuted. The Pentecostal outbreak at Azusa Street, whose fruits now encircle the world, was born in the midst of severe persecution and hostility. Yet God was pleased to own and multiply each one.

Certainly, we must labour with all our energies for unity, but to argue that God's hands are tied until we sink our differences for the sake of a 'tribal get-together' remains unconvincing.

Many of us have longed for revival for years and will continue to pray, asking for God's intervention. Some feel that they have specific promises. My friend Mike Sprenger, having attended meetings in Pensacola, felt that God promised him that revival was coming to the UK and that as a sign of confirmation he would find that on his return flight to the UK the wind speed outside the plane would change dramatically as they passed over New England. As he made the journey he recalled the promise and at the geographic point he raised his hand in faith (many modern flights display a map and tell you exactly where you are on the flight, as well as wind speed). Although he had to several times refuse the attention of air hostesses as they saw his raised hand, he continued to adopt this position of faith. To his amazement and delight, sure enough, as they flew over New England the wind speed of the plane dramatically changed. Mike returned to us in England thrilled at the promise he had received and the confirmation that took place.

Some months later, he returned to Pensacola and stood on the platform giving that testimony to the gathered crowd. When he did so, there was an outbreak of the Holy Spirit that surpassed anything that had happened in recent months. God came powerfully once again, owning the promise of revival.

In longing and praying for revival, we stand in a great Christian tradition. Two voices from the past must suffice to encourage us. Alexander Whyte said:

> I may not live to see it. But the day will come when there will be a great Revival over the whole earth . . . He has it in His seven-sealed book that there will be a time of refreshing till all the ends of the earth shall see the salvation of God. (G. F. Barbour, *Life of Alexander Whyte*, Hodder & Stoughton, 1923)

William Jay (1769–1853) shared the same testimony:

> We have many and express assurances in the scriptures which
> cannot be broken, of the general, the universal spread and reign
> of Christianity, which are not yet accomplished. Nothing has
> yet taken place in the history of divine grace, wide enough in
> extent, durable enough in continuance, powerful enough
> in energy, blessed enough in enjoyment, magnificent enough in
> glory, to do anything like justice to these predictions and
> promises. Better days, therefore, are before us, notwithstanding
> the forebodings of many. (Quoted from Iain Murray's *The
> Puritan Hope*, Banner of Truth, 1971)

Let us stay full of faith that God will come and, though the
vision tarry, let us wait for it praying with all our hearts and
serving him with all our energies, while making every effort
to maintain the unity of the Spirit and attain to the unity of
the faith (Ephesians 4:3, 13).

# 29

# Millennium Year

I wonder how you saw in the new Millennium? I, together with some of my family, fought my way through London's phenomenal crowds (later estimated at three million), and managed to stand overlooking the Thames, opposite Big Ben. The atmosphere was extraordinary. Numbers grew ever greater until the crush was reminiscent of old football crowds that used to stand packed together in the terraces. As people forced their way through, my family became somewhat separated, but people were extraordinarily friendly and all those around us became like a huge family together, sharing jokes and laughing. Whereas you might often see people with a can of beer in their fist, tonight champagne was the chosen beverage. I have never seen so many bottles of it in my life!

Eventually, Big Ben's hands were coming together to celebrate the midnight hour. The crowd began to shout the countdown, 'Ten, nine, eight . . .' We all joined in, until the explosive moment when the skies lit up with the greatest firework display I have ever seen. It lasted for ages and filled the sky with light and beauty. Suddenly, it was all over and we made our way back to my son Ben's home in the East End. No vehicles were allowed in the city centre, so many groups were walking arm in arm, singing and shouting through the streets of London. Although alcohol was flowing freely, in God's mercy I never saw one ugly incident. Everybody seemed to be good-natured. I later heard from a friend that the police were so incredibly outnumbered on the night that if things had become hostile they would have been incapable of handling it.

As we made our way home, I found myself thinking, 'Aren't people wonderful!' I know they are sinners, I know they are lost, but they are wonderful. God so longs to bring the crowds to himself. They are his crowds, made in his image. They are not Satan's crowds. Satan didn't make them. He has nothing to offer them. He is an intruder and a liar and a thief. These are God's crowds. Don't you long for crowds to fill God's kingdom? Don't you long for Jesus to be popular on the streets of your town? That night was an amazing celebration. We were all celebrating the Millennium, AD2000, but somehow Jesus hardly got a look in. Jesus, the actual centre of the meaning of the date, was pushed to the margins of the celebration.

The next day, we watched the TV review and the world-wide party was a sight to behold. Starting east of New Zealand, on a remote island just on the right side of the International Date Line; going on to the breathtaking Sydney harbour explosion of colour; then to Asia and Europe, with the superb Paris display lighting up the Eiffel Tower. Then we saw the Thames lit up, no longer from our restricted view in the crowd but from the magnificent aerial views captured on TV. Finally, across the Atlantic, we saw the celebrations in the States. The world was rejoicing. The biggest international party ever seen, but Jesus was hidden.

For me, the lasting impact was the great reminder that Jesus loves people, crowds of people, and though they may choose to marginalise him, he has given us the awesome responsibility of telling them who he is and who they are, and how they can find him, repent and receive eternal life.

At the church in Brighton (and many other NFI churches) our year began with a week of church prayer, including fasting for many. It was a good time and, having just completed our faith project of paying all our bills on the Clarendon Centre by the end of the century, we wanted to face a new and realistic faith goal. Brian, one of our members, came to the front of the prayer meeting and suggested that we believe for one person to be saved each week through the coming year. When I think of the 120 pouring forward for salvation every Sunday in Bangkok when I was there, it seemed so pathetic. But for us it was honest and real. We prayed for it in faith, and in God's mercy, as the year went by, we saw it happen. Progress is slow, but progress is there. Numbers attending Alpha increased steadily (with the occasional blip). There is no question that evangelism is our preoccupation. Our year's programme is now shaped with evangelism in view.

Having said that, we must obey Christ's commission, which was not simply to evangelise, but to make disciples. The need for us to develop greater skills at making apprentices is ever before us. 'Teaching them to observe all that I commanded you' (Matthew 28:20) is still part of the Great Commission. Jesus is obviously interested not only in numbers but also in transformed lifestyles that bring honour to his name and see him as the focal point of all their joys and hopes.

To my dismay, when I visited the USA towards the end of 1999 I was often asked about my expectations for the forthcoming Millennium. It became clear that the questions were not focused on evangelistic opportunities that the Millennium might afford, but the question of Christ's imminent return, or the fear of inevitable chaos that the Millennium bug would cause. I heard of people hoarding food and taking other steps based on fear. Attitudes to the end time for many are rooted in a sensational approach to isolated passages of Scripture rather than a sober submission to its whole teaching. Jesus told us, 'This gospel of the kingdom shall be preached in the whole world for a witness to all the nations, and then the end shall come' (Matthew 24:14). The book of Revelation tells us that every tongue, tribe and ethnic group will be present in the eternal kingdom and there are manifestly more peoples to be reached before Christ's return. Although we must always have an attitude of preparedness for Christ's return, which in one sense will be as unexpected as a thief in the night, surely God does not want us in panic mode, but rather busy and active in reaching the lost.

For me, Millennium year underlined the urgency of the day, especially for the vast crowds outside of Christ. Any temptation for the church to be simply in maintenance mode must be overcome as we give ourselves to the vital role of world evangelisation. Though I was saddened by questions I was asked in the US, nevertheless they expressed the fact that the door of salvation will not be open for ever and this is no time for complacency but for wholehearted commitment to prayer, evangelism and the building of strong churches.

Our desire to be increasingly outward-looking was reflected in the speakers invited to Stoneleigh 2000. George Verwer, that great missionary statesman, held his audience spellbound as he spoke, not only with humour and grace, but also with great passion about world evangelisation. His energy and capacity for sustained hard work is legendary. I remember when he first appeared on the evangelical scene with such burning intensity for the lost that you expected that he wouldn't be around for long! But like Moses' bush he's burning on and hasn't burnt out! What a man! What an example of godliness and holy passion. I was moved at the end of his session when I saw how many individuals approached him to express love and appreciation. Most of them seemed to introduce themselves by recalling the dates when they served God on Operation Mobilisation. Often George remembered them individually. His capacity is phenomenal. His knowledge of the nations compares with most people's knowledge of their own kitchen. His very clothing reflects his passion for the nations. Not many people have the map of the world built into the design of their jackets!

Our style of operation would differ from George's but we gladly sit at his feet, hoping to catch something of his zeal for Christ and his urgency for world evangelisation, not to mention his wonderful humanity, friendliness and enduring commitment to individuals.

We were also delighted to have Steve Chalke on our platform, as he challenged us about getting the gospel into today's marketplace. His own pioneering style of breaking into the media for Christ's sake is very provocative. He has courageously followed *Star Trek*'s famous split infinitive 'to boldly go' where no one has gone before! With humour and great candour, he stripped away any fantasies his hearers might have about the glamour of being on TV or in the media. Having heard him, we realised how he has had to be tough, patient and willing to take risks. He has been willing to be vulnerable to the misunderstanding of other evangelical believers by bravely entering hostile territory, sometimes having to agree to walk into it with one hand tied behind his back. If we are going to get out of the safety of well-worn paths, we may have to do things that we would rather not do and get into situations we would prefer not to be in. It goes with the risk factor of following Jesus outside the normal safety areas.

David Oliver from Salt and Light's Basingstoke Community Church also came to challenge us at Stoneleigh about the workplace as a context not for frustration and mere endurance but for light-bearing and kingdom advance. He strongly challenged the sacred/secular divide and urged us to be 100 per cent alive to Christ in every place. Often pastors wonder how they can get their church members to mingle among the sinners and not get cut off from the world, forgetting that most of them spend nearly all of their life precisely in that setting. It is 'full-timers' who so easily get separated from ordinary secular people. Church members spend every day with them in the workplace. David's challenge was punchy and provocative without being merely sensational. It was an honest, biblically based appeal to be on our toes to the opportunities that come every day. He urged us not to put God in a box of Sunday meetings, or even specially arranged evangelistic occasions.

At Brighton 2000, our International Leaders' Conference attended by about 1,800 delegates, we were further exposed to provocative men on the move. Nicky Gumbel, in his inimitable way, continued to urge us into evangelism, backed by remarkable statistics from the growing impact of the Alpha programme. He is always a joy to hear and his warm, disarming style draws you along and inspires you to believe that you also could see many saved if you got among neighbours and friends with the gospel.

Another guest speaker was New York's Bill Wilson. His

reputation had gone before him and he didn't disappoint us! What a man and what a ministry, particularly among 22,000 children in New York. I was moved by his obvious transparency and longing for the lost to be saved. I sat in the front row as he spoke, watched the tears flow down his cheeks and knew I was being exposed to a raw, authentic pioneer; a man who has stepped outside of the norms that so often dictate our actions. He lives with daily physical danger, has looked death in the face but keeps pressing on. He said that if people don't know what your passion is you haven't got one! Such men are rare. It is a great privilege to meet them and feel the impact of their inner burnings. They are not the products of consensus. Bill's attitude to committees was not exactly flattering, describing them as 'the unfit chosen by the unwilling to do the unnecessary'!

David Connolly, who is doing similar work to Bill Wilson in Liverpool's Frontline Church, accompanied Bill. I met the same Holy Spirit fire, but wearing different clothes and coming through a different channel. Gentle humility and a northern British accent contrasted with Bill's abrasive New York style. But the same Holy Spirit was impacting the hushed crowd as he spoke. What has been built in Liverpool under his oversight is profoundly impressive.

I also made sure to get to Andy Hawthorne's seminar. I had heard so much about him and the Worldwide Message Tribe. I had also met him at Stoneleigh, but this was my first chance to actually hear this firebrand evangelist from Manchester. At Stoneleigh Bible Week, the gathered thousands rocked with Stuart Townend's recent 'The Lord our God is breaking out'. As he is doing so, the Lord is catching up some choice servants and Andy is certainly among them. He boasts of his Salvation Army roots and is a modern day replica of their early pioneers. He is an action man who has inspired the younger generation to follow Catherine Booth's advice to 'thrust yourself on the attention of men'. As Bill Wilson said, 'If you want something you have never had before, you have to do something you've never done before!'

The call to break out of the mould has clearly grabbed those named in this chapter. They have become modern heroes of the faith, though some are better known than others and some have been on the road longer than others. As we press on into the new Millennium, such people will often provide keys that will unlock the future for the church's success. Much has taken place in the last few years to reinvigorate the church. It could be said that the church in the West, and in particular in the UK, is dying, but if you look more carefully you will discover that there are many churches which have come alive. The problem is that most people in the world don't know about it. Most who come to Alpha or get close enough to see what is happening in such churches are attracted before they even hear the preaching. They are impressed by the warmth and friendliness, the enthusiasm and joy, the sense of community and personal devotion to a God that these people seem to know intimately. They are also pleasantly surprised by the freedom from the religious trappings that they had expected to encounter.

Rather tongue-in-cheek, we called our Brighton 2000 conference 'Does the Future Have a Church?'. In spite of present statistics of decline filling our newspapers, we are left in no doubt regarding the future. The future will see a glorious church. Only God can fill her sails and propel her into a full display of glory, but we remain convinced that he will do it and that all the developments of recent decades are preparatory to a mighty breakthrough of great proportions.

Brighton 2000 held one more surprise for the delegates who gathered. Though the future undoubtedly has a church,

I announced that it would not necessarily have a Stoneleigh Bible Week and that Stoneleigh 2001 would be, as far as we knew, the last. Many were shocked and the *Christian Herald* newspaper rushed for an interview and filled their next edition's front page with the news. Why did we stop? How did we arrive at such a decision?

# 30

# No Well-Worn Paths

I was as amazed as anybody when God led us to close the
Stoneleigh Bible Week. Probably I was more aware of its significance than most. Tens of thousands had been blessed in
so many ways. Hundreds had been saved and healed, and
thousands baptised in the Holy Spirit. Over the years, many
had had their vision of God's purpose for the church and for
their own individual lives clarified. Whole churches had
been transformed as a result of exposure to its life and
teaching.

Children loved Stoneleigh and countless numbers received
Christ there and enjoyed being built up by the wonderful
children's ministry. Hundreds of young people were called to
full-time service and were encouraged by being alongside
thousands of their contemporaries in a context of wholehearted worship. Being on site with tens of thousands of
believers was an experience in itself. Some of us actually live
in towns smaller than Stoneleigh Bible Week crowds. It was
quite a phenomenon to see acres of believers playing, talking, praising and enjoying their identity together. Thirty per
cent of those attending were not from NFI churches and for

them it provided great exposure to our life, vision and values.

Worshipping together with thousands was a breathtaking experience. Also, enjoying the ongoing impact of that worship throughout the year from the annual CD or cassette and Stoneleigh songbook was a wonderful bonus. Each year, the CD went around the world and gained us friends in many nations. Prophetic preaching in the main meetings sharpened our vision and stirred our motivational commitment to the vision, and excellent teaching in the seminars supplied backup and practical application, leading to transformed lives and churches.

In addition to that, our international mission was strengthened through exposure to many overseas guests. Through the excellent evening videos, our work overseas and throughout the UK was magnificently represented, inspiring many to contribute to offerings that in the last years exceeded £1 million.

So why on earth did we stop Stoneleigh? Simply, because we really believe that God told us to. If I had made a decision based on weighing up the pros and cons I would never have reached that conclusion, but God impressed his will upon us in such a way as to leave us in no doubt.

When we stopped the successful 8,500-strong Downs Bible Week after ten years we had never heard of Stoneleigh. We did not know that God was getting us ready for 25,000. We stopped meeting at a small racecourse in the south of England, not knowing that within two years God would lead us to the massive Royal Agricultural Showground at Stoneleigh in the heart of the nation. We did not know that we would go from what was essentially a southern English camp to an international conference, attended by people not only from all over the UK but also from well over 40 nations. We simply obeyed the Lord. I remember at the time being asked why on earth we were closing such a successful conference. My only answer could be that God was clearly guiding.

So how did our decision to close Stoneleigh come about?

Initially, the showground briefly stopped us in our tracks by intimating that they were not interested in granting us a new contract (our previous ten-year contract had just run out). But that hiccup was soon overcome as we re-negotiated the use of some small sections of the grounds and they were very happy for us to go ahead.

However, during the brief time of uncertainty it was as though the Lord caught our attention and made us consider a previously unasked question: should we continue the Bible week? Within the space of a few short weeks, and in the context of much fervent prayer, we received a succession of prophetic words and visions that led us to a settled and peaceful conclusion. We should stop! One of the words which strongly impacted us was 'Unless a grain of wheat falls into the ground and dies it abides alone, but if it dies it brings forth much fruit.' Another prophetic word called us to leave the safety of the bank and launch out onto the fast-moving river that was about to move us into God's greater purposes.

Of course, both of these pictures left me with a mixture of excitement and uncertainty. Falling into the ground and dying didn't sound the most exciting thing in the world to do. Also, after eleven years of experience of Stoneleigh Bible Weeks, we had built a phenomenal team of hundreds of workers, all knowing the part that they had to play. We had developed experience each year as we had grown larger and larger. Stoneleigh had become something of great strength and significance, strong and secure. But as far as I was con-

cerned, God had spoken and I was freshly gripped by a
sense of adventure. Stoneleigh had become established, but
did God want it to be part of the Establishment? I think not.
God had taught us that there were no well-worn paths
ahead of us. Our very title, New Frontiers International,
aims to reflect that conviction and keeps us looking
forward.

The final Stoneleigh years saw more people saved than
ever before. Did that reflect a greater preoccupation with
evangelism on our part? Were we being drawn into a fresh
awareness of the harvest? If so, and if evangelism was to be
our main preoccupation, Stoneleigh Bible Week was not the
best place to be. We had recently been impacted by the ministry of the Indian evangelist Rambabu. Two of my sons had
asked me, 'Are you going to get Rambabu preaching at
Stoneleigh?' I told them that of course I was not. He's an
evangelist! Stoneleigh was not really an evangelistic context.

Surely you could have done both, you could argue. We
could have evangelised and continued Stoneleigh. Yes, this
must be true. But the fact was that Stoneleigh absorbed an
extraordinary amount of time and energy for many throughout the year. Certainly the dividends it paid were phenomenal but nevertheless the expenditure of time and manpower
was so great that it would have been very hard for us also to
commit ourselves to major evangelistic endeavour in addition to Stoneleigh itself. If God wanted us to be committed
to major evangelistic programmes, if God wanted us also to
join hands more with people in other streams and settings,
Stoneleigh probably would have got in the way.

God led us to get ready; to clear the ground for what he
was preparing. Like Joshua, we were about to cross Jordan.
We were to move out of dwelling in tents and into invading
cities. It was time to mobilise.

One of the strongest prophetic pictures that God impressed on me was that of Joseph. I felt that God said to me that the days of Joseph's storing resources were over. It was time to start feeding the dying and hungry, time to start moving out to the needy rather than continuing to fill Stoneleigh's barns every year. As I spoke to the thousands of teenagers packed into their meetings, I felt that God impressed on me that it was time to set them loose! We were on the move. There were no well-worn paths ahead. We were not even fully sure of the shape of things to come, but had a growing sense of expectation in our hearts that God would make the way clear and replace all the joys, delights and fruitfulness of Stoneleigh with something even more glorious.

Conferences can be helpful, but they are not essentially what we are. They help us on our mission, but they do not constitute our mission. Our mission in the world is to go and make disciples of all the nations. God has brought a group of churches together in NFI to accomplish what we as individual churches could never accomplish alone. He has developed strong bonds of love and friendship, and he continues to raise up the Ephesians 4 ministries of apostles, prophets, evangelists and pastor/teachers through our ranks.

We also acknowledge our indebtedness and dependence upon the whole body of Christ, having received so much from people from many diverse backgrounds. Across the UK, a growing tide of expectation grips many and the need for the nation to be re-evangelised and for hundreds of churches to be planted must take priority. We must become more mobile and embrace mobility as a lifestyle. Pastoral mode and 'celebration' mode must give way to evangelism mode.

It is reported that Smith Wigglesworth brought the following remarkable prophecy in 1947:

During the next few decades there will be two distinct moves of the Holy Spirit across the church in Great Britain. The first move will affect every church that is open to receive it, and will be characterised by a restoration of the baptism and gifts of the Holy Spirit.

The second move of the Holy Spirit will result in people leaving historic churches and planting new churches.

In the duration of each of these moves, the people who are involved will say, 'This is a great revival.' But the Lord says, 'No, neither is this the great revival, but both are steps towards it.'

When the new church phase is on the wane, there will be evidence in the churches of something that has not been seen before: a coming together of those with an emphasis on the word and those with an emphasis on the Spirit. When the word and Spirit come together, there will be the biggest movement of the Holy Spirit that the nation, and indeed the world has ever seen. It will mark the beginning of a revival that will eclipse anything that has been witnessed within these shores, even the Wesleyan and Welsh revivals of former years. The outpouring of God's Spirit will flow over from the United Kingdom to mainland Europe and, from there, will begin a missionary move to the ends of the earth.

Prophetic people in our own ranks tell me that everything we have experienced thus far is simply preparatory to the greater things that lie just ahead. What has been achieved thus far must not keep us from the biggest and most significant thing yet, the task that everything experienced hitherto has paved the way for. We are sure that co-operation with other groups of churches will hasten that process. Increasing amounts of my time are being spent beyond the borders of NFI, in widespread and diverse opportunities for fellowship and ministry.

When Abraham was called he obeyed by going out from

his secure home and city to receive an inheritance, though he did not know where he was going. There were no well-worn paths ahead of him and he was the father of all who believed. When Jesus invited Peter and his companions to abandon their nets and follow him, the shape of the future was unknown. Their call was to follow him. He in himself claimed to be the way. Their responsibility was to be in touch with him. Like Moses, they had to learn to be ready to pitch camp or move on as he dictated.

The early believers were called followers of the Way (Acts 9:2). It seems that static familiarity can constitute danger for the Christian pilgrim. It lessens your need to hold on tightly to him. Repetition and force of habit can rob you of your sense of adventure and dependence on your guide. A well-worn track easily becomes a rut. Boredom can begin to paralyse the next generation, especially if there are no goals to score and no mountains to climb! If you simply have to learn the rules and sit in your pew you will look elsewhere for your highs and even be vulnerable to insubstantial novelties that blow through Christendom; anything to break out of the groove!

God wants us stable in doctrine but mobile in practice! Many who are not actually going anywhere for God can find novelty in fanciful doctrinal experiments. The New Testament church was essentially on the move but strongly rooted in unchanging truth. Prior to the Wesleyan revival, the church had lost its sense of certainty regarding the content of the gospel. But when Wesley, Whitefield and others rediscovered the wonder of the new birth and the liberating certainties of justification by faith, they covered not only the UK but also the developing American colonies with their message, releasing armies of preachers and planting churches in virtually every town and village. The Salvation

Army started from a tiny group in London but encircled the world in one generation!

We sometimes hear the illustration that God is looking for empty vessels so that he can fill them. But the Holy Spirit wants not so much to fill your empty glass, but to fill your open sail – fullness on the move, filling your sails with dynamic energy and mobility, rather than simply filling your static cup!

Jesus, aged 30, probably called contemporaries or younger men to accompany him. I was 23 when I took the plunge. David Holden was 22 when he began to lead the Sidcup church. The extraordinary growth of the Chinese church is being overseen in many places by young people and 80 per cent of Kriengsak's workers were in their 20s when I visited Bangkok. We must not consciously or unconsciously communicate that exceptional levels of maturity are required before it is possible for God to use us. Simon Peter and the other apostles were not exactly exemplary but they were immediately enlisted on a mission. They left all to follow him. He corrected them as they moved on together. He knew Simon's weakness and knew he could make him into the rocklike 'Peter'; but he reshaped him on the journey.

Jesus was not a stationary figure. He was constantly on the move. To join him meant to be available and to move with him. Sometimes churches reach to the NFI team for our help. In their minds might be the desire for us to help sort out some foundational matters, or even help them make some necessary transition in embracing the presence of the Holy Spirit in their midst, or developing a discipleship programme. These are worthy motives and not to be dismissed, but increasingly our desire, if we become involved with any existing churches, is to catch them up on a mission with us, as Paul did with the church in Rome (Romans 15:23–24).

Moses' invitation to Hobab (Jethro), 'Come with us and we will do you good' (Numbers 10:29), seems most apt. Our goal is not so much to 'come *to you*' or even to get people 'to come *to* us' (at Stoneleigh, or anywhere else) but to come *with* us. Moses was motivated by promises for the future. 'We are setting out to the place of which the Lord said, "I will give it to you" . . . For the Lord has promised good concerning Israel.' He had a glorious history of God's providential care and mercy. He had seen a vision. He was on a journey and invited Hobab to join them. The good that God promised Moses could be shared with others. Hobab was welcome.

Hobab was also honoured and respected as a potential functioning team member. 'You will be as eyes for us.' In other words, 'You don't come just to be added to the back row of the marching column; you can tell us where we can camp' (see Numbers 10:31). Moses honoured Hobab's gift and unique ability to contribute to their success with his local knowledge of the area. Moses was following the cloud. There were no well-worn paths across the wilderness but it seems that Hobab knew something of the terrain and could advise them. When the cloud stopped Hobab could step in and speak. He did not usurp the cloud's authority to guide, but he could nevertheless 'be eyes' for them. Every new member of growing churches can be quickly taught that they have a part to play. They can be 'eyes' for us, or indeed 'ears' or 'hands', as Paul makes clear in 1 Corinthians 12 and Ephesians 4. People must be added to a functioning living body and learn to play their part, not simply make up the audience that watches the platform artists perform.

The way ahead is unknown. The paths are not well worn, but the promises are bright. We believe that more awaits us than we have seen thus far. Let us invite people to join us on the adventure.

I don't put high value on nostalgia, but it is wonderful to look back and honour God for his mercies thus far, convinced that the best is yet to come. The call to plant 1,000 churches in the UK draws us forward. Opening doors in Europe, the Middle East, Africa, Asia, the Americas and even Australasia provide massive challenges. As John Piper says, 'Mission is not the ultimate goal of the church; worship is. Mission exists because worship doesn't.' God is seeking worshippers and we have the high privilege of involvement with him in his great cause.

A vision that a dear friend of mine shared recently as we prayed together was of a very small child seated on the lap of his father, his tiny hand too small to turn the large page of the book before him. But the large hand of the father was taking the page and beginning to turn it. God knows what all our next chapters will bring and we wait with expectation for the pages to turn.

# New Frontiers International

**International Office**
New Frontiers International
17 Clarendon Villas
Hove
East Sussex BN3 3RE
United Kingdom
Phone:  (+44) 1273-234555
Fax:     (+44) 1273-234556
Email:  nfi@n-f-i.org
Web page: http:/www.n-f-i.org

**UK Office**
NFI (UK)
24 Station Road
Sidcup
Kent DA15 7DU
Phone:  (+44) 20-8309-9060
Fax:     (+44) 20-8302-4260
Email:  nfi-uk@dial.pipex.com

**South Africa**
NFI (South Africa)
21 Nelson Road
Observatory 7925
Cape Town
South Africa
Phone: (+27) 21-447-3630
Fax:     (+27) 21-447-3613
Email: jubilee@nfi-in-africa.co.za
Web page: www.jubilee.org.za

**India**
NFI (India)
Frontier Management Centre
3rd Main, Hoysala Nagar,
Bangalore 560 016
Karnataka
India
Phone: (+91) 80-565-3170
Fax:     (+91) 80-565-3170
Email: nfiblr@vsnl.com

**USA**
NFI (USA)
C/o Jubilee Church
700 Tuxedo
Webster Groves
MO 63119
USA
Phone: (+1) 314-918-1699
Fax:     (+1) 314-918-1572
Email: nfiusa@fastlynx.net

# Enjoying God's Grace

## by Terry Virgo

God's grace is almost too good to be true – a wonderful answer to the drudgery of condemnation that so many Christians seem to endure.

*Enjoying God's Grace* is an interactive book – questions and suggestions throughout the text keep things practical and help you to explore the relevance of God's grace to your life.

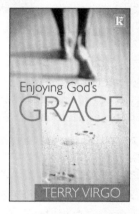

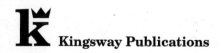

**Kingsway Publications**

# A People Prepared

## by Terry Virgo

*Wake up!* That's what the Holy Spirit is saying. There is a new day coming and God wants us to step into it, alert and ready for all that he has for us.

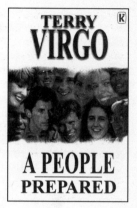

*A People Prepared* offers a vision of a church inspired by the grace of God, informed by the word of God, and empowered by the Spirit of God.

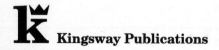

**Kingsway Publications**

# Sarah: Mother of a Nation

## by Wendy Virgo

Sarah was prophetic and very relevant to the present age. Her life, entwined with Abraham's, was about response to progressive revelation and moving on in the purposes of God. It was about the power of God's word to produce faith, and about how the response of individuals to the call of God can affect history.

She was an ordinary woman who became extraordinary: a pioneer, and the mother of a nation.

**Kingsway Publications**

# Mary: the Mother of Jesus

## by Wendy Virgo

From the first Christmas to the first Easter and beyond, we follow Mary, the mother of Jesus.

Wendy Virgo's skilful and moving narrative brings to life the dilemmas and dangers, the price and the pain, of being mother to the most special Person in history.

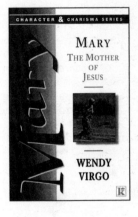

**K** **Kingsway Publications**